THE LIBERAL AND TECHNICAL
IN TEACHER EDUCATION

A Historical Survey of American Thought

Merle L. Borrowman, Ed.D.

GREENWOOD PRESS, PUBLISHERS
WESTPORT, CONNECTICUT

Library of Congress Cataloging in Publication Data

Borrowman, Merle L
    The liberal and technical in teacher education.

    Reprint of the ed. published by Teachers College,
Columbia Unviersity, New York, in series: Teachers
College studies in education.
    Includes bibliographical references and index.
    1. Teachers, Training of—United States. 2. Education
—Philosophy. I. Title. II. Series: Teachers College
studies in education.
LB1715.B66 1977   370'.73'0973   77-24026
ISBN 0-8371-9737-6

Copyright, 1956, by

Teachers College, Columbia University

Originally published in 1956 by Teachers College, Columbia
University, New York

Reprinted with the permission of Teachers College Press -
Columbia University

Reprinted in 1977 by Greenwood Press, Inc.

Library of Congress catalog card number 77-24026

ISBN 0-8371-9737-6

Printed in the United States of America

Preface

ONE NEED NOT DWELL ON EVIDENCE THAT MODERN LIFE IS "OUT OF joint." The United States faces awesome responsibilities for which it is ill-prepared, and these responsibilities come at a time when our value-systems are in a state of profound reconstruction.

In these conditions the American turns, as he has turned throughout his history, to such institutions as the school. Sometimes he turns in anger, asking why education has not prevented the deep social crisis and making the school a scapegoat for many difficulties. Sometimes he turns in naïve faith, believing that a bit of superficial tinkering with the school curriculum or administration will bring an end to the troubled times. Sometimes he turns in quiet determination, recognizing that the school, limited though its power may be, is yet one of his best tools for increasing deliberate control over the forces which sweep him.

When he looks at his schools, however, the American finds the same struggles between competing power groups, competing value-systems, and competing methodological theories which mark other dimensions of his common life. He finds the experts, in whom he is inclined to place great faith, deeply divided by controversy.

The sharp clash of ideas between men who understand each other and who share a common devotion to the critical search for truth is the central process of collective human thought. It requires a continual re-definition of issues and positions. Moreover, there is an ever-present danger that those involved in controversy will become so attached to their own ideas that institutions to which they share a common loyalty

v

will be destroyed. One task of thought, in education as in every other field, is to keep issues sharply defined and to see that controversy moves toward the resolution of action-inhibiting problems.

Current issues are not resolved by historical analysis—nor are they completely defined. History is but one of several tools which can and should be brought to bear. There is, however, a facet to every situation which is missed unless recourse is had to the historical view.

This facet is especially critical where attitudes are concerned, since these, of all cultural patterns, seem to have greatest continuity. Frequently, a point of view, arrived at through trying social experiences and well conceived to give meaning to those experiences, lives on when the cultural patterns which made it valid have completely changed. Such a point of view imposes form on institutions like education which tend to recreate the original attitude in people of a later age in which that attitude promotes only tension. Thus the attitude and the institution oscillate and become useless in a society which they no longer fit. Sometimes they become worse than useless, for a tradition out of harmony with the rest of a culture can be a dangerous source of disintegration.

On the other hand, some traditions of great antiquity repeatedly prove themselves serviceable in spite of changes in the culture. It is not necessarily to be expected that they will always be useful. If they have not been rechallenged severely in each age, they may have great antiquity and also great irrelevance. They should then be eliminated. If, on the contrary, they have met test after test, and if, moreover, an analysis of the present culture shows them still to be useful, they should not lightly be abandoned. They are priceless assets.

If a tradition can be either a priceless asset or a grave threat to society, then tools to analyze the record of traditions are extremely important. Probably the best such tool is history.

American formal education has been paradoxically vulnerable to the evil of two excesses. The first, which it shares with institutionalized education the world over and at all times, is an irresponsiveness to change. This is particularly marked in higher education. The second is a tendency to faddism, a characteristic which it shares with most of the American culture. This has been apparent in the tidal sweep of the Oswego movement, Herbartianism, progressive education, the elective system, and the current general education movement. The clash of fad

with tradition has been the American educational dialectic out of which
has come significant change.

A balancing factor—the perspective which helps to disclose excess—
is always needed. This perspective is history. One who follows closely
the history of education in America is conscious of the need to guard
constantly against the extremes of both the hobbyist and the entrenched
traditionalist.

The responsibility of the educational historian in a professional school
is primarily a functional one. Among his major concerns is the continued search through the records of the past for new meanings in current problems and new light on their solution. Ultimately his efforts
must be measured in terms of the extent to which they make formal
education more effective. The present study is, therefore, problem
oriented. It is focused on the search for balance between two educational functions, both of which are essential in a technologically advanced society. On the one hand is the necessity to train individuals to
perform efficiently the specialized technical tasks assigned to them. On
the other hand is the need to make certain that each person systematically considers the far-flung implications of his vocational and
avocational decisions.

A study of this problem could be made in relation to professional
groups other than teachers, and the same issues are involved in the conflict between general education and the specialized offerings of the high
school and college. However, to trace the issues as they have developed in teacher education has several advantages. From the standpoint
of educational reform, improvement in teacher preparation spreads most
rapidly throughout other units in the educational system. If, in their
own professional education, teachers become acutely sensitive to the
issues involved, and highly appreciative of both the liberal and technical functions of education, they are less apt to ignore either in their
own teaching and in making educational policy. Moreover, there is currently wide agitation and a spirit of experimentation in teacher education circles. If this spirit is to be most profitable it must be informed
by all the disciplines which provide channels into relevant knowledge.

In gathering information for this study I have relied largely on the
published records of the leading educational organizations and on the
published opinions of individuals who have been actively concerned
with some phase of collegiate education. I have felt that, in an impor-

tant sense, anyone actively concerned with higher education in America shares a responsibility for the teacher's *professional* competency. There has, of course, been long and sometimes bitter controversy between those representing the so-called academic disciplines and those in departments of education. One of the most damaging aspects of much of this controversy has been the lack of real communication between those holding divergent views. Controversy without communication can contribute little to the advance of truth. For this reason I have tried to see the ideas of both of these groups as related and worthy of consideration. I have also tried to recognize differences of philosophical point of view within these major groups. However, it will be readily apparent that I write from a frame of reference which is generally that of experimentalist educational philosophy.

One humbling experience in writing a preface is that of recognizing assistance without which the study could not have been completed. When one subtracts those elements which must in honesty be credited to others there is little left to claim but the shortcomings—the failure to achieve the standards which such inspiration and assistance seem to promise. Moreover, one despairs of naming all whose influence has been large; only those directly involved can be mentioned. My sincere gratitude is extended to Professor R. Freeman Butts for guidance, inspiration, and assistance going far beyond the present study; to Professor Lawrence A. Cremin, who has been a close friend and adviser in the dozens of minor crises and the several major problems which attend such a project; to Professors Ralph R. Fields and Florence B. Stratemeyer, who have drawn from their broad experience and deep insight into teacher education problems to guide me on some of the major concepts here discussed; and to my wife, Ona Borrowman, who, besides working tirelessly on the manuscript, has been a constant source of encouragement.

M.L.B.

Contents

THE LIBERAL AND TECHNICAL
IN TEACHER EDUCATION

A Historical Survey of American Thought

chapter ONE

Some Problem Areas in the Education

of American Elementary and

Secondary School Teachers

RECENT IMPORTANT STUDIES [1] TESTIFY TO THE WIDENING AREAS OF agreement about some of the traditionally most provocative issues in teacher education. The increasing interest of liberal arts colleges in teacher preparation and the conversion of many teachers colleges into multipurpose institutions hasten this trend. However, a number of problems and attitudes, deep-rooted in our history, continue to impede the degree of progress which is needed.

[1] American Council on Education, Commission on Teacher Education, *The Improvement of Teacher Education: A Final Report by the Commission on Teacher Education* (Washington, D.C.: The Council, 1949); Warren Lovinger, *General Education in the Teachers Colleges* (Oneonta, N.Y.: American Association of Colleges for Teacher Education, 1947); and Van Cleve Morris, *The Education of Secondary School Teachers in the Liberal Arts Colleges* (unpublished doctoral project, Teachers College, Columbia University, 1949; summarized in Association of American Colleges, *Bulletin*, 36:511–528, December, 1950).

1

General Considerations

Since the turn of the century the issues have been defined largely in terms of the liberal arts college versus the teachers college. Even in the universities the conflict has tended to pit those having a teachers college viewpoint against those representing the liberal arts outlook. This distinction has always been somewhat misleading, as will be seen. Yet there are real problems in the search for balance between the objectives that are traditionally emphasized by both the liberal arts college and the teachers college.

The real issues have been hopelessly entangled with status ones—the teachers college seeking academic recognition, the teachers of the classical liberal subjects fighting to maintain their pre-eminence, the advocates of the educable elite resenting the infringement of mass education, those committed to the research ideal opposing time spent in other disciplines or in the pursuit of other vocational goals, and all types of institutions competing for students and popular support.

Ill-defined and untested slogans and clichés have become the weapons with which the fight has been waged. Within their own circles all groups have recognized the lack of agreement over definitions of words which they have thrown as profoundly meaningful at their opponents. The long controversies in university circles over the meaning of "liberal education" and in the teachers college circles over the meaning of a "teacher's knowledge of subject matter" may be offered as cases in point.

Theoretically, most college educators now recognize the need for adequate *technical and liberal* preparation of teachers. Logically they are quite free to welcome their erstwhile opponents as part of the same "we" group. Psychologically, however, the structured thinking and the attitudinal patterns imposed by the intellectual climate in which they have grown and worked continue to prevent a full partnership. They still accept, uncritically, the old distortions of other points of view; they still reject, blindly and resentfully, criticism of their own practices. Bias, misconception, and conceit dictate opinion far more often than does considered judgment. One thing needed is a continuing effort to redefine issues so there will be more objective thinking by all concerned.

SOME TERMS DISCUSSED

Words which lie at the heart of a controversy inevitably become so funded with bias, so confused by redefinition, and so misunderstood by careless thought that their use is open to question. Yet people who have long used them to express vital thought cannot abandon them. No other words carry the meaning which must be conveyed. The writer who must use such words can only define them as carefully as possible and trust his readers to accept the definitions in good will for the purposes of his presentation. Four concepts are at the heart of the present study, and the meaning of what follows depends on their being understood in the author's frame of reference.

Two of the four concepts refer to the *function* of an educative experience, not to a segment of the curriculum, as such. These two concepts are *liberal* and *technical*. The two other terms, *general education* and *professional education,* refer primarily to administrative arrangements by which the total pre-service curriculum is divided into segments.

The liberal function of education.—The idea of a liberal education as contrasted, or related, to a technical education once had, perhaps, a commonly accepted meaning. This meaning included the Aristotelian concept of education for leisure as opposed to education for use. Its objective was to produce the free man—a man who, relieved from the need to produce goods or artisan services directly, could spend his time in speculative thought concerning the problems of philosophy and government. Education in the speculative arts was thought to differ fundamentally from training in the practical arts. The latter was considered to be properly a plebeian concern best satisfied by apprenticeship.

By the medieval period, liberal education had come to have an agreed-upon content composed of the classical seven liberal arts. Shortly after the opening of the American experience it gained a psychological rationale: the theory of formal discipline and faculty psychology. The antiquity of its tradition and the fact that its basic premises were often so impressively stated by writers in earlier historical eras predisposed its modern advocates to a perennialist philosophy.

As the controversy in American higher education heightened, the term "liberal" came to be completely identified in the mind of some with this specific program of education. Certain of its aspects have, however, been under constant fire. These include the assumption that a fixed curriculum, based largely on the thinking of the past, can be adequate for modern times, the claim that there is a necessary dichotomy between education for use and education for leisure, the concentration on intellectual training as the sole function of higher education, and the belief in faculty psychology—in one form or another.

Yet, transcending any specific curriculum there is a liberal function of education which must not be ignored. This function is implicit in virtually every statement of the aims of liberal education. In a word, this function is perspective. And perspective must be seen as having at least three dimensions—time, community, and methodology.

The liberal function of education is to make certain that the individual sees every problem of living, *including the professional ones,* in the broadest scope possible. This includes a concern for what went before and for what is to follow. It also includes an understanding of the forces which the community—local and world—is bringing to bear on the situation and of the possible consequences of a given decision on the community. These are the time and the community perspectives.

The problem of providing breadth in terms of methodology is different. It is assumed that the most intelligent decisions are based on the consideration of all the relevant data which can reasonably be assembled. These data usually include facts as revealed by the scientific laboratory, by scholarly research in the libraries, and by the techniques of the social scientists. They also include facts revealed by the emotional and aesthetic insight of sensitive people and generalizations arrived at by the rational processes of disciplined intelligence.

Obviously no one person, or group of persons, has the time or ability to gather every relevant fact in every situation. Education functions liberally to the extent that it seeks to ensure the greatest achievable breadth. It is to be hoped that reasonable competence in using some tools of analysis can be developed in every person. It is also to be hoped that everyone can be made sensitive to the areas where other tools are most productive, and can develop the habit of seeking the advice of experts in using those tools when is it important to do so.

The technical function of education.—Technical, when viewed functionally, is not the antithesis of liberal. The two are complementary and may even in some cases be alike in kind, differing only in purpose. Education functions technically when its purpose is the cultivation of skill in the actual performance of a previously determined task. It is less concerned with the determination of purpose and policy and more concerned with their implementation. Education which aims at technical proficiency generally places a premium on the reduction of specific tasks to effective routine.

As the words are here used, there is also an element of specialization attached to the technical which is not so characteristic of the liberal function. For example, detailed instruction and practice in the techniques of historical research and criticism constitute for the potential historian an important part of his technical equipment. The same experience, however, may have for the prospective elementary school teacher the liberal function of making him sensitive to the proper uses of history in the general analysis of problems. In the case of the historian such training serves to give him skills in the routine tasks which define his specialized competency; in the case of the elementary school teacher it broadens his perspective by making him sensitive to another tool of intellectual analysis. While the functions are not mutually exclusive the instruction is primarily technical in the one case and primarily liberal in the other.

So far as the prospective teacher is concerned, education is here defined as functioning technically when it cultivates skill in such matters as classroom management, test construction, lesson presentation, grading, and reporting to parents.

It must be re-emphasized that, for this discussion, the liberal and the technical are not viewed as different curricular offerings. A given course should provide systematic attention to the achievement of both liberal and technical ends. They are in opposition only when the concern for one leads teachers and students to forget the importance of the other. However, some educative experiences do function *primarily* in a liberal *or* a technical manner.

The general education sequence.—One of the major educative tasks of our time is to maintain effective communication between groups of people becoming ever more specialized. For this reason, and for administrative convenience, there are grounds for having students with different specialized objectives living and learning together, or in the same manner, as long as possible. There are some understandings and competencies which are demanded for effective living and for the successful discharge of specialized or professional duties irrespective of the vocation one chooses. That portion of the curriculum which brings together these common learnings and can logically be offered simultaneously to students with divergent occupational goals makes up the general education sequence.

General education is more and less than liberal education as the terms are here used. Both because it is more and because it is less, its use as a synonym is dangerous. Some experiences offered in the general education program function technically for each student. The big danger in seeing general and liberal education as synonymous is that it then becomes too easy to equate the whole of the professional or specialized sequence with the technical function. In teacher education the danger is particularly acute. The historical tendency of both the liberal arts people and certain educationists has been to keep all professional considerations out of the liberal education program, and to assume that the professional program should concern itself largely with the tricks of the trade.

The professional education sequence.—This is a misleading term because it seems to imply that everything having to do with professional competency is to be offered within the specialized sequence. This is not the case. Among the professional objectives of teacher education this sequence assumes responsibility only for those which are most effectively achieved if the students share a fairly common occupational goal. The professional sequence is here thought of as that section of the curriculum which is so specialized that only those preparing for professional work in education or related fields find it profitable.

As was noted of general education, the professional sequence also serves both the liberal and the technical function. There is no less need to bring perspective to bear on professional decisions than on other problems of living. Obviously, the lines between the general and professional sequences are hard to draw.

AREAS OF CRITICAL DECISION

The ideal of the skilled teacher–craftsman, capable of making educational decisions illumined by broad knowledge and an acute sense of ultimate consequences, is probably shared by all. A central problem in the education of teachers has been to make certain that the search for craftsmanship and the efforts to ensure breadth complement, rather than compete with, each other. The ensuing historical analysis of thought focuses on this problem.

There are three areas in planning the collegiate program of prospective teachers where crucial decisions respecting the relationship of the liberal to the technical function are made: (1) the concept of general education; (2) the relationship of the general education sequence to the professional education sequence; and (3) the relationship of the liberal and the technical functions within the professional sequence. No decision can be made intelligently in reference to any of these without considering the others. The attitude which prevails with respect to the first will, for example, condition the thinking of students and faculty in respect to the third, and will compel those responsible for the professional sequence to adopt a particular type of program.

These three areas provide the framework for each of the ensuing chapters. After an introductory discussion of the general climate of opinion which prevailed in American society during each period, there is an analysis of the way different people were looking at the purposes of general education. Obviously, for much of the time the phrase "general education" was not used and is here imposed. Those who think of liberal education and general education as synonymous have been an important group in every historical era.

The discussion of varying concepts of general education in each period is followed by a description of different conceptions of the ideal relationship between the professional and the general sequences. Finally, there is an analysis of how people have conceived the professional sequence itself, in so far as the relationships between the technical and liberal functions are concerned.

Current Issues in Thought Concerning
Teacher Education

In this section current thought about teacher education will be reviewed. Certain issues involved in the three problem areas mentioned above will be defined.

THE CONCEPT OF GENERAL EDUCATION

There are two closely related problem areas concerning general education programs for prospective teachers. The first is the question of the relative emphasis to be given to the development of intellectual skills. The second involves the wisdom of using a functional base (either problem-centered or vocation-centered) for organizing the sequence.

General education and the development of intellectual skills.—Perhaps no problem is more basic to the controversy about general education than that involving the emphasis to be placed on the cultivation of intellectual skills, and the most effective method of such cultivation. At one extreme of thought is that position, so well represented by Robert M. Hutchins, which makes the cultivation of intellectual ability the sole obligation of the school, and considers such functions as character building, training in social graces, and body building the responsibility of other agencies. In its extreme form this position relies largely on faculty psychology and formal discipline. It posits such independent faculties as will, reason, and memory, and implies that the intellectual faculty of reason can be developed largely in isolation from the emotional–psychic dimensions of the student's life as well as from the peculiar cultural conditions of a specific age and society.

At the other extreme is a position which has very little sympathy even for talk of "intellectual" activities—a position so exclusively concerned with meeting the emotional needs of students that it denies more than a casual glance to developing techniques of disciplined thought. Recent attacks on education by representatives of some of the other university disciplines have not infrequently cited this tendency as characteristic of professors of "education."

One of the most outspoken of such critics is the historian, Arthur E. Bestor, of the University of Illinois. In a number of periodical articles, and on the floor of the American Historical Association's 1952 convention, Bestor repeated the old charge that professional educators have little respect for intellectual development and for the academic disciplines.[2]

While Bestor's particular concern was with the program of the secondary schools, he has clearly implied that only teachers who have

---

[2] See Arthur E. Bestor, "Liberal Education and a Liberal Nation," *The American Scholar,* 21:139–149 (Spring, 1952); "Aimlessness in Education," *The Scientific Monthly,* 75:109–116 (August, 1952); " 'Life-Adjustment' Education: A Critique," American Association of University Professors, *Bulletin,* 38:(3) 413–441 (Autumn, 1952); and "Schools Criticized on Basic Learning," *The New York Times,* December 28, 1952. Since this was written Bestor has made a more detailed and explicit statement of his position, especially in respect to the preparation of teachers, in *Educational Wastelands* (Urbana: University of Illinois Press, 1953).

learned in their professional education to take the cultivation of intellectual skills lightly could be responsible for such programs. This implication was made explicit on a number of occasions, and Bestor pointed to utterances and policies of professional educators to back it up. One statement offered in evidence was that of a junior high school principal, A. H. Lauchner, who said:

When we come to the realization that not every child has to read, write, and spell . . . that many of them either cannot or will not master these chores . . . then we shall be on the road to improving the junior high school curriculum.

Between this day and that a lot of selling must take place. But it's coming. We shall some day accept the thought that it is just as illogical to assume that every boy must be able to read as it is that each one must be able to perform on a violin, that it is no more reasonable to require that each girl shall spell well than it is that each one should bake a cherry pie. . . .[3]

Bestor pointed to other evidence purporting to show that professional educators consider the development of the intellectual skills as of little more importance than the "problem of acquiring the ability to select and enjoy good motion pictures."

There are a number of problems in providing universal secondary education which Bestor ignores, and he betrays grave limitations in his knowledge of the learning process. Moreover, there may be gross exaggeration and distortion in his generalization of the attitude he condemns.[4] Nevertheless, the basic allegation that *some* educationists hold an extreme position and place little importance on the building of intellectual skills, especially verbal skills, is true.

The point is that one problem of general education grows out of differing values placed on the development of these intellectual skills, and positions are held at all points on a continuum between the extremes here suggested. Communication among those holding differing views frequently breaks down because of changing and confused terminology. For example, the academically minded educators frequently

[3] A. H. Lauchner, "How Can the Junior High School Curriculum Be Improved?," *Bulletin of the National Association of Secondary-School Principals,* 35:299 (March, 1951).

[4] For a carefully documented rebuttal of Bestor's charges see Harold C. Hand and Charles W. Sanford, "A Scholar's Documents," *Bulletin of the National Association of Secondary-School Principals,* 37:460–488 (April, 1953). These authors, besides giving a point-by-point refutation of Bestor, cite numerous examples of his careless and misleading use of evidence.

appeal to "discipline," a term which many education specialists immediately associate with the theories of formal discipline and faculty psychology or with a rigidly defined and carefully guarded body of information. Such associations are not inaccurate when related to the ideas of some academic professors, but are misleading in respect to others.

Bestor took time from his attacks on the professors of education to remind his colleagues in other fields that an academic discipline ". . . is not the same as a subject matter field. The one is a way of thinking, the other an aggregation of facts." [5] He pointed out that higher education had lost repute because of its failure to make this distinction.

Bestor's argument was not the traditional one about formal discipline. He stated that the race has developed certain tools for attacking problems as they arise. These can be considered simply effective ways of looking at practical situations and of improving the quality of behavior used in meeting them. To Bestor, the communication of the ability to use these tools was the prime responsibility of organized education. Of this power he said:

That it cannot be communicated by someone who does not possess it—by a teacher who is not also a scholar—is self evident. But neither can it be communicated by scholars and scientists if they pay too much attention in their classes to what they have learned and too little to how they learned it. Academic courses which teach men to perform mathematical computations but not to think mathematically, to manipulate laboratory apparatus but not to think scientifically, to remember dates but not to think historically, to summarize philosophical arguments, but not to think critically—these advance no man toward a liberal education. Courses may bear the respected labels of academic discipline and yet be, in reality, no more than the subject matter fields about which educators prate.[6]

Bestor's disciplines are not faculties to be developed indirectly by exposure to subject matter. They are specific ways of behaving which can be learned. There is room for sharp controversy about how they can best be taught.

Others who speak of intellectual discipline as the prime objective of education do use the terminology of formal discipline, though they claim to recognize its technical obsolescence. Mark Van Doren, for

[5] Bestor, "Liberal Education," p. 145.
[6] *Ibid.*, p. 147.

example, suggested that the old ways of describing the process by which one comes to have well-ordered emotional responses and sharp, critical thinking ability are useful descriptive tools, regardless of their technical accuracy or lack of it. He recognized the psychological evidence which opposes these old concepts, yet he insisted that "Even in the old terms, the theory [of faculty psychology] made more sense than it is given credit for." [7]

The basic issue about intellectual skills is not one of value. It involves the methodological problem of how best to develop them. The philosophical position of John Dewey, which provides the rationale for much of the theory of the educationists, was not anti-intellectual. On the contrary, as one of the leading experimentalist philosophers, John L. Childs, has pointed out, ". . . it was concern for cultural and intellectual values, not indifference to them, that led Dewey to experiment with an activity, or experience curriculum." [8]

Childs also insisted that the new emphasis on the all-round growth of the child did not deny the primary place of intellectual development among educational ends. An essential point of those who oppose an exclusive concern with intellectual skills is simply that experience cannot be so divided. Harold Taylor, in discussing the position, pointed out that

Reason and emotion, that is, knowing and wanting, are described as parts of an organism at work in ways natural to itself, and the emphasis is placed upon integration and continuity—the integration of the passions and the intellect, of thought and action, of heredity and environment, of the individual and society, of the past and present, of knowledge and values, of matter and mind.[9]

It should be noted that the opposition to programs which divorce intellectual development from the rest of the student's ongoing experience is not restricted to the experimentalist school of educators. Recently, Edward A. Fitzpatrick has, from a basically Thomist position,

[7] Mark Van Doren, *Liberal Education* (New York: Henry Holt & Company, Inc., 1943), p. 121.

[8] John L. Childs, *Education and Morals, An Experimentalist Philosophy of Education* (New York: Appleton-Century-Crofts, Inc., 1950), p. 149.

[9] Harold Taylor, "The Philosophical Foundations of General Education," *General Education*, Part I, Fifty-First Yearbook of the National Society for the Study of Education, Nelson B. Henry, ed. (Chicago: The University of Chicago Press, 1952), p. 36.

re-emphasized the integral relation of experience, knowledge, and action.[10]

Attitudes toward the development of intellectual skill thus vary broadly. A number of positions could be placed on a continuum. On one extreme is the position of Hutchins and others who see the cultivation of the faculty of reason through the traditional program of liberal arts and the great books as the prime objective and content of education. A second position, which shares with the first a conviction that the school ought not concern itself with educative tasks other than the cultivation of intellect, is that represented by Bestor. Here the emphasis is on training in the use of the disciplines as intellectual tools.[11] A third position, held by the instrumentalists and others, agrees that the development of intelligence is a prime end of education, and defines intelligence in terms of a whole human organism responding effectively in lifelike situations. To its advocates the idea of developing intelligence outside the context of problems recognized as meaningful to the student is unacceptable. They reject, too, any idea that the intellectual dimension of life can be separated from the emotional or aesthetic dimensions. Finally, there seems to be a fourth position so intent on meeting student needs, and so confident that intelligence will automatically develop if students are kept active, that little systematic thought is given to directing this activity. The cultivation of intelligence is thus left largely to chance.

Traditional versus functional general education programs.—One's attitude toward the purposes of general education naturally predisposes him toward a specific organizational pattern for that program. In 1947 the Executive Committee of the Cooperative Study in General Education discussed approaches to this problem of organizing general education. At one extreme, growing logically from the position of those who emphasize the intellectual faculties, were the Great Books programs like that of St. John's College of Annapolis. The second, which in a sense stressed the academic disciplines as fields of learning, was the traditional liberal arts college approach of having students take formal courses in each of several disciplines. The third, which showed concern

10 Edward A. Fitzpatrick, *How to Educate Human Beings* (Milwaukee, Wisc.: The Bruce Publishing Company, 1952), pp. 61 ff.

11 In his article, "On the Education and Certification of Teachers," *School and Society,* 78:81–87 (September 19, 1953), Bestor reveals clearly the extent to which his concept of education reduces to training in the disciplines as such.

lest the specialized disciplines, as such, become too controlling, was that based on surveys of fields of knowledge. The fourth involved individualized instruction, a position which seems to suggest that the most effective organization of knowledge is achieved if the individual, rather than specific courses or disciplines, is made the determining factor in curriculum planning. The Committee saw these four as closely related. Each, the Committee thought, presupposes organization in terms of subject matter which is not functionally defined by current needs or problems.[12]

The Committee saw a crucial issue separating the above four from the fifth type of program which organized general education in terms of social problems or of human needs. This crucial issue was to determine whether to use the traditional classifications of knowledge to organize general education or to use a functional approach. Actually, this issue does not sharply separate the fifth position from the other four. The third and fourth approaches also suggest a search for new organizational patterns. Implicitly, they reveal increased willingness to consider current social factors and individual needs in planning the general education curriculum.

The attitudes held by the general education faculty on these issues becomes a decisive factor in planning the professional sequence. They define the bounds of what is possible in relating the professional to the general sequence and determine the kind and amount of liberal education which the student will bring to his specialized study.

THE RELATIONSHIP OF THE GENERAL
TO THE PROFESSIONAL SEQUENCE

Closely paralleling the ideas of different groups about general education are their concepts of how best to relate it to the professional sequence. While the lines are hard to draw it may be useful to distinguish three positions, each having important subdivisions. The *first* holds for a complete separation of the general from the professional sequence. The *second* seeks to harmonize the two under a single all-embracing theme of social and individual needs. In practice this second

---

[12] American Council on Education, *Cooperation in General Education,* A Final Report of the Executive Committee of the Cooperative Study in General Education (Washington, D.C.: The Council, 1947), pp. 38–43. The phrases qualifying each position are those of the present author, not of the committee. Moreover, the order of discussion is rearranged.

concept frequently leads to a program which is largely general in the early years, becoming largely professional in the later ones. However, it avoids the implication that education for the vocational dimension of life is different in kind or dignity from general education. The *third* position also opposes any conceived dichotomy between the two sequences. It attempts to integrate the entire collegiate program around the professional objective. This approach constitutes the logical rounding out of the historical demand for "professional treatment" of all subjects in the pre-service program.

The general and the professional as discrete sequences.—In 1945 the pages of *School and Society* carried a series of letters and articles concerning the proper place of the department of education in the college. In one of these J. Leonard Sherman voiced the perennial cry of the conservative liberal arts college when he said:

This educational institution has one sole function to perform, and that function is to offer a broad general culture through the teaching of the liberal arts. . . . When it attempts to add to this function specialized training in any one of the professions it must divert its energy from this sole legitimate function. . . . No educational institution can serve two masters.[13]

Sherman went on to argue that the only place for instruction in education is in the graduate school, and to insist that no part of professional training should be allowed to interfere with the general education of the college.

This position is well known. It is essentially that which seems to lie behind the current experimental program being developed in Arkansas under sponsorship of the Fund for the Advancement of Education. The details of the Arkansas experiment remain to be worked out, although C. M. Clarke, chairman of the executive committee which will direct the project, has indicated clearly that there will be a "sharp dichotomy of general and professional preparation" and that no professional courses as such will be offered during the first four years.[14]

The general and the professional as parallel and harmonized sequences.—The extreme positions—that which argues for a rigid separation of the general and the professional, and that which places the

---

[13] J. Leonard Sherman, "Shall the Liberal Arts College Be Liberalizing or Nondescript?," *School and Society*, 62:327 (November 17, 1945).

[14] C. M. Clarke, "The Ford Foundation–Arkansas Experiment," *The Journal of Teacher Education*, 3:260–264 (December, 1952).

professional role at the center of the entire pre-service program—are rather easily definable. Each of these positions provides for a single reference point or purpose for every segment of the curriculum. Between these two, however, there is a large body of teacher educators who see the need for some sort of balanced approach to the curriculum as a unit but who are unwilling to make the professional objective itself the determining factor.

Those holding this central ground differ significantly among themselves, but they share a common feeling that it is unsound to imply, even by patterns of curriculum organization, that general education and professional education are basically different in kind and largely unrelated. They are anxious to ensure the greatest possible carry-over of each into the other. A similar concern is felt by some of those responsible for the professional training of other specialized groups. A belief that there should be a "blending of general education and specialized training" was expressed in the 1950 National Conference on Higher Education, at which such areas as medicine, dentistry, aeronautics, biology, chemistry, forestry, and accounting were represented.[15]

In keynoting the 1952 meeting of the Council on Cooperation in Teacher Education, Agnes Snyder, chairman of the department of Education at Adelphi College, and Francis Keppel, then dean of the Faculty of Education at Harvard University, both attacked the artificial separation of professional instruction from general education. Keppel and Snyder seemed to speak from a common concept, each considering the collegiate program an integrated attempt to prepare the student for his total destiny—a destiny which included but was not limited to the professional role as that role is usually understood.

Snyder suggested that

If we assume that a vital learning experience in all fields is the basis of sound teacher education, not only will the sharp demarcation between general and professional education disappear, but the attempt to parcel each out on a quantitative basis will likewise fall into discard. Instead, there will be the effort so to interpret the learning experiences of the student in all fields as will help him see the relationship between his studies and his personal and professional problems. This means that a sound education in all fields of knowledge—the arts, the biological

---

[15] See Cora E. Taylor, "Current Issues in Education for the Professions," *Current Issues in Higher Education, 1950,* National Conference on Higher Education (Washington, D.C.: National Education Association, 1950), p. 93.

and physical sciences, the social sciences, and philosophy—is needed as a basis for both the personal development and the professional competency of the teacher.[16]

Keppel stressed a related idea in maintaining that

. . . the study of education is the study of a central aspect of our society and requires the highest level of philosophical, sociological, psychological, and historical capacities. A sharp division between courses in these aspects of human knowledge and courses in education seems meaningless.[17]

The concept of a harmonized program demands that professional considerations enter somehow into the planning of general education. Keppel pointed out that the prospective teacher must come to grips with the problems of education at an early period in the collegiate program. He had previously suggested that for many students this coming to grips might better occur in courses in philosophy and the social sciences. "I suspect," he said, "that our success in this effort will depend on the extent to which the faculties of liberal arts colleges are sensitive to the challenge that the problems of American education present, particularly to the departments of philosophy and the social sciences." [18]

Apparently the essence of the Harvard position Keppel had in mind is that while the professional objective should play some part in determining the content of general education courses, it should not be stressed, as such, until after the completion of a four-year general education program.

Snyder noted that the timing of a student's introduction to the professional sequence should be determined largely in terms of specific individuals. However, she emphasized that the earlier the professional goal, as such, was recognized, the better.

Though they have much in common, these two points of view suggest one issue which divides those who argue for harmonizing the general and the professional sequences. It is the problem of how early and how explicitly the professional objective should be allowed to enter the general program.

[16] Agnes Snyder, "Conflicting Points of View and Challenges in the Education of Teachers," The Journal of Teacher Education, 3:(4)243–248 (December, 1952), p. 246.

[17] Francis Keppel, "Contemporary Issues in the Education of Teachers," The Journal of Teacher Education, 3:(4)249–255 (December, 1952), p. 252.

[18] Ibid., p. 252.

In 1951 Hollis L. Caswell, then Dean of Teachers College, Columbia University, argued that the professional sequence should be started as soon as the student recognized a vocational goal and should parallel the general education sequence throughout. He implied that the beginning of the third collegiate year was "late."

Caswell's reasons for this position included two that were largely professional—the need for better selection and guidance of prospective teachers and the need for a longer period of professional maturation. His proposal was also aimed at improving general education. He suggested that the strength of the professional objective could enrich meaning and provide a dominant purpose around which to integrate learning. The early beginning of the professional sequence, he argued, provides "a desirable directive influence on general education." [19]

The vocational objective does in fact develop early in American students. This has been cited by educational sociologists as argument for its early and explicit recognition in patterning the general education curriculum.[20]

However, W. Earl Armstrong, reporting for a discussion group in the 1950 National Conference on Higher Education, suggested that the pressure to make an early vocational choice and to modify general education accordingly may actually be driving capable students away from preparing for elementary school teaching. The group seemed to feel that ". . . many who are interested in their own education first and what they will use it for second tend to shy away from the curricula for the preparation of elementary school teachers." [21]

Something of the same concern has been expressed in recent years by such pioneers in teacher education as Charles H. Judd and William C. Ruediger.[22] Both of these men are strong advocates for closely relating

[19] Hollis L. Caswell, "The Professional Sequence in Teacher Education," American Association of Colleges for Teacher Education, Fourth Yearbook, 1951 (Oneonta, N.Y.: The Association, 1951), p. 84.

[20] See Robert J. Havighurst, "Social Foundations of General Education," *General Education*, Part I, Fifty-First Yearbook of the National Society for the Study of Education (Chicago: The University of Chicago Press, 1952), p. 85.

[21] W. Earl Armstrong, "Current Issues in the Preparation of Teachers for the Elementary and Secondary Schools, Section A," *Current Issues in Higher Education*, National Conference on Higher Education, 1950 (Washington, D.C.: National Education Association, 1950), p. 97.

[22] Charles H. Judd, "Should University Schools of Education Cease to Exist?," *School and Society*, 62:141–142 (September 1, 1945); William C. Ruediger, "The Sins of 1839," *School and Society*, 62:294–295 (November 3, 1945).

the general to the professional sequence, but both have seen a danger in permitting the professional objective to play too dominant a role in general education.

Professionalized general education.—The search for an all-embracing concept around which to integrate the whole pre-service program has led some teacher educators to urge that the professional goal itself serve that function. The idea that a singleness of purpose constitutes the greatest value and advantage of the normal school and teachers college is, as will be seen, deeply rooted in the tradition.

The basic idea of professionalized general education is that the competencies, personal and professional, needed by the effective teacher include the legitimate aims of general education. This position has evolved through a long effort to provide for the "professional treatment of subject matter." In its evolution it has meant many things. Some indication of the practical implications of the concept as currently held is found in the program of the Montclair State Teachers College which is among the schools moving in this direction.

At Montclair the instruction which corresponds to general education in other colleges is offered as "professional–cultural background." It includes a sequence of survey type courses, oriented around contemporary problem areas, providing a total of forty semester hours of credit. The courses are jointly planned by the departments of social studies, English, science, geography, and "integration" (roughly comparable to the usual "education" department). While some of the courses in the major and minor fields of subject-matter specialization are discipline oriented, those in the professional–cultural background are not so focused.

In the formal statement of the rationale for its curriculum the college clearly emphasizes the controlling position of the professional objective. For example, one of the "fundamental principles" listed in its *Bulletin* reads:

The relative value of the curricular materials used in a teachers college should be judged by the nature and needs of the schools and communities which it serves. *Though teachers are exponents of broad culture, yet the selection of the necessary materials for a prospective teacher must be made on the basis of professional service.*[23]

[23] See New Jersey State Teachers College, *Bulletin of Information and Catalog of Courses, 1952–1954* (Montclair, N.J.: The College), p. 16, *passim.*

When the Montclair *Bulletin* turns to the justification of its background courses the professional objective is again clearly cited as the controlling one. It is noted that if the teacher is to recognize and use the many-sided interests of high school pupils and to be aware of the relationships between his area of specialization and social events he must have a broad education. It is ostensibly in order to meet these "professional needs" that the professional–cultural sequence is required.

There is no denial of worthy nonprofessional goals to be derived from general education, but the professional treatment position assumes that these can be included in an adequate concept of professional competency, and require no special focusing.[24]

Something which approaches closely the professionalized general education position was suggested for the universities by Frederick E. Bolton in 1945.[25] Bolton, who had served as head of a number of colleges of education in American universities, suggested that the entire collegiate program of prospective teachers should be determined by the college of education in the light of professional as well as general education considerations. This control, he suggested, should include the right to designate which academic courses taught outside the college of education would be creditable and to specify those academic instructors whose offerings were acceptable.

THE LIBERAL AND THE TECHNICAL FUNCTIONS
WITHIN THE PROFESSIONAL SEQUENCE

Among the problems in organizing the professional sequence are three which have particular bearing on the present discussion. One is the search for a more rewarding way of handling certain important theoretical materials and experiences which do not lead directly to techniques. Such materials and experiences will here be referred to as the foundations—psychological, social, and philosophical—of education. The second problem area involves the search for more effective ways of building the teacher's technical skill. The third, closely related to the other two, involves the place of so-called direct-experience programs.

[24] For a defense of this approach in terms of widely accepted goals for general education, see Mowat G. Fraser, "Advantages of a Teachers College Education," *The Journal of Higher Education,* 23:(6)308–312, 343–344 (June, 1952). Fraser is head of the department of integration at Montclair.

[25] Frederick E. Bolton, "What to Do About University Schools of Education," *School and Society,* 62:432–433 (December 29, 1945).

The foundations of education.—In addition to technique, professional education has long concerned itself with certain limiting and directing factors imposed on the educative task by the biology of the student and the pressures of the culture. The disciplines and the subject matter used to make the prospective teacher aware of these factors have been those of the academic community at large—psychology, biology, philosophy, and the social sciences. The findings of all these disciplines have implications not only for what and how the child *can* learn but also for what he *ought* to learn. The findings have typically been fed into orientation courses, into child development courses, into courses on the school and society, and into courses in history of education, educational philosophy, educational sociology, and educational psychology.

Some of the materials—for example, those dealing with group dynamics and those concerned with an understanding of the learning process—do bear directly on technique. They are defended even by people who ask only of the professional sequence that it pay off in producing skilled craftsmen. But the foundational materials have a further function which can be defended only if one holds a broader concept of the teacher's role. Three developments in educational and social theory have led to such a broadened concept.

The first of these developments has been the growth of understanding about the emotional patterns of human life. This new understanding has resulted in the school assuming greater responsibility for promoting psychological as well as intellectual maturity—if the two can be separated. It has made it necessary for the teacher to carefully choose techniques in the light of their incidental emotional impact on the pupils concerned as well as of their contribution to increased verbal skill. Needless to say, the increased emotional tensions brought on by industrialization and urbanization make this responsibility acute.

A second development which has changed the concept of the teacher's role has been a more sophisticated understanding of the school's strategic position as an instrument in the making of public policy. The school has always been not only an area in which pressure groups and other social and intellectual forces contend, but also a significant agent in that contention. However, educators have only recently begun to investigate the full implications of their social responsibilities and opportunities in this respect.

Finally, the idea that teachers, even school administrators for that matter, should play a major and professional part in making basic educational policy is comparatively young. Yet current thought suggests that the classroom teacher should participate in a continuing revision of the curriculum and in making other important educational policy decisions. These decisions constitute, to a significant though not overwhelming degree, the making of social policy.

The problem of educational foundations in the professional sequence is to focus the maximum available knowledge on these policy decisions. The historical approach to this problem was that of other university disciplines, namely, to pyramid specialized course upon specialized course and to permit the student to elect, on the basis of personal and often extraneous factors, from among these courses, none of which were functionally oriented.

The solution inherent in the thinking of some members of the academic community, including some educationists, is to deny that those directing the professional sequence have responsibility for this liberal function. Thus Bestor defended the oft-heard position that the proper preparation of teachers involves "liberal education" plus the "tricks of the trade." [26] If Bestor had used "liberal education" as it is here used, his position would have allowed for liberal emphasis within the professional sequence. However, his discussion as a whole seems to indicate an identification of the professional sequence with the "tricks of the trade."

From the camp of the educationists, Edith E. Beechel, disturbed at recommended cutbacks in student teaching programs, gave some indication of the opinion which certain "practical" educators hold for educational theory. In an address to the Association for Student Teaching Beechel said, "Since in student teaching more than in any other professional course the need for knowledge is linked with the need for action, why not, as an economy measure, dispense with a few high-salaried theorists—those who profess to teach! They really wouldn't be missed. . . ." [27]

Some authorities who insist that the prospective teacher does need to view educational problems from the standpoint of the foundational disciplines suggest that this be done as part of the general education

[26] Bestor, "Liberal Education," pp. 141–142.

[27] Edith E. Beechel, "The Challenge of the Future," *Practicing Democracy in Teacher Education,* Twenty-Fifth Anniversary Yearbook of the Association for Student Teaching (Lock Haven, Pa.: The Association, 1946), p. 11.

sequence. Keppel's analysis of the policy underlying one of the Harvard University plans has already been cited in this respect (see above, page 16). This plan provides for the professional faculty to administer appraisal examinations to measure the prospective teacher's grasp of the social, psychological, and philosophical implications of basic educational policy decisions. Whether or not an instructor responsible for general education courses in foundational disciplines is willing and prepared to give adequate attention to educational problems is the crucial question, as Keppel recognized.

The current trend, however, seems to be toward incorporating foundational materials into "practical" courses in education.[28] The crucial question about such an approach is whether or not the teachers of these practical courses are prepared and willing to give adequate attention to the rather involved philosophical, sociological, historical, or psychological problems involved. The adequate handling of such materials on more than a superficial basis would seem to demand considerable training.

In 1951 Caswell saw the solution as that of organizing "foundations" courses around basic problem areas. He recognized that miseducation would result if the teachers handling such courses were inadequately prepared in the disciplines from which they drew their materials. To forestall this threat he insisted that teachers colleges or departments of education must make certain that the faculty members assigned to teach such courses be thoroughly trained in their respective academic disciplines. In cautioning against superficiality, Caswell pointed out that teacher education, though recognizing the need for "substantial intellectual content," had still not penetrated the full meaning of the need in planning the professional sequence.[29]

One problem in handling foundational materials is that of keeping the optimum distance between theory and direct utility. There are two equally-to-be-feared dangers in educational theorizing. One is that theory can become so far removed from real problems that it becomes meaningless in their solution; the second is that it becomes so closely tethered to immediate utility that perspective is lost. The theorist himself can be so out of touch with practice that he is completely insensitive to

---

[28] Walter S. Monroe, *Teaching–Learning Theory and Teacher Education, 1890–1950* (Urbana, Ill.: University of Illinois Press, 1952), pp. 536–538.

[29] Caswell, *op. cit.*, p. 87.

practical issues, or so concerned with immediate action that he neglects the discipline and understanding needed for adequate judgment concerning underlying problems.

In some respects those handling the foundational materials are in the position of many peacemakers who find themselves turned upon by both parties to a dispute which they attempt to mediate. Their task is to bring the disciplines of the academic community to bear functionally on the problems of the educational practitioner. Yet from the side of the practitioners there is evidence of a revolt against an intellectual approach,[30] while from the side of the learned disciplines there are serious threats of alienation. The support given to Bestor's attack on public education and the educationists by the five hundred respected scholars reported to have signed the petition backing his argument before the American Historical Association's 1952 convention is an example of this latter threat.[31]

If educational theory fails to have the support of either the academic departments upon whose disciplines it depends, or of the practitioners with whose problems it is concerned, it is apparent that something is critically wrong with the theory, the academicians, the practitioners, or with all three.

Education for technical competency.—Implicit in the above discussion was the idea that educational theory operates in two dimensions. The theory which is of special concern to the foundations areas is that which serves as a base for educational policy decisions. These decisions are involved in such activities as designing the curriculum, grouping students, determining the nature of special treatment required by atypical students, and relating the educational program to the community. Foundational theory should provide a series of sensitivities and understandings which the teacher carries in mind as background for his policy decisions, but which will probably not provide a blueprint for technique. In this sense it is liberal rather than technical theory.

There is, however, a dimension of theory which is more directly related to how to teach. Educational research and experimentation have

[30] E. Graham Pogue, "Improving Undergraduate Programs of Teacher Education," *Addresses on Current Issues in Higher Education,* National Conference on Higher Education (Washington, D.C.: National Education Association, 1951), pp. 177–182.

[31] "Schools Criticized for Basic Learning," *The New York Times,* December 28, 1952.

resulted in a vast body of information on techniques of lesson organization and presentation, of group activity, of test construction and administration, and of teaching many skills and subjects. This body of technical theory has constituted the content of courses in general methods of teaching and in special methods of teaching specific levels or subjects.

Some foundational materials do function both technically and liberally, as has been suggested. Yet the distinction between the two functions of theory is important, not because either is more valuable than the other or because they are mutually exclusive, but because if the distinction is neglected the total value of educational theory is reduced.

One of the traditionally most provocative problems has been that of relating instruction in technique to the practical experience held by everyone to be important in developing technical competency. Currently, there are few areas in teacher education about which there is less basic controversy. Few teacher educators today would quarrel with Snyder's statement that "As to techniques of teaching, these can be learned effectively only in the classroom. Courses of method divorced from practice are notoriously ineffective." [32]

Snyder went on to suggest that the "cooperating teacher" is the teacher of techniques and that the study of principles underlying method and of method itself should grow out of the practical classroom experience. The wide acceptance of this position has led to an extensive development of programs for off-campus student teaching and for apprenticeship. This element of teacher education has become, perhaps, the most rapidly growing edge in the whole movement.[33]

Direct-experience programs around which is organized instruction in principles and techniques of teaching have become the heart of technical education for teachers. However, those responsible for such programs have broader ambitions than to serve only in this technical function. The use of direct experience as the core of the entire collegiate program, certainly of the entire professional program, is being seriously explored. The question of whether or not the traditional preoccupation

---

[32] Agnes Snyder, "Conflicting Points of View," p. 246.

[33] See Association for Student Teaching, *Off-Campus Student Teaching*, 1951 Yearbook of the Association for Student Teaching (Lock Haven, Pa.: The Association, 1951); and American Association of Teachers Colleges, *School and Community Laboratory Experiences in Teacher Education* (Oneonta, N.Y.: The Association, 1945), for examples of developments in this field.

of such programs with technical, and even illiberal, concerns can be escaped seems to be a major one.

The uses of direct-experience programs.—The thinking of many people concerned with direct experience in teacher education has been explained by Florence B. Stratemeyer of Teachers College, Columbia University, as follows:

Studies in the field of psychology and human growth and development point out that what is learned in a situation is in terms of the elements in the situation to which the learner *responds* and which he uses in other situations. That to which the individual responds in a situation is that which has or can have *meaning* for him in terms of his *purposes*. For an experience to have meaning for the learner two things are necessary: (1) the learner must have had sufficient experience related to the situation at hand so that when the situation is presented he recognizes it, and (2) he must be mature enough so that he can be helped to deal with the situation with some degree of satisfaction to himself.

The first factor has special significance for direct experience in the professional program for teachers. The danger of meaningless verbalization is especially marked in the case of the prospective teacher since he has had so little previous experience with the ideas and concepts with which he is dealing in the professional program.[34]

Growing out of this basic position have been proposals for giving a vastly extended role to direct experience throughout the collegiate program. The currently developing experimental curriculum at Adelphi College is indicative. This plan provides for travel and for periods of work in communities. Around such experiences learning is organized. How much time should be devoted to such programs and the relative effectiveness of direct as opposed to vicarious experience in specific cases are major problems which will demand continuing attention.[35]

Historically, as will be seen, the concept of laboratory experience has sometimes been differentiated from that of apprenticeship. The basis of the distinction has been that the laboratory experience functions liberally to provide a broader understanding of basic principles, while an

[34] Florence B. Stratemeyer, "The Expanding Role of Direct Experience in Professional Education," Association for Student Teaching, *Off-Campus Student Teaching*, pp. 5–6.

[35] Arthur I. Gates, in "Language Activities as Experience," *Teachers College Record*, 54:417–423 (May, 1953), has noted the inadequacies and dangers of the common distinction, in terms of reality, between "direct" and "vicarious" experience. He suggests that this distinction, which is leading to a de-emphasis of language activities in the educative process, may have been pushed to the point where sound educational policy is threatened.

apprenticeship program focuses on the development of routine technical skills. The question of whether the newly developing direct-experience programs will be of the laboratory or the apprenticeship nature according to this distinction is the crucial one. There is no doubt that many of their advocates hope for the former.

The tradition of direct experience in teacher education is one which focuses on the training school technique, and this tradition continues strong. The previously cited *Bulletin* of the New Jersey State Teachers College at Montclair, for example, states as one of the "fundamental principles" that "The demonstration school should be the laboratory and integrating center of all courses and all curricula." While technical theory can well be expected to prove itself in the classrooms of the demonstration school, the wisdom of expecting foundational theory and general education to do so on a short-term basis remains doubtful. The continued effort to broaden the base of direct experience by providing for participation in such matters as faculty meetings, community surveys, industrial work, and work in nonschool youth agencies seems more promising.

Summary

In current attitudes toward general education, toward the relationship of the general to the professional sequence, and toward the professional sequence itself, issues have been noted in which the relationship of the liberal to the technical function of teacher education is involved. Contemporary decisions concerning these issues are being made in differing climates of opinion, in each of which historically rooted convictions loom large. It is the purpose of the ensuing chapters to help objectify some of these historical forces which operate unnoticed in institutions and individuals.

chapter TWO

American Teacher Education
Prior to 1865

TEACHER EDUCATORS VARY IN THEIR SENSITIVITY TO THE UNDERLYING forces which move society. Yet inevitably they reflect these forces, and their thoughts must be judged accordingly. The formative years of the American normal school called for innovation in many dimensions of life, particularly in our formal educational institutions.

General Forces Influencing
Educational Thought

This is not a story of beginnings. Indeed, the significant issues and practices in teacher education are so deeply rooted in the Western tradition that one can but arbitrarily choose a point at which to pick up certain threads from a most involved pattern.

Those threads which deal specifically with the beginnings of formal teacher education in Europe and America have been traced again and again. A recognition of the work of Ratich, whose pedagogical seminary is reported to have opened in 1619 at Koethen; of Jean Baptiste de la Salle, who established his Seminary for Schoolmasters at Rheims in 1684; and of Francke, whose Seminarium Praeceptorum was founded at Halle in 1696, is needed only to keep in mind the fact that American teacher education came late, and drew upon older European experiences.

In some respects the larger philosophical and educational tradition of the West is more directly related to this study. The classical concept of a liberal education, given early form by Plato and Aristotle, and elaborated, institutionalized, and even dogmatized in the ensuing centuries, provides at the same time great assets and major problems. The struggle to maintain and extend the vital values of this tradition in the face of an equally vital need to train competent specialists is the dilemma of modern education. Since this particular story of teacher education in America is but one phase of that larger struggle we will return to the American version of the liberal tradition again and again.

Most of the other thorny problems of educational philosophy which have risen have long traditions. Not the least of these is the basic question of *how one knows*. The relative roles and merits of reason, intuition, empirical observation, and faith in authority have occupied the attention of man for ages. When educationists in the early decades of the present century were arguing the relative importance of empirical science and philosophy in determining educational aims, they repeated arguments already old when formal American teacher education began. As early as 1651 Thomas Hobbes had expressed the idea that a science of human nature and conduct—as exact and rigorous as the science of physics—was possible. The line of thinking pioneered by Hobbes gave birth to many of the assumptions which have since been used by some sociologists and psychologists in trying to create an exact science of education.

THE EUROPEAN HERITAGE

When nineteenth-century American educationists argued, as they were wont to do, about the "true theory" of the normal school they betrayed their deep roots in the absolute philosophical idealism of European thought. When they raised questions about educational method and organization, here, too, they turned to European authorities.

In spite of differences in technical philosophy, Western civilization, at the time the American public school system was receiving its early impetus, showed unanimity on a number of basic issues. John Herman Randall has noted that the early beginnings of the intellectual chaos which marked the late nineteenth and the twentieth centuries were clearly discernable in the "trim and well-ordered alleys of the Enlightenment gardens." Nevertheless, he pointed to the existence of a "fairly definite, coherent, and systematically organized body of beliefs and ideals, to which the great majority of the intellectual classes gave assent." [1] Though the formative years of American teacher education cover the period of disintegration, there was some agreement previous to this period of chaos.

For example, the romantic protest against the Enlightenment did not in any serious manner challenge the faith of Europeans and Americans in the ultimate progress of mankind toward a better world. Moreover, whether men claimed to follow the path of pure reason, of faith, or of Newtonian science, they were led to conclude that the world and human life were governed by thoroughly reliable and unchanging laws, a true knowledge of which, once gained, could be depended upon as a guide to all human conduct. Finally, in most schools of thought at the beginning of the nineteenth century were found notable humanitarians willing to devote their efforts to the improvement of the conditions of living of the many.

The American scene was influenced by other than philosophical currents from Europe. The repeated social, political, and economic issues which Europe faced in the first half of the nineteenth century had important indirect effects on the development of American society. The constant influx of immigrants from abroad, the comparative freedom from the threat of attack, the intellectual stimulus of European political and economic controversy, and the growth of nationalistic fervor were reflected on this side of the Atlantic and had their bearings on our educational thought.

GENERAL POLITICAL AND SOCIAL CONDITIONS

The period around 1830 was clearly an agrarian period in America. In 1830 less than 7 per cent of our people lived in cities of more than

---

[1] John Herman Randall, Jr., *The Making of the Modern Mind* (Boston: Houghton Mifflin Company, 1940), p. 389.

eight thousand inhabitants, and by 1840 the figure had risen only to 8.5 per cent.[2] Yet it was a period in which the old patterns of economic organization were changing significantly, the old political philosophies were becoming inadequate, the traditional bodies of knowledge in the technical fields as well as in the humanities and the pure sciences were expanding at a phenomenal rate, and the social institutions—family, school, church, technology, and government—were already moving into eras of such rapid change that the old patterns would be scarcely recognizable a few decades later. The revolutionary liberalism of 1776, the oligarchic Federalism of Hamilton, and the "Arcadia" of Jeffersonian agrarians, were already either gone or in process of basic intellectual reorganization. The Jacksonian revolution, widely hailed as the emergence of the common man to power in America, was under way. Its dependence on class-conscious labor groups in the populous eastern states has seemed anachronous even to historians who have but recently recognized the great influence of these groups.[3]

The period after 1830 was one of great expansion. Under pressure of social and economic conditions in the older states, and aided by a liberal land policy and constantly increasing immigration, the western movement continued at great speed. The population increased from thirteen million in 1830 to seventeen million in 1840, and the total number of inhabitants increased by 35 per cent and 36 per cent respectively in the two decades following. Only a half-dozen American cities, concentrated on the Atlantic and Gulf coasts, had passed the twenty-five thousand mark in 1830. By 1860 such inland cities as Chicago, St. Louis, and Cincinnati had passed the hundred thousand mark.[4] Industry, agriculture, and commerce grew apace.

Critical political problems occupied the center of national attention. The slavery question, the Americanization of immigrants, the National Bank issue, territorial expansion, and tariff policies caused much concern. Each of these, of course, involved competing sectional and class interests, and each raised a question of the meaning and adequacy of the Federal Constitution.

In spite of this change and of these crucial problems, however, indi-

---

[2] Louis Hacker, *The Shaping of the American Tradition* (New York: Columbia University Press, 1947), p. 332.

[3] Arthur M. Schlesinger, Jr., *The Age of Jackson* (Boston: Little, Brown & Company, 1945), *passim*.

[4] Hacker, *op. cit.*, pp. 331-332, 455.

vidual Americans lived in a fairly coherent world. The church had recovered from its bout with eighteenth-century deism, and from the narrow confines of Edwardian Calvinism. God was seen as essentially benevolent and progress as obviously inevitable. Moreover, change occurred at a pace which still enabled the father to understand the world in which his son was growing. The family was still quite largely self-sufficient in most respects. The New England textile industry had turned to a factory system and had seen the birth of industrial capitalism by 1830, but the bulk of manufacturing was still being done on a cottage basis. Most of our economy was either mercantile or agrarian, rather than industrial, even as late as 1850. The government in Washington was still far removed from the daily life of the average citizen, although local issues, capable of being resolved by a public meeting of those involved, frequently arose. True, there was much ado at the time of national elections, and, in fact, very complex questions of economics and political science were sometimes involved. But these issues were easily reduced to slogans for the citizen, and if he voted wrong he was seldom highly conscious of any direct result in his day-by-day life. He lived most of his time in the neighborhood, which, save in the largest cities, was homogeneous and closely knit.

THE AMERICAN CHARACTER AND SOCIAL THOUGHT

Attempting to describe the American character has been a favorite pastime of visitors and natives for many generations. Only a few of the more pertinent characteristics need mention here. Ralph Barton Perry described the period under discussion as one of which the "harsh self-assertion of the individual" was partly characteristic.[5] He suggested further that it was also a period in which romantic humanitarianism "represented democracy's benevolent and universalistic aspect." The blending gave rise to a spreading movement for self-culture and for increased educational opportunity for all classes. The early normal school was partly the result of this movement.

Another central feature of the American character in the Jacksonian era, and the ensuing ones, was that cited by Ralph Henry Gabriel when he said, "The core of American life was activism; citizens of the United

[5] Ralph Barton Perry, *Puritanism and Democracy* (New York: The Vanguard Press, 1944), p. 139.

States had little time or training for contemplation." [6] This "activism" covers a broad range of meanings. At one extreme is the philosophical attitude of a Peirce, James, or Dewey which insists that a theory has meaning only in terms of what happens when it is acted upon. At the other extreme this activism becomes openly anti-intellectual, hostile to theorizing of any kind, and totally unconcerned with "book-learning." It has characterized some Americans in every age.

As early as 1831, in the period when the normal school was being developed, Alexis de Tocqueville noted this activism and sought an explanation. Of the Americans he said:

Their strictly Puritanical Origin, their exclusively commercial habits, even the country they inhabit, which seems to divert their minds from the pursuit of science, literature, and the arts, the proximity of Europe, which allows them to neglect these pursuits without relapsing into barbarism, a thousand special causes, of which I have only been able to point out the most important, have singularly concurred to fix the mind of the American upon strictly practical objects.[7]

In further explanation, Tocqueville added:

Everyone is in motion, some in quest of power, others of gain. In the midst of this universal tumult, this incessant conflict of jarring interests, this continual striving of men after fortune, where is that calm to be found which is necessary for the deeper combinations of the intellect?

.   .   .   .

Men who live in democratic communities not only seldom indulge in meditation, but they naturally entertain very little esteem for it. A democratic state of society and democratic institutions keep the greater part of men in constant activity; and the habits of mind that are suited to an active life are not always suited to a contemplative one. *The man of action is frequently obliged to content himself with the best he can get because he would never accomplish his purpose if he chose to carry every detail to perfection. He has occasion perpetually to rely on ideas that he has not had leisure to search to the bottom; for he is much more frequently aided by the seasonableness of an idea than by its strict accuracy* [italics added]; and in the long run he risks less in making use of some false principles than in spending his time in establishing all his principles on the basis of truth. The world is not led by long or learned

[6] Ralph Henry Gabriel, *The Course of American Democratic Thought* (New York: Ronald Press Company, 1940), p. 26.

[7] Alexis de Tocqueville, *Democracy in America*, Phillips Bradley, ed. (New York: Alfred A. Knopf, Inc., 1945), Vol. II, pp. 36–37.

demonstrations; a rapid glance at particular incidents, the daily study of the fleeting passions of the multitude, the accidents of the moment, and the art of turning them to account decide all its affairs.[8]

Whether Tocqueville was right in considering this "activism" an inherent characteristic of democratic life or not, he did describe the action philosophy of many of the early normal school people. Forced, as they were, to compete with other interests for funds appropriated by the state legislatures and with other educational units for students, they lived close to the people and close to the moment. If the theoretical results of their policies were logically contradictory, adaptations were made only when the contradiction became evident in practice.

In so far as they had a conscious and systematic philosophy these early normal school men were idealists. Yet their habits of acting were, in common with those of most Americans, pragmatic.

American "activism" has, in many cases, gone to extremes of anti-intellectualism. Lawrence A. Cremin cited the effects of this tendency in opposition to the common school revival during the first half of the nineteenth century.[9] He considered the tendency "inherent in the equality of the frontier." Tocqueville noted that American equalitarianism compelled the privileged classes to mask the symbols of their opulence.[10] To some Americans in the century of the normal school a preoccupation with intellectual pursuits tended to be such a symbol— or else the mark of a fool. Merle Curti has documented this tendency by pointing out that learned men, particularly if they had political ambitions, often found it expedient to feign ignorance.[11]

It should be noted that the tendency toward anti-intellectualism was strongest among the rural groups and the lower economic and social classes from which the students of the normal schools, and later the teachers colleges, were largely recruited.

However, American equalitarianism did not consciously seek a leveling down process. While the laborer or the farmer might speak disdainfully of the classical intellectual education, and be suspicious of

[8] *Ibid.*, pp. 42–43.

[9] Lawrence A. Cremin, *The American Common School: An Historic Conception* (New York: Bureau of Publications, Teachers College, Columbia University, 1951), pp. 67, 120–121, 125.

[10] Tocqueville, *Democracy in America,* Vol. I, pp. 179–180.

[11] Merle Curti, *The Growth of American Thought* (New York: Harper and Brothers, 2nd ed., 1951), pp. 268–269.

those who talked in abstract terms, he insisted that his own children have access to this type of schooling.[12]

The typical nineteenth-century American was a man with a mission. To him, God had saved the American continent for a final noble experiment in liberty and self-government, which might well be the last best hope of man. "And this doctrine of the destiny of America," according to Gabriel, "held up before the humble democrat, whose drab world rarely extended beyond the main street of his village, a romantic vision in which he could see his inconspicuous efforts after righteousness invested with a world significance." [13]

This sense of mission, turned outward, frequently led to the boastfulness and ethnocentrism which foreign observers have considered characteristic of the American. It contributed to our aggressive attitude toward Mexico in the 1840's.

Turned inward, this sense of mission helped to make the first half of the nineteenth century one of reform in virtually all dimensions of life. There was a revival of the evangelical spirit in religion, and Americans were, perhaps, more self-consciously religious than at any subsequent period. Religious issues, of a bitter sort, were often involved in political and educational conflicts. Cremin has pointed to the desire to make good Christian Americans of both the new immigrant and the old resident as a major cause for the growth of the common school.[14]

The American of the early normal school era was aware that he faced an epoch of crisis—moral, political, and economic. Characteristically, he turned to education, and, as was his habit, he preferred to improvise new institutions rather than to reform the old.[15] The common school and the normal school were such institutions.

---

[12] See Cremin, *The American Common School*, pp. 41 and 121; and R. Freeman Butts and Lawrence A. Cremin, *A History of Education in American Culture* (New York: Henry Holt & Company, Inc., 1953), pp. 418–419. The latter points to the significant, though often unnoticed, fact that the Kalamazoo decision hinged on the question of using tax funds for a "classical" education. The affirmative decision thus confirmed the belief that all classes of citizens should have access to the "highest" type of education.

[13] Gabriel, *The Course of American Democratic Thought,* p. 25.

[14] Cremin, *The American Common School,* pp. 44–47.

[15] Ralph Barton Perry, in *Puritanism and Democracy,* pp. 210–211, has noted that "Instead of appealing to established institutions and profiting by their prestige, the American has been traditionally accustomed to improvise his social mechanisms, multiplying them or allowing them to lapse as the situation may require."

TENTATIVE BEGINNINGS OF AMERICAN
TEACHER EDUCATION

The thesis that teachers require a type of preparation somehow different from that provided other citizens, and that specialized institutional patterns are needed to furnish this preparation, gained acceptance in America largely between 1820 and 1865. Systematic programs to test this thesis awaited the foundation of public normal schools after 1839. There were, however, tentative but important beginnings earlier. For example, Benjamin Franklin is credited with having noted in 1750, that the country was "suffering at present very much for want of good Schoolmasters." One value seen in his proposed academy was that "a number of the poorer Sort will be hereby qualified to act as Schoolmasters." [16]

In the years following this suggestion a number of academies and colleges made some efforts specifically to prepare teachers. Among the earliest were Zion Parnassus Academy, near Salisbury, North Carolina (1785), and Westtown Boarding School (1799), Nazareth Hall (1807), and Washington College (1831), all in Pennsylvania. As the nineteenth century got under way a number of academies and small colleges offered special instruction for teachers.

It was in the Northeast that the American common school and the normal school first took root. They came with the renaissance in which New England found herself between 1830 and 1850. The leaders of this renaissance, men like Emerson and Thoreau, were the spokesmen of America's highest aspirations.

It is paradoxical that Americans—materialistic, anti-intellectual, and pragmatic—should flock by the thousands to the lyceum and the chautauqua to hear Emerson, their self-appointed critic, attack these characteristics. Yet in him they found expressed their basic faiths in equality, in individualism, and in progress. His emphasis on the unconquerable self, his tendency to consider social institutions relatively unimportant, and his glorification of a simple life close to the soil struck responsive

---

[16] *Minutes of the Common Council of Philadelphia, 1704–1776,* under date of July 31, 1750, quoted by Francis N. Thorpe in *Benjamin Franklin and the University of Pennsylvania,* U. S. Bureau of Education, Circular of Information, 1889, No. 2 (Washington, D.C.: Government Printing Office, 1889), pp. 245–246. The minutes do not record the actual authors. James P. Wickersham, in *A History of Education in Pennsylvania* (Lancaster, Pa.: Inquirer Publishing Company, 1886), p. 60, gives credit to Franklin but without documentation.

chords. The transcendentalist reign, though brief, gave impetus to the educational reform which swept from New England's shores to the West and South. It has been of lasting importance to American education.

However, it is a mistake to assume that all New England was motivated by high equalitarian principles. As late as 1838 Noah Webster was still pleading that the Federal Constitution be revised to give a permanent recognition of the distinction between rich and poor and to save the country from democracy by granting the rich a permanent role in government.[17]

The class structure of modern America had already begun to take shape in Massachusetts in 1830. The old leading families had established themselves through mercantile activities and were turning to industry. When George Bancroft, born of the "natural aristocracy" in New England, deserted the Whig Party to consort with wage earners "from the halls of infidelity and atheism," [18] there remained little doubt that issues of economic class had begun to burn in Boston.

Some leaders saw in the conditions of the Jacksonian and post-Jacksonian eras a crucial threat to the cohesiveness of the American community. In the face of this threat they conceived a school commonly attended by all groups and classes, commonly supported and controlled by the entire community, and providing the knowledge commonly required for Christian virtue and for economic and political competency.[19] Almost without exception the pioneers of the common school saw the need, in connection with it, of a special institution for the preparation of teachers for the new classrooms. [20]

---

[17] Noah Webster, *Letter to the Hon. Daniel Webster, on the Political Affairs of the United States,* cited by Arthur Schlesinger, Jr., in *The Age of Jackson,* pp. 267–268.

[18] Quoted from the *Boston Atlas* by Schlesinger in *The Age of Jackson,* p. 163.

[19] This formulation of the common school ideal is from Cremin, *The American Common School,* pp. 81–82. Cremin's entire analysis of the forces which gave rise to the common school is highly pertinent to normal school history since the latter was intimately related to the former.

[20] See James G. Carter, "Outline of an Institution for the Education of Teachers," *Boston Patriot,* February 10, 15, 1825, reprinted by Henry Barnard in *Normal Schools, and Other Institutions, Agencies, and Means, Designed for the Professional Education of Teachers,* Part I (Hartford, Conn.: Case, Tiffany and Co., 1851), pp. 91–100; Calvin E. Stowe, "Normal Schools and Teachers Seminaries," *Common Schools and Teachers Seminaries* (Boston: Marsh, Capen, Lyon and Webb, 1839); and Horace Mann, "Remarks at the Dedication of the Bridgewater State Normal School," *Educational Writings of Horace Mann,* Vol. V of

In response to these conditions Samuel R. Hall opened his private normal school at Concord, Vermont, in 1823. Shortly thereafter, in 1827, James G. Carter opened a similar school at Lancaster, Massachusetts. In 1834 New York State provided grants of public money to promote professional teacher education in the academies. Finally, in response to the untiring efforts of such men as James G. Carter, Charles Brooks, Calvin Stowe, Horace Mann, and Edmund Dwight, Massachusetts established, in 1839, the first of the public single-purpose normal schools.

Critical decisions concerning the relationship of these schools to the common schools and to the colleges were made in these early years. The pattern chosen has been profoundly important in the whole atmosphere and program of professional teacher education since that time. To understand why the particular choice was made and some of the consequences of that choice it is necessary to look at the conflicting conceptions of general education which were then held.

The Concept of General Education

In America's pre-Civil War period the gradation of elementary school, secondary school, and college was ill-defined. The professional preparation of teachers on every level, from the immediate post-elementary school to the college, was responsibly advocated. Prevailing concepts of general or liberal education at each of these levels must, therefore, be considered.

THE CONSERVATIVE COLLEGE AND THE
CULTIVATION OF INTELLECT

In 1828 the Fellows of Yale College, under pressure to provide a more practical education and to relax the emphasis on the "dead" languages, asked their faculty for an opinion about the need to revise the curriculum. The Report of the Faculty,[21] in response to this assign-

---

The Life and Works of Horace Mann, Mary Mann, ed. (Boston: Lee and Shepard, 1891), p. 219.

[21] Yale Faculty, "Original Papers in Relation to a Course of Liberal Education," *The American Journal of Science and Arts,* 15:(2)297–351 (January, 1829). This report is in two parts; the first, from which the extracts here used were taken, was written by President Jeremiah Day, the second by Professor James L. Kingsley.

ment, provides a classic statement of the purposes and meaning of collegiate education as conceived by the conservative college. It has been recognized as describing the ideas which tended to dominate American higher education until nearly the end of the last century.[22]

The type of person which the Yale faculty hoped to develop would have had many of the qualities sought by all modern educators. They wanted to train people to habits of concentration, of nicely balancing evidence, and of thoroughly controlling an awakened imagination. "The great object of a collegiate education," according to President Jeremiah Day, ". . . is to give that expansion and balance of mental powers, those liberal and comprehensive views, and those fine proportions of character, which are not to be found in him whose ideas are always confined to one particular channel." [23]

The goals explicitly sought by Yale were exclusively intellectual, and intellect was defined in terms of faculty psychology and conceived of as being developed by formal discipline. The objective of each offering in the curriculum was to discipline a specific power of the mind. The value of a subject was found primarily neither in its contribution to the immediate solution of problems nor in its appeal to the interest of the student, but in its use in training the intellectual faculties. The powers to be developed were conceived of as limited in number, and the proper subjects for their training were thought to be clearly known. A one-to-one relationship between each subject offered and the specific mental power thereby cultivated was implied. The subjects offered were mostly the traditional ones.[24]

The report did recognize that new sciences were being developed and

[22] For a detailed analysis, see R. Freeman Butts, *The College Charts Its Course: Historic Conceptions and Current Proposals* (New York: McGraw-Hill Book Company, Inc., 1939), pp. 118–125; see also Richard Hofstadter and C. DeWitt Hardy, *The Development and Scope of Higher Education in the United States*, published for the Commission on Financing Higher Education (New York: Columbia University Press, 1952), pp. 15–16.

[23] Yale Faculty, "Original Papers," pp. 308–309.

[24] It should be noted that in many respects the liberal arts college has been profoundly concerned with moral training, training in the social graces, and the development of wholesome personalities. It has attempted to secure these ends by a multitude of practices—compulsory chapel and control of nonclass activities, for example—many of which have been poorly integrated with the instructional program itself. It seems a bit misleading, therefore, that in designing and defending their course of study the Yale faculty, and many who have followed, operated so largely in terms of training the faculties of intellect. The cultivation of intellect, which was ideally considered only instrumental to character development, seems to have become in fact the end-in-itself.

that there was need for periodic reviews of the curriculum. The recently added courses in chemistry, mineralogy, geology, and political economy were cited as evidence of Yale's responsiveness to this need.

The Yale faculty thought of their program as providing general education for the leadership classes in all areas of vocation. It was recognized that the traditional college program had been considered preparatory especially for the higher professions. However, the report insisted that the program offered and the goals sought at Yale were equally needed by leaders among the farmers, merchants, and manufacturers.

The spirit of the entire report was hostile to any modification in the interest of specific occupational preparation. It was argued that the consideration of professional problems and duties before the liberal concepts were firmly planted would prevent the latter's ever taking root. President Day insisted that once a man entered the practice of his profession his mind was necessarily given over to these duties, leaving little energy for the cultivation of liberal views unless the habit of such cultivation was already firmly fixed.

In the college catalogue for 1829–1830 the Yale faculty again stressed the idea that "The object, in a proper collegiate department, is not to teach that which is peculiar to any one of the *professions;* but to lay the foundation which is common to them all."

Noting the existence of professional schools of law, theology, and medicine, the catalogue pointed out that the undergraduate course was not intended to interfere with these. On the contrary, it was argued:

It [the undergraduate course] contains those subjects only which ought to be understood by everyone who aims at a thorough education. The principles of science and literature are the common foundation of all high intellectual attainments. They give that furniture [factual knowledge] and discipline, and elevation of mind, which are the best preparation for the study of a profession, or of the operations which are peculiar to the higher mercantile, manufacturing, or agricultural establishments.[25]

BEGINNINGS OF COLLEGIATE REFORM

Under the influence of Yale, Princeton, and others, the conservative point of view continued to dominate collegiate education in America

[25] *Catalogue of the Officers and Students in Yale College, 1829–30* (New Haven, Conn.: Baldwin and Treadway, Printers), pp. 27–28.

until after the Civil War. Nevertheless, there were important early efforts to make the program more functional and more responsive to the changing demands of American life. During the period in which the normal school took root the possibility of such a reorientation seems to have been significant.

The idea that a single list of subjects, well insulated from utilitarian considerations, was needed to provide liberally educated people had been under attack by Thomas Jefferson since his affiliation with William and Mary in 1779. By 1825 his ideas bore some fruit in the new University of Virginia.

Jefferson was joined in 1825 by George Ticknor who, under the influence of recent developments in the German universities, began to experiment with an elective program at Harvard. Ticknor's early reforms were continued by Josiah Quincy, although a more conservative trend set in at Harvard after 1846.[26] The seed planted by Ticknor really flourished in the later regime of President Charles W. Eliot.

The work of Jefferson and Ticknor was significant in a number of ways. For one thing they added to the curriculum a number of subjects, especially in the natural sciences, whose obvious utility would help to undercut the old idea that subjects pursued for their usefulness had no liberalizing value. Moreover, once the university research ideal was introduced, it inevitably led to an expansion of knowledge which could not conceivably be encompassed in a single prescribed curriculum. Even by the time the normal schools were established the hope that collegiate students could adequately study all the higher branches of learning was vain.

In the first half of the nineteenth century a number of colleges followed the tentative leads of Harvard and the University of Virginia. R. Freeman Butts has illustrated this trend with examples from fifteen different colleges.[27] One of the most influential reformers in this movement was Francis Wayland of Brown University, whose vision of teacher education and of higher education in general was most advanced.

Wayland, like virtually all thinkers of his time, accepted the concept of formal discipline and faculty psychology which ran through the Yale report. He had the same concern for "generous knowledge and vigorous

---

[26] For a discussion of the early efforts of Jefferson, Ticknor, and others, see Butts, *The College Charts Its Course*, Chapter VI.
[27] *Ibid.*, pp. 131–155.

mental discipline." Yet he deeply challenged the argument that the same liberal course was equally satisfactory for all occupations. The colleges, as then organized, were, according to him, "merely schools preparatory to entrance upon some one of the professions." [28]

Wayland argued that, though the colleges provided adequate pre-professional training for the professions around whose needs its curriculum had grown, they were of little service to the rest of the community. He saw the "very choicest portions" of the community—the merchant, mechanic, and manufacturer—as having no place to send their sons for an adequate higher education. He proposed the establishment of liberal education programs specifically tailored to the needs of these other groups. Such programs, Wayland thought, should parallel the traditional one.

The attacks of Wayland and others on the traditional collegiate idea of general liberal education implicitly denied (1) that there was a single course of study uniquely suited to the liberal function of education, (2) that liberal education beyond the academy and the common school was needed only by the so-called higher professions, and (3) that functional or practical courses were inevitably illiberal. Such thinking among college leaders necessarily preceded the development of functionally oriented general education programs in which professional considerations were deliberately brought into the design of the total collegiate program.

THE ACADEMY CONCEPT OF GENERAL EDUCATION

Such men as Jefferson, Ticknor, and Wayland strove to make the collegiate program more directly functional in the lives of those aspiring to vocational goals other than the professions. At the same time other leaders of the American community turned to the academy. This institution, which had deep historical roots in the courtly academies of the Renaissance and in the "dissenter's academies" of the English Puritans, had among its most effective supporters Benjamin Franklin and the Phillips family. Franklin's 1749 "Proposals Relating to the Education of Youth in Pennsylvania" [29] and the Phillips Academies at And-

---

[28] Francis Wayland, *Thoughts on the Present Collegiate System in the United States* (Boston: Gould, Kendall and Lincoln, 1842), p. 143.

[29] Benjamin Franklin, "Proposals Relating to the Education of Youth in Pennsylvania," cited by Edgar W. Knight and Clifton L. Hall in *Readings in American Educational History* (New York: Appleton-Century-Crofts, Inc., 1951), pp. 74–80.

over and Exeter provided patterns for many subsequent schools of this type.[30]

The academy was designed by Franklin, as stated in his "Proposals," to provide an opportunity for students to learn "those things that are likely to be *most useful* and *most ornamental*. Regard being had to the several Professions for which they are intended." [31]

Neither Franklin nor the Phillipses were unconcerned with the development of intelligence. However, neither defined the function of their academy in terms of the development of intellectual faculties alone. To Franklin the usefulness of a subject was a prime recommendation. For example, though he extolled the beauty of the classics and the pleasure of reading them, he insisted only on their being studied by those who could turn them to professional use.

This emphasis on utility is not so clear cut in the constitution of the Phillips Academies, where college preparation was somewhat emphasized. Nevertheless, the curriculum was also designed to be functional for those having nonprofessional vocational goals. Moreover, the important aims of the institution were stated in terms of character and moral attitudes rather than of intellectual faculties. The *first* and *principal object* of the academy was, according to John and Samuel Phillips, "the promotion of true piety and virtue."

The academy was the earliest logical extension of the common school program, and in many states it was subsidized as part of that system. Ultimately it became a high school, either making way for the public secondary school or developing into an independent preparatory school. It was also, as noted above, the predecessor of the normal school and the major rival of that institution until after the Civil War.

The New England high school was, in its beginning, a public academy. It was founded in recognition of the fact that the college and the college preparatory grammar school did not provide the type of education needed by many students. Thus the committee which recommended the formation of the Boston English Classical School, commonly recognized as the first public high school, reported:

The mode of education now adopted, and the branches of knowledge that are taught at our English grammar schools, are not sufficiently ex-

---

[30] *The Constitution of the Phillips Academy in Andover* (Andover, Mass.: Flagg and Gould, 1828), contains a statement of the purposes of this academy as conceived by the founders.

[31] Franklin, "Proposals," pp. 76–77.

tensive nor otherwise calculated to bring the powers of mind into operation nor to qualify a youth to fill usefully and respectably many of those
stations, both public and private, in which he may be placed. A parent
who wishes to give a child an education that shall fit him for active
life, and shall serve as a foundation for eminence in his profession,
whether Mercantile or Mechanical, is under the necessity of giving him
a different education from any which our public schools can now
furnish. Hence, many children are separated from their parents and
sent to private academies in this vicinity, to acquire that instruction
which cannot be obtained at the public seminaries.[32]

Here again the emphasis was on the useful subjects, and the idea
of developing intellectual faculties without respect to the functional
value of the curriculum received less stress. While college preparation
soon became one of their major functions, the high schools were also
thought of as alternatives to college. They were designed to provide
terminal education for many of their students, and such education had
both its liberal and technical functions.

THE COMMON SCHOOL AND GENERAL EDUCATION

To a significant extent it seems accurate to think of the public educational systems of New England as having been dual systems in the
early decades of the nineteenth century. It is quite true that the lower
grades of the common school fed students into the high school or academy from which some went into the colleges. Nevertheless, the secondary schools and colleges tended to constitute something of a closed circle
so far as educational theory and purpose were concerned. Teachers
for the secondary schools were very largely recruited from the colleges, and the college preparatory function very quickly came to dominate these schools. Moreover, there was, at the time the normal school
movement started, a general feeling that secondary and higher education were designed to train only the leaders of society and those who
had some special interests or abilities.

The common school, on the other hand, was at first thought to have
responsibility only for that training which was universally needed by
citizens of the United States. There was constant pressure to expand
the curriculum, but in the early period the only subjects whose inclusion brought general agreement were the so-called "common

---

[32] Minutes of the Boston School Committee, 1821, cited by Ellwood P. Cubberley in *Readings in Public Education in the United States* (Boston: Houghton
Mifflin Company, 1934), p. 229.

branches"—the three R's, plus spelling, geography, grammar, and, perhaps, a bit of physiology, history, and ethics or religion.[33] To this system and curriculum the normal school was originally tied. Just as the secondary school and college formed an inbred system feeding on itself, so, too, did the elementary and normal school. Students tended to go directly to the normal school after a few years of elementary education and then return to teach in the lower grades.

A teacher-preparing institution must be close enough to the school which it serves to understand the problems involved and to provide opportunities for practical experience. Such a relationship does not, however, demand that the prospective teacher limit his general education to that of the lower school. Yet, partly by force of circumstance and partly by the deliberate intent of some school leaders, such a limitation resulted in the early normal schools.[34]

Many of the normal school people opposed this limitation. For example, Nicholas Tillinghast, the first principal of the Bridgewater (Massachusetts) Normal School described his ideal to Henry Barnard as follows:

My idea of a Normal School is, that it should have a term of four years; that those studies should be pursued that will lay a *foundation* on which to build an education. I mean, for example, that algebra should be thoroughly studied as the foundation for arithmetic, [and] that geometry and trigonometry should be studied, by which, with algebra, to study natural philosophy. . . .[35]

Another who bowed reluctantly to the exclusive emphasis on elementary subject matter was William F. Phelps, the first principal of the Trenton (New Jersey) State Normal School. He was to be heard many

---

[33] See Cremin, *The American Common School*, pp. 64–72. Cremin's analysis covers only the original formulation of the ideal, which was rather quickly extended, especially in the West, to include the high school and the state university. One reason why western normal schools more quickly and generally turned to the training of secondary as well as of elementary school teachers might be that a more extended concept of the common school prevailed in this area where private higher education had not so thoroughly dominated the secondary school.

[34] Some teacher educators have held that elementary subjects treated in terms of their organizational logic and with the thought of their being later retaught are essentially and profoundly different from the same subjects as presented in the elementary school. To those holding this position the manner of treatment rather than the content determines the level of intellectual challenge. To the extent that this position is accurate the above classification of normal school general education as elementary is unfair.

[35] Henry Barnard, *Normal Schools*, Pt. I, p. 80.

times repeating the plaintive cry, "How are you to teach them how to teach that of which they know nothing?" [36]

The first report of Phelps to the trustees of the Trenton school revealed the sharp conflict between hope and stark reality.[37] The curriculum he proposed included a number of the so-called "higher branches" which were usually offered in the academies and colleges. These included algebra, geometry, natural science (chemistry, geology, and physics), and moral philosophy. This was surely not an overly ambitious hope. Yet, when Phelps came to describing the instruction actually provided, it was limited, so far as general education was concerned, to spelling and word analysis, reading and elocution, arithmetic, geography, drawing, and music.

School people did not all consider the stress on the lower branches unfortunate from the standpoint of general education. On the contrary, Horace Mann, for example, thought it essential. In his 1839 *Annual Report* he noted that the enrollment of the Massachusetts normals could have been greatly increased had they been willing to add instruction in such subjects as algebra, geometry, astronomy, and chemistry. Of their refusal to do so he said:

One of the most cheering auguries in regard to our schools is the unanimity with which the committees have awarded sentence of condemnation against the practice of introducing into them the studies of the university to the exclusion or neglect of the rudimental branches. By such a practice a pupil foregoes all the stock of real knowledge he might otherwise acquire; and he receives, in its stead, only a show or counterfeit of knowledge, which, with all intelligent persons, only renders his ignorance more conspicuous. . . . For these and similar considerations, it seems that the first intellectual qualification of a teacher is a critical thoroughness, both in rules and principles, in regard to all the branches required by law to be taught in the Common Schools; and a power of recalling them in any of their parts with a promptitude and certainty hardly inferior to that with which he could tell his own name.[38]

[36] American Normal School Association, *American Normal Schools, Their Theory, Their Workings, and Their Results, as Embodied in the Proceedings of the First Annual Convention of the American Normal School Association* (New York: A. S. Barnes and Burr, 1860), p. 43.

[37] William F. Phelps, "Report of the Principal," *First Annual Report of the Board of Trustees of the New Jersey State Normal School to the Legislature for the Year, 1855* (Philadelphia: King and Baird, Printers, 1856), pp. 20–79.

[38] Horace Mann, "Report for 1839," *Annual Reports of the Secretary of the Board of Education* (Boston: Rand and Avery Co., 1868), p. 60.

These common branches, when taught in the manner of the normal school, were thought by some to yield the same type of intellectual discipline claimed for the classical languages in the colleges. Phelps, although he consistently decried the low academic standards of the normal schools, nevertheless stated as a major premise of the normal school curriculum ". . . the conviction that a thorough and scientific knowledge of the so-called Elementary Branches, is absolutely essential to good scholarship, and that *they are better adapted when properly used, to secure those habits of attention, order and method* so conducive to the future progress of the pupil, *than any other means* [italics added] at the disposal of the teacher." [39]

The theories of faculty psychology were easily applied to the common branches. Thus Phelps's Board of Trustees at Trenton explained that the "true principles" of arithmetic were there unfolded so that students were freed from dependence on a multiplicity of technical rules. The utility of learning these principles was found not so much in the knowledge of arithmetic gained, "as in being the means of disciplining the mind, of cultivating the habit of attention, and of developing the faculties of abstraction and of reasoning." [40]

In a sense the common branches may, in fact, have provided a more adequate general education for teachers of the pre-Civil War era than does that offered in colleges preparing teachers for service in contemporary society. These were times when social problems were comparatively simpler and where nonschool agencies of education were far more adequate. Tocqueville, in attempting to explain the practical wisdom of the American and his understanding of political institutions, described this time as one in which:

> The citizen of the United States does not acquire his practical science and his positive notions from books; the instruction he has acquired may have prepared him for receiving those ideas, but it did not furnish them. The American learns to know the laws by participating in the act of legislation; and he takes a lesson in forms of government from governing. The great work of society is ever going on before his eyes and, as it were, under his eyes.[41]

[39] William F. Phelps, "Report of the Principal," *Second Annual Report of the Board of Trustees of the New Jersey State Normal School, to the Legislature, for the Year Ending February Ninth, 1857* (Trenton, N.J.: Printed at the Office of the "True American," 1857), pp. 113–114.

[40] *Ibid.,* p. 20; also see above, pp. 37 to 39, Yale Faculty, "Original Papers."

[41] Tocqueville, *Democracy in America,* Vol. I, p. 318.

In any case Horace Mann and other advocates of the normal school and the common school seemed confident that these lower branches provided adequate general education. In Massachusetts alone a number of distinguished Americans supported the movement. They noted that the curriculum was to concentrate primarily on the elementary branches, yet they had apparently great faith that well-prepared teachers for the citizen body would emerge. Those holding this opinion included Edward Everett, then governor of Massachusetts, and possibly William E. Channing, and Daniel Webster.[42]

It has been frequently charged that Mann and his followers were misled by their enthusiasm for the Prussian normal school system into establishing American professional teacher education on an elementary and, hence, superficial basis. The most prominent of those who have recently maintained this position is Charles H. Judd,[43] but the argument goes back well into the nineteenth century. In fact, Mann's opponents in the Massachusetts legislature accused him of trying to Prussianize the school system as early as 1840.[44]

Mann met the charge by granting that the Prussians had perverted the great instrument of public education to despotic ends. Yet he saw their success in creating despotism as evidence of the power of education. Under republican institutions where the spirit of liberty prevailed he insisted that it could be made "one of the noblest instrumentalities for rearing a nation of free men." [45]

However, Prussian teacher education had a social class basis which Mann apparently failed to perceive; and the normal schools whose pattern he chose were those designed to train teachers from the lower class *for* the lower class. The Prussian teachers' seminaries took students directly from the *volksschule,* the lower-class school, trained them thoroughly in techniques of teaching and in the common branches, and sent them back to teach under the supervision of the clergy. The lat-

---

[42] Edward Everett, "An Address at the Opening of the Normal School at Barre, September 5, 1839," Barnard, *Normal Schools,* Pt. I, pp. 179–194; William E. Channing, "Remarks of William E. Channing on Education and Teachers," *ibid.,* pp. 115–122; and "Proceedings of an Educational Convention in Plymouth Country in 1833," *ibid.,* pp. 154–156.

[43] Charles H. Judd, "Should University Schools of Education Cease To Exist?," *School and Society,* 62:141–142 (September 1, 1945), and *The Evolution of a Democratic School System* (Boston: Houghton Mifflin Company, 1918).

[44] *Massachusetts House of Representatives Document No. 49, 1840,* p. 3.

[45] Mann, "Report for 1843," *Annual Reports of the Secretary of the Board of Education* (Boston: Rand and Avery Co., 1868), p. 242.

ter, having been trained in the *gymnasium* and the university, generally represented a higher social class.

Mann and others were impressed by the status of the schoolmaster whose prestige among the Prussian masses did seem great. This prestige was derived partly from the fact that schoolmasters were state officials and that they were among the few lower-class people who held such positions.

At the time of Mann's visit to Prussia liberal Germans were quite aware that the schoolmaster was trained for a lower-class role. I. L. Kandel has described them as already arguing that future teachers must have an intellectual training not limited to the subjects which were taught in the elementary school. These Germans insisted, according to Kandel, that "The teacher of the future must be taught to think and not trained as a machine." [46]

It is interesting to note that by the time Mann became president of Antioch College in 1853 he had apparently come to believe that college-level education was required by a vastly greater number of people. Perhaps by this time he would have been less content with the elementary nature of the normal curriculum. He argued that

Another respect, in which our College is bound to meet the advanced and advancing wants, is in the solidity and breadth of the foundation which it lays, not only for the professions, but for all the business vocations of afterlife. It requires a vast deal more knowledge now to give a man a respectable and safe standing in any condition of life than it did a few years ago.[47]

The decision of Horace Mann and others to support a general education program which was primarily that of the elementary school was based on many factors besides their faith in German teacher education practice. The realities of the educational situation combined to make exalted visions of professional teacher education seem farfetched. These

[46] I. L. Kandel, *The Training of Elementary School Teachers in Germany,* Contributions to Education, No. 31 (New York: Bureau of Publications, Teachers College, Columbia University, 1910), pp. 11–12.

[47] Horace Mann, "Demands of the Age on Colleges," *Life and Works,* Vol. V, p. 410. The present author suspects that when Mann and political leaders like Edward Everett placed such emphasis on the "common branches" in the normal school they were motivated by the political necessity to reassure the academies and colleges that the normal school was not a competitor. To the extent that this is true a theory developed on the basis of political expediency gave form to a major educational agency.

realities included the low salary and low social status of the elementary school teacher, the inadequate supply of teachers with any specialized training, the competition among public agencies for state support at a time when governmental budgets were very limited, the uncertain success of the idea of universal, free, public education, and an exalted view of the potentiality of the school combined with a naïve view of educational and social theory. Moreover, the attitude of the academic community and the prevailing concepts of the ideal relationships between general and professional education (which will be discussed shortly) tended to force a close allegiance between the lower schools and the normal school.

The normal school was thus doomed to modest beginnings in practice. What was to be important to history, however, was the vision toward which it moved. In respect to general education we have seen that three alternative theories were available: (1) that of the conservative college which stressed formal discipline and insisted on the continued use of the classical languages and the traditionally non-utilitarian liberal arts, (2) the more flexible position, closely related to the rationale of the early academy and high school, of college reformers anxious to use the newly developing scientific and practical subjects on openly utilitarian as well as on disciplinary grounds, and (3) the theory of the Prussian teachers' seminary which restricted the curriculum largely to the common branches and depended on the very thorough and analytical treatment given such subjects to provide the mental discipline considered necessary. We have noted that those who selected the latter position by choice, as opposed to such men as Phelps and Tillinghast who merely bowed to the apparently inevitable, originally considered the common branches adequate to the task of educating for American citizenship and Christian morality.

The Relationship of the General
to the Professional Sequence

From the very beginning of formal teacher education in America there were several clear-cut points of view concerning the relationship of the general to the professional sequence. In this section we will examine three of these positions.

THE GENERAL AND THE PROFESSIONAL
AS DISCRETE SEQUENCES

The position of the conservative college and academy.—We have already noted the position of the Yale faculty which held that liberal education was possible only if the student were free from the immediate demands of vocational preparation. According to this view, that which is now called the general education sequence would have to be finished before professional considerations were allowed into the program.

This ideal was clear cut. One went to college for liberal education, after which he turned to the professional school or to apprenticeship for occupational training. Well-defined and rationalized, this view provides one of the most nearly fixed points in the history of American educational thought.

In the early period the leaders of the conservative colleges did not consider teaching a profession for which specialized training was needed. Pedagogy, as a proper subject for research, did not gain recognition in the major universities or colleges until the post-Civil War era. The technique of teaching was thought by those holding the perennialist view to be an art best developed by apprenticeship. When the need for professional instruction was accepted, however, these people naturally placed it in the pattern previously set for older professional schools.

The position which dominated colleges in the conservative tradition was also held by many of their graduates who taught in the better grammar schools, the high schools, and the academies. This group included some of the bitterest enemies of the normal school movement.[48]

The ideal of a strictly professional normal school.—The conservative liberal arts advocates were anxious to keep the general and professional sequences apart in order to preserve the purity of the liberal arts from what they considered the taint of professionalism. Some of

---

[48] Opposition to the normal schools, based partly on this attitude, was involved in the complex and acrimonious dispute between a group of thirty-one Boston schoolmasters and Horace Mann, growing out of the latter's "Report for 1843." See *Remarks on the Seventh Annual Report of the Hon. Horace Mann, Secretary of the Massachusetts Board of Education* (Boston: Charles C. Little and James Brown, 1844); and Horace Mann, *Reply to the "Remarks of the Thirty-One Boston Schoolmasters on the Seventh Annual Report of the Secretary of the Massachusetts Board of Education* (Boston: Wm. B. Fowle and Nahum Capen, 1844). Three other documents complete the series in this rather long-lived controversy.

the normal school people, in like spirit, argued that there must be a sharp separation in order that the normal school be free to concentrate on building teaching skill.

So long as normal school students were deficient even in mastery of the common elementary subjects it was obvious that instruction in these subjects must be provided. However, some of the normal school people believed that the "true theory" of the institution called for concentrating exclusively on professional education. The growing hope of these people was that students would complete their general education elsewhere. In this spirit the Salem (Massachusetts) Normal School urged prospective students to go first to another school, and added:

When you have thoroughly completed their courses of study and acquired maturity and discipline of mind, if you wish to become teachers, come to us, and engage for our brief term, with the aid and companionship of others having the same end in view, or already in the work, in the special study of the philosophy and art of teaching, and in the practical exercises tending to an immediate preparation for this noble work.[49]

Among those stressing this position as ideal in 1859 were Phelps and Richard Edwards.[50] Although Edwards later shifted his position, the "strictly professional" ideal was to gain increased strength in the 1870's and 1880's, as will be seen. These men shared the conviction of the conservative college that a single focus must dominate each sequence in the curriculum. In a sense, the purists from both sides— those wanting to protect general education from professionalism and those wanting to free professional education from the distraction of what they called academic subjects—were logical allies from the beginning. In addition to developing arguments which are still heard, they helped to strengthen verbal habits which tend to direct the thinking even of those who reject the purist theories. By 1865 teacher education circles habitually talked in terms of the "academic versus professional" dichotomy.

There were those in both college and normal school circles who, though accepting a distinction, refused to grant the opposition of the

[49] *Semi-Annual Report Made July 22, 1858, to the Board of Visitors for the Salem State Normal School,* quoted by Alpheus Crosby in "The Proper Sphere and Work of the American Normal School," American Normal School Association, *American Normal Schools,* p. 24.

[50] American Normal School Association, *American Normal Schools,* pp. 41–44, 73–77.

general to the professional sequence. There was also, among the normal school people, a group which considered the distinction itself undesirable. The following sections are concerned with these groups.

THE GENERAL AND THE PROFESSIONAL AS
PARALLEL AND HARMONIZED SEQUENCES

It has been noted that there were tentative starts toward professional teacher education in the colleges before the founding of the normal schools, and that, in the early decades of the nineteenth century, a spirit of experimentation flourished briefly. A few of the college leaders faced and denied the assumed incompatibility of general and professional education for teachers. For example, the faculty of Amherst College, in 1827, noted that a large share of their students actually went into teaching. As a professional aid to these students the faculty recommended the addition to the curriculum of a course in the "science of education." [51] The faculty defended such a course on the grounds of its liberalizing effect on the students, with no apparent thought that such a specialized course was hostile to the liberal spirit of the general education program.

Another who suggested that the college might provide professional education without destroying its ability to function liberally was Wayland. His suggestion was based on an uncommonly high conception of the teacher's role in the community which he described as follows:

I by no means suppose the whole duty of a teacher to be fulfilled by the performance of the labors of the school room. If a suitable person be engaged for this, and if the station be rendered permanent and sufficiently attractive by the social consideration which properly belongs to it, a multitude of indirect benefits will naturally follow. Such an instructor would be the friend and companion of his pupils after the relation of master and scholar had terminated. He would encourage and direct the studies of those who wished to pursue their investigations by themselves. He would cultivate science and stimulate his neighbors to literary acquisition by the delivery of lectures, the formation of libraries and every other means of popular improvement. In this manner a class of professional men would be raised up among us whose influence would be felt most benignly over every class of society, and of whose labors the benefit would be incalculable. Such a system there-

---

[51] Amherst Faculty, *The Substance of Two Reports of the Faculty of Amherst College, to the Board of Trustees, with the Doings of the Board Thereon* (Amherst, Mass.: Carter and Adams, Printers, 1827). The proposals were rejected.

fore, in order to be successful, involves the necessity of a class of higher seminaries, seminaries capable of teaching teachers, in other words institutions for professional education.[52]

Wayland seems to have taken it for granted, as had the Amherst faculty, that whatever was offered in the professional sequence would be compatible with the liberal emphasis of the college program as a whole.[53]

Within the normal school movement there were also those who by 1859 were arguing that teachers must have the same type of general education as other leaders in society. One of these was Alpheus Crosby, who, in addressing the first national normal school convention, stressed the need for professional leaders who combined rich general education with professional training. Crosby asked:

But shall the higher branches of study be introduced into our Normal Schools farther than a liberal and truly scientific preparation for the work of common school instruction requires? . . . If they are not so introduced we may expect in the future, as we have observed in the past, the following consequence. Those who have been professionally educated for the work of teaching, who have made it a science, will, for the most part, be confined to what are regarded as the lower, or as only medium positions in the work; while the highest places, the most influential and the most lucrative, will be chiefly occupied by those who, however well educated in other respects, have never made the science of teaching a distinct object of study . . . who perhaps even scout the idea that any professional training is needed by the teacher. The evils of such a state of things I need not attempt to describe; of so unnatural a divorce between educational science and educational influence, between didactic skill and high literary attainment, between professional preparation for the work of teaching and favorable position in the work.[54]

Crosby proposed to solve the problem either by adding the higher branches to the normal school or by adding a thorough course in "didactics, theoretical and practical" to the college. Like Wayland, he saw no incompatibility here.

THE PROFESSIONAL TREATMENT POSITION

In 1837 Calvin E. Stowe outlined in considerable detail a plan for a normal school or teacher's seminary. He suggested that it should admit

[52] Wayland, *Thoughts on the Present Collegiate System*, p. 5.
[53] *Ibid.*, pp. 153, 155.
[54] Crosby, "The Proper Sphere and Work," *American Normal Schools*, p. 29.

only those who were already thoroughly grounded in the common branches and should concentrate largely on professional training. The course of study he proposed was, so far as the professional elements were concerned, ahead of anything actually achieved in teacher education for many years thereafter. It included history of education, the philosophy of mind, the "peculiarities of intellectual and moral development in children, as modified by sex, parental character, wealth or poverty, city or country, family government [etc.]. . . ," along with the science of education, and the art of teaching.[55]

In respect to the subjects which were to provide the general education of the normal school he suggested that the curriculum include:

A thorough, scientific and demonstrative study of all the branches to be taught in the common schools, *with directions at every step as to the best method* [italics added] of inculcating each lesson upon children of different dispositions and capacities, and various intellectual habits.[56]

The key concept here was that method of teaching was to be considered "at every step" as academic subject matter was presented. In other words, the instruction in all classes was to proceed from a professional point of view. In 1924 Edgar D. Randolph wrote the history of this idea as if it constituted the guideline of all effective teacher education.[57]

The early practitioner who has become the symbol of this "professional treatment of subject matter" was Cyrus Peirce, the principal of the first public normal school at Lexington, Massachusetts. In applying the concept Peirce suggested, at different times, two guiding principles: (1) that instruction in academic subjects, art of teaching, and practice teaching be thoroughly intermingled,[58] and (2) that "The art of teaching must be made the great, the paramount, the only concern. It must not come in as subservient to, or merely collateral with anything else whatever." [59]

[55] Calvin E. Stowe, *Common Schools and Teachers Seminaries* (Boston: Marsh, Capen, Lyon, and Webb, 1839), p. 85.

[56] *Ibid.*

[57] Edgar D. Randolph, *The Professional Treatment of Subject Matter* (Baltimore: Warwick & York, Inc., 1924).

[58] Cyrus Peirce, Letter to Henry Barnard, dated January 1, 1841, reprinted in Arthur O. Norton, ed., *The First Normal School in America: The Journals of Cyrus Peirce and Mary Swift* (Cambridge, Mass.: Harvard University Press, 1926), pp. 1–11.

[59] Cyrus Peirce, Letter to Henry Barnard, 1851, *ibid.*, p. 284.

With this singleness of purpose no conflict between the academic, or general, and the professional was possible. The selection of academic material and the manner of its presentation to the student was to find justification solely in increased classroom proficiency. The plan avoided the troublesome dichotomies between the academic and professional and between theory and practice. It did so, however, by focusing on a narrowly technical concept of the professional.

It should be noted that, in addition to the common branches, especially stressed, Peirce gave frequent lectures in natural history, moral philosophy, physiology, algebra, bookkeeping, mental philosophy, and geometry.[60] The extent to which these were actually made instrumental to the technical art of teaching is not clear.

Randolph maintained that the professional treatment position was largely in eclipse from Peirce's time until it was revived after 1870.[61] He seems to have been correct so far as explicit statement of the theory is concerned, although there are strong indications that in practice the Stowe–Peirce theory was dominant throughout the early period. This point was held by Vernon Mangun who based his conclusions on studies of practice in Albany State Normal School [62] and in the Massachusetts normals.[63] Moreover, Wellford Addis attributed the "renaissance" of the normal school movement in the 1870's to the fact that the "stamp . . . given the normal school by a Peirce . . . began to want unanimous consent by 1870." [64]

Philosophical positions are frequently given explicit statement only when they are seriously challenged by the *status quo* which they seek to replace or by new theories threatening to supplant them. The failure of the early normal school people to give explicit formulation to the "professionalized treatment" idea may simply indicate that it was, in fact, widely accepted. When it began to be restated after 1870 it was in opposition to a growing tendency to emphasize the academic subjects for

[60] See Norton, *The First Normal School in America, passim.*

[61] Randolph, *The Professional Treatment,* p. 77.

[62] Vernon Mangun, "Early Normal School Practices," *Educational Administration and Supervision,* XI:25–38 (January, 1925).

[63] Vernon Mangun, *The American Normal School, Its Rise and Development in Massachusetts* (Baltimore: Warwick & York, Inc., 1928).

[64] Wellford Addis, "The Inception and the Progress of the American Normal School Curriculum to 1880," *Report of the Commissioner of Education for the Year 1888–89,* Vol. I (Washington, D.C.: Government Printing Office, 1891), p. 295.

their own sake. Similarly, when, in the 1920's, the position was again emphasized it was as a reform movement.

The idea that a teacher education institution must have this singleness of purpose, that the demands of the professional task must dictate the whole pre-service program, was central to the very concept of the normal school. More than any other idea it led to their establishment, and it remains until the present the major argument for a single-purpose institution.

Between 1820 and 1850 the choice between a single-purpose normal school and the multipurpose academy or college was made. The subsequent development of teacher education theory has been deeply influenced by that choice which deserves a further examination.

There were in these decades a considerable number of leaders in the colleges, the academies, and the normal schools who apparently felt that an adequate professional program, harmonizing the professional sequence with the liberal sequence but making neither completely dominant, was possible. These people, of whom the Amherst faculty, Wayland, and Crosby were representative, had, as we have seen, an exalted concept of the role of the teacher. They shared the belief that a general education similar to that provided other students of the college was needed by the teacher. They were convinced of the importance of some specialized instruction of a professional nature, although they tended to emphasize philosophical considerations rather than the actual techniques of teaching. In the colleges and academies, however, they were bitterly opposed by the liberal arts purists. The establishment of the normal schools which relieved the colleges of the responsibility for at least elementary school teacher education may have made the purist victory easier.

Had the beginnings of professional education been worked out under the leadership of such men in the college, or even the academy, perhaps a broader view of it would have prevailed. Such was not the case. The colleges, for the time, virtually abandoned the field, and the academies were widely reported to have failed in their efforts.

This alleged failure has been challenged periodically.[65] On theoretical

---

[65] Judd has consistently maintained that the adoption of the normal school pattern was unnecessary and un-American; see his article, "Should University Schools of Education Cease to Exist?," *School and Society*, 62:141–42 (September 1, 1945). John C. Almack, basing his thesis on the New York situation, specifically charged that "the normal schools were 'put over' on the American people

grounds the most powerful advocates of "professional" education assumed that only a single-purpose school, i.e. the normal school, could succeed, and, accordingly, they campaigned vigorously for public support of their contentions. Actually, teachers for the common schools continued to be trained by the academies and high schools for many years, though the majority of them prior to 1865 had neither secondary nor normal training. No extensive statistical comparison of the merits of normal-trained teachers, as opposed to those trained in the academies, was made, or is possible.[66] The enthusiastic support of the educational reformers who backed the normal school might, if turned in favor of the academies or colleges, have resulted in those institutions developing a more effective program.

The question is, however, academic. Horace Mann, Henry Barnard, James Wickersham, State Superintendent Thomas H. Burrowes of Pennsylvania, State Superintendent Samuel Young of New York, and many others threw their weight behind the normal school movement and argued that the academies had either proved their inability or were logically doomed to do so. Thus Northrup, in his *Fourth Annual Report,* suggested that New York's "costly mistake" in attempting to provide adequate professional education through the academies did not prevent its repetition in Kentucky and Maine. He added that "The early failure of the experiment both in Maine and Kentucky was no matter of surprise to the intelligent friends of education." [67]

These men, and those of similar opinion, were highly respected leaders in the educational revival of the period. With the principals of the normal schools they organized the associations which were most concerned with the education of teachers. They were men of action, and, in the

---

in the first place by a little group of educational theorists and propagandists who had had no real contact and no real experience with them"; see "The Issue in Teacher-Training," *Educational Administration and Supervision,* XI:267–75 (March, 1925).

[66] Testimonials somewhat in the manner of present-day advertising were frequently published to sell the "normal method" to the state. For example the Trenton (New Jersey) State Normal School reported fourteen endorsements from different districts in 1860. Characteristic of these was the Tom's River response, "Our school has been under the direction of Normal teachers for almost two years. An entire revolution in the school has been the result." *Fifth Annual Report of the Board of Trustees,* p. 33 (Trenton, N. J., 1860).

[67] *Fourth Annual Report of the Superintendent of Schools of Connecticut,* cited by Wellford Addis in "The Inception and the Progress of the American Normal School Curriculum to 1880," p. 281.

manner which Tocqueville had described as characteristic, they took the best ideas they could find and turned them to account. Whether their belief that nothing but the single-purpose normal school could be perfected in time was correct or not, they succeeded in establishing the deep conviction that the college and the academy had been tried and had failed. This conviction has, from the beginning, been at the heart of much teacher education thought.

To the extent that the conservative spirit prevailed in the colleges and the academies it was to be expected that the professional program would receive little enthusiastic support. Such a lack of support is precisely what the advocates of the normal school idea reported when they observed the academies in action. In state after state, the chief school officers reported to legislators that the attempt to train teachers in any institution but the single-purpose normal school was failing. The almost universal complaint was that in the college, the academy, or the university, the teacher training department was considered an appendage which lacked single-minded support, the overarching professional spirit, and the unity needed for successful teacher education.[68]

The decision to make the professional task the measure and guide for the entire program of the teacher educating school, whether or not it offered professionalized subject matter, generally prevailed. This made the question of how liberally one viewed the function of the professional sequence in some respects more crucial than if parallel programs of general and professional education had been established.

The Liberal and the Technical Functions
Within the Professional Sequence

Granted the need for some kind of specialized education for teachers, there existed from the beginning of the normal school differences of opinion about how to relate and what relative emphasis to place on the liberal and the technical functions. These differences were partly related to one's concept of the role of the teacher and of the school.

[68] See Otto Welton Snarr, *The Education of Teachers in the Middle States: An Historical Study of the Professional Education of Public School Teachers as a State Function* (Chicago: The University of Chicago Press, 1945), pp. 99–117; James P. Wickersham, *A History of Education in Pennsylvania,* p. 608; and Henry Barnard, *Normal Schools,* Part I, p. 21.

PREVAILING CONCEPTS OF THE ROLE OF
THE TEACHER AND OF THE SCHOOL

Perhaps no generation of American educators has had a greater faith in education as an instrument of social policy than did the early fathers of the common school and normal school movements. Steeped in the Enlightenment faith in the infinite perfectibility of men and institutions, and inspired by the dream of an equalitarian society and government, it seemed to them that only an effective school system was needed to lead directly to Utopia. The indispensable role of the normal school in this process was clearly spelled out time and again. For example, William F. Phelps argued (1) that free government was totally dependent on intelligence and virtue, universally diffused, (2) that such virtue and intelligence could only be secured through the common schools, (3) that the common school's effectiveness depended on a supply of well-trained teachers, (4) that a supply of teachers fitted to the duty of rearing a nation of intelligent free men could be secured only through the normal schools, and, finally, that ". . . when these self-evident truths come to be fully understood and acknowledged, Normal Schools will become co-extensive with the wants of the people, and co-equal with the power, dignity, and the importance of the government itself." [69]

The early normal school leaders were at great pains to exalt the role of the teacher, and to imbue him with a keen sense of mission. So successful were they in this respect that as early as 1848 Baynard Rush Hall [70] thought it necessary to plead for tolerance on the part of normal school graduates toward other young teachers who had been denied the opportunity for professional education in the normal schools. The word "professional" became the symbol of a new gospel, and the need to make of teaching a "true profession" was invariably cited as one of the prime reasons for the normal school movement.[71] The danger of turn-

---

[69] William F. Phelps, "Relations of Normal Schools to Society," *Second Annual Report of the New Jersey State Normal School*, pp. 109–110.

[70] Baynard Rush Hall, *Teaching, A Science: The Teacher, an Artist* (New York: Baker and Scribner, 1848), pp. 213–214.

[71] It is an instructive experience to follow the nineteenth-century deliberations of normal school people in such sources as the National Educational Association *Proceedings* wherein the phrase "professional" seems to appear in almost every sentence, always in connection with instruction in "education," and then to turn to such sources as reports of meetings of the Association of American Universities in which discussions of "professional education" never concern teacher education until well into the present century.

ing over the task of teaching to people who were not motivated by a deep love of the work and a profound sense of responsibility toward it was always stressed.[72]

Yet, though the teacher's importance was largely acclaimed in orations and though the friends of education placed tremendous faith in what he could accomplish, both the faith and the early program of teacher education were naïve. The concepts and knowledge that guide and inspire modern teacher education were not yet developed, and the life of the nation neither supported nor required the preparation of teachers competent according to modern demands. The usual common school teacher was a part-time person with limited responsibility and even more limited prestige. He accepted as natural the low salary, the patronizing attitude, and the social restrictions which the community dictated.[73]

The idea that instruction could be anything but subject-matter centered had, for practical purposes, not entered the thinking of educators. The curriculum, even on the elementary level, was traditionally defined, and such recent notions as a continually evolving curriculum would have seemed strange indeed. By the same token the thought that the young man or girl teaching a few weeks in the country school was really a significant agent in determining public policy, save in a very mechanical manner, would have seemed farfetched.

The idea of professional leadership in the making of educational policy was just beginning to be sensed by perceptive leaders in the states and larger cities. The real leaders in educational thought were still amateurs, except for an occasional college president or professor. Many of the leaders—including Cyrus Peirce—were ministers. Others, like Horace Mann, had originally been trained for the law. The function of the secretary or the treasurer of the board of education was in the process of evolving into that of the modern school superintendency on the state and city level.[74] The first national organization of men who were

[72] Typical of many speeches and articles stressing this point was David P. Page's discussion in 1849 of the "Teacher's Relation to His Profession," *Theory and Practice of Teaching: or the Motives and Methods of Good School-Keeping,* twenty-fifth edition (New York: A. S. Barnes and Burr, 1860), pp. 270–291.

[73] For a discussion of the economic, social, and political status of teachers in this period, spiced with some rich anecdotal material, see Willard S. Elsbree, *The American Teacher, Evolution of a Profession in a Democracy* (New York: American Book Company, 1939), pp. 271–305.

[74] The rise of professional supervision paralleled in time the growth of the normal school. Probably the first city superintendent was appointed in Buffalo,

professionally concerned with the making of policy for the public schools was the National Association of School Superintendents which first met in 1866. Most of these men were probably trained in the liberal arts colleges and had received no formal education in a professional sequence.[75] Thus a dualistic system was quickly established in practice. The graduates of the normal school did not at first assume policy-making responsibility; those who did were educated in the liberal arts colleges.

THE LIBERAL FUNCTION IN THE EARLY
PROFESSIONAL SEQUENCE

Before a more sophisticated view of the role of the school and the teacher could prevail it was necessary for the analytical tools of the natural and social sciences to be turned upon the nature of human development, the interrelationships among cultural patterns, and the educative process itself. If the classroom teacher were to play more than a simple mechanical role in the school program he had to learn to look at his professional decisions and activities in the light of these disciplines. This required the greater development of the newer natural and social sciences—sociology, psychology, anthropology, political science, and social psychology. It also required the more systematic application to educational problems of such older disciplines as philosophy, history, and the humanities.

Prior to 1865, these newer university disciplines either had not differentiated themselves enough from philosophy, or had not focused clearly enough on contemporary problems, that a clear concept of their function in the professional sequence was possible. The humanities, whose unique and essential values lie in creating an all-embracing sense of community and in providing insight into human behavior, remained in the control of those who were most opposed to any thought of a utilitarian or professional use for their discipline. Though the place of lit-

---

New York, in 1837, and the number of such reached only twenty-nine by 1870. See Elwood P. Cubberley, *Public School Administration*, rev. ed. (Cambridge, Mass.: Houghton Mifflin Company, 1922), pp. 34–84, for the evolution of the local and county superintendency.

[75] Even as late as 1883 William H. Payne reported that of those holding the more important school superintendencies in Michigan, which boasted of one of the leading normal schools, sixteen were educated in the university as compared with five educated in the normal school. These sixteen had apparently received no professional instruction as such. See William H. Payne, *Contributions to the Science of Education* (New York: Harper and Brothers, 1887), p. 336.

erature and language was always considered when educators philoso-
phized about the curriculum there was then, as now, little development
of the implications of these subjects for the professional sequence itself.
When humanistic studies were offered is was for their general value to
the student as a person and not because they were thought to have professional significance for teachers, except as content to be retaught.

So it was with history. As early as 1827 Vermont had required that
history of the United States be taught in the public schools, and other
states followed. The course was introduced into the normal schools
simply so that teachers could know enough to teach the subject effectively. The purpose of this instruction was almost entirely patriotic, and
most of the available texts were more notable for their sentiment and
dramatic excellence than for a careful regard for facts. The influence of
German scientific history was not to become great until after 1880,
while the new history of James Harvey Robinson and Charles Beard
awaited another century.

History of education, as such, began to secure a place in the normal
school curriculum after 1860, and by 1875 had become fairly common.[76] The early texts by H. I. Schmidt and L. P. Brockett [77] were
strictly narrative histories attempting to cover too much, of which too
little was known, in far too brief a space. That such materials could
have brought significant new meanings to the analysis of educational
problems seems doubtful, particularly since the students had so little
previous liberal education.

The other social sciences were even less well developed. In sociology
the impact of August Comte was only vaguely sensed. The influence of
Herbert Spencer was just beginning, and the work of Lester Frank
Ward, William Graham Sumner, and Albion Small was yet to come.
Lewis Henry Morgan did not publish his *Ancient Society,* the pioneer
work in cultural anthropology, until 1877. Public administration, in-

---

[76] It appears that much historical material was used by earlier teachers in connection with their lectures on theory and art of teaching (see Norton, *The First
Normal School in America, passim*). A limited survey of normal school catalogues suggests, however, that formal courses were introduced in the western
normal schools between 1859 and 1870 and were first offered in the older eastern
schools, e.g., Bridgewater and Westfield, Massachusetts, and Trenton, New Jersey,
between 1870 and 1880.

[77] H. I. Schmidt, *History of Education* (New York: Harper and Brothers,
1842); and Linus P. Brockett (pseud. Philobiblius), *History and Progress of
Education from the Earliest Time to the Present* (New York: A. S. Barnes and
Burr, 1860).

ternational relations, public law, government, and economics were yet to be differentiated from the original catchall course in political economy which itself had only recently gained a place in the college curriculum. Experimental psychology and social psychology were also undeveloped.

It is most significant that teacher education theory had been worked out before these disciplines, which are particularly suited to liberalizing the concept of the professional task, were well developed. The old emphasis on the art of teaching and on subjects to be taught in the common schools had gained a strong hold on the attitudes of the normal school people before these new concepts arose to challenge it. When the new disciplines were developed they were promoted by the university people who tended to look down on the normal school. The stage was thus set for the bitterness which has marked the attitude of the technicians and theoreticians toward each other.

The modern professional sequence has evolved largely out of the early courses in the theory and art of teaching, and of the older collegiate courses in intellectual philosophy or the science of mind. Thus Peirce's students at Lexington studied John Abercrombie's *Mental Philosophy* reportedly to understand the mental faculties possessed by the child and the proper ways of disciplining them.[78] Such texts as Abercrombie's and Wayland's *Intellectual Philosophy* constituted the major sources of information concerning the "science of the mind" from which modern instruction in psychology and philosophy of education have grown.

A somewhat limited set of principles, partially differentiated from intellectual philosophy and from the art of teaching, began to develop early as a "science of education." From a methodological standpoint the concept of science was not in any clear sense different from that of philosophy. Both, as applied to the study of mind and of education, were still largely introspective and rationalistic in nature. For example, the graduates from the Trenton Normal School were asked, in their science of education examination, such questions as:

What is education in its most comprehensive sense?
In what order do the intellectual powers come to maturity?

[78] Cyrus Peirce, Letter to Henry Barnard, January 1, 1841. Perhaps Peirce referred to Abercrombie's *Inquiries Concerning the Intellectual Powers, and the Investigation of Truth,* Jacob Abbott, ed. (Boston: Otis, Broaders, and Co., 1839); see also Norton, *The First Normal School in America,* p. 86.

What is the rational order of development of the five great sciences? In what order should they be introduced as the studies of the human spirit? [79]

Philosophically, most of these early normal teachers were idealists. Starting with their concept of the ideal each of the early "scientists" tried to work out a complete system to guide their policies. In their desire for a unified system, their concern for the harmonious development of the whole child, and their moral emphasis, the influence of Pestalozzi was apparent.[80]

By 1859 some of these mental philosophers had come to be concerned over the great emphasis being placed on techniques in the teacher education program. Alpheus Crosby expressed this concern at the first Normal School Convention as follows:

> It seems obvious that any course of professional training which is not merely mechanical or empirical, must have for its basis a thorough consideration of the principles of the profession, of its philosophy, and that this should underlie and give form to all the attention which may be paid to practical methods. Methods must be constantly changing accordingly as circumstances change; and these change more or less each successive day. . . . But principles are in their nature eternal. . . .
>
> In most professional schools, the fundamental importance of the study of principles upon which the profession is based has been recognized and practically regarded. . . . Why has it not been equally seen that in a Normal School, for the training of educators, the prime subject of study should be the principles of Education, and that the most earnest effort of the student should be directed, not to the solution of a miscellaneous question in Mr. Blank's arithmetic, but to answer for herself such questions as these, "What is Education?   What does it comprise? . . ." [81]

At this same convention John Ogden, insisting that normal school people must quickly and adequately define the science of education, pointed out that a mere grouping of practical hints about teaching subjects was not science.[82] Ogden went on to develop his concept of the

---

[79] William F. Phelps, *Documents Accompanying the Fifth Annual Report of the Principal of the Normal School* (Trenton, N. J., 1860), p. 61.

[80] The early influence of Pestalozzianism on teacher education theory is discussed by Obed J. Williamson, *Provisions for General Theory Courses in the Professional Education of Teachers* (New York: Bureau of Publications, Teachers College, Columbia University, 1936), pp. 9–19.

[81] Crosby, "The Proper Sphere and Work of the American Normal School," *American Normal Schools*, pp. 25–26. .

[82] *Ibid.*, pp. 60–73.

science as being composed of absolute laws and axioms capable of definite classification and arrangement and of being studied independently
of other subjects. He defined the science of education, in the manner
then customary, as embracing (1) the nature of man's educational capacities, (2) the nature of educative forces or instrumentalities (i.e.,
the subjects), and (3) the modes of teaching.

This type of educational science did not reach its greatest development until the end of the century. In its earliest form it was dogmati-
cally handed to students who were perhaps not equipped to consider it
critically or to develop any real talent for philosophical analysis.

While Ogden and Crosby were rather confident that their science had
arrived others were not so certain. The lack of real confidence was apparent at this first convention. As if to clinch the argument for all time
these assembled normal school people, protesting too much, solemnly
resolved "That education, as based upon the nature of man, and having
fixed principles, is truly and eminently a science. . . ." [83]

A more realistic estimate of educational "science" as it was, and as it
perhaps ought to be, was given by Richard Edwards:

The science of education is only in its formative state. Its principles
have never been arranged and digested with the care and precision we
find in some departments of knowledge hitherto more devotedly cultivated.

Not but that it would be quite possible, and comparatively easy, to
frame a theory of education that should be more or less complete in all
its parts, and measurably satisfactory to ourselves, perhaps; but this is
not the method of building up sciences that has been highly valued since
the time of Lord Bacon; and nowhere ought our theories to be founded
upon a more careful induction than in this matter of education.

Every principle, before it is deemed trustworthy, should be subjected
to a rigorous process of verification, and the system finally adopted
should be the result deduced from the experience of many, continued
through many years.[84]

PROVISIONS FOR TECHNICAL INSTRUCTION

The idea that the "art of teaching" could be taught was not easily
accepted by some early educators, even in the normal school itself. For
example, Nicholas Tillinghast, who was principal of the second public

[83] *Ibid.*, pp. 106–107.
[84] *Ibid.*, p. 82.

normal school [at Bridgewater, Massachusetts] had serious doubts.[85] He seems to have believed that the normal school had discharged its duties when it had provided a good academic background and a continuing example of effective technique. Among the normal school people this position was apparently not common after the first years, although as late as 1859 C. E. Hovey of Illinois Normal University seems to have partly accepted it.[86] The same attitude was apparently accepted in the New York City normal schools.[87]

The early texts, as well as the early practice, were overwhelmingly concerned with instruction in techniques. One of the most popular of these texts was written by David P. Page, principal of the Albany, New York, Normal School,[88] who was among those placing great emphasis on an extended general education for teachers. His book, nevertheless, was filled with practical suggestions on such items as proper punishment, school arrangements, and "right modes of teaching." Like Peirce, Page felt that the art of teaching should not be presented as distinct from educational principles or subject matter.[89] But, also like Peirce, he centered his instruction on the art.

Where the Peirce ideal of professional treatment prevailed, there was a close intermingling of instruction in educational theory with instruction in techniques of teaching and with direct experiences in practice situations. The flavor of this blend is suggested by the following entry in the diary of one of Peirce's pupils, Mary Swift:

This morn, Mr. Peirce wished to try the experiment of having one of the scholars hear the recitation in N. [natural] Philosophy. Accord-

[85] There has been some controversy over Tillinghast's position. The above analysis is based primarily on a letter to Barnard and on the testimony of Edwards who was for some time a student and assistant of Tillinghast. See Richard Edwards, *Memoir of Nicholas Tillinghast* (Boston: James Robinson and Company, 1857); American Normal School Association, *American Normal Schools*, p. 50; and Barnard, *Normal Schools*, Part I, pp. 79–80.

[86] American Normal School Association, *American Normal Schools*, pp. 50, 53.

[87] See Henry Kiddle, Assistant Superintendent of New York City Schools, Letter to William Phelps dated December 26, 1856, *Second Annual Report of the Board of Trustees of the New Jersey State Normal School to the Legislature, for the Year Ending February Ninth, 1857* (Trenton, N.J.: Printed at the Office of the "True American," 1857), p. 162.

[88] Page, *Theory and Practice of Teaching*. See also Samuel R. Hall, *Lectures on School Teaching* (Boston: Richardson, Lord & Holbrook, 1829).

[89] Page, in his *Theory and Practice of Teaching*, p. 4, suggested the logical possibility of separating the "art" from the "science" of education which he rejected as undesirable. Nevertheless, as the professional curriculum began to expand, precisely this distinction was first to become general.

ingly he gave to me the charge of the recitation. The feeling caused by asking the first question tended rather to excite my risibles, but feeling the necessity of sobriety—I was enabled to play the teacher for a short time. I think that he can judge very little about our idea of teaching from the example which we give him in hearing a recitation for the manner in which it is carried on depends very much upon the interest felt by the teacher in the scholars & in their study.[90]

The Peirce technique of having the pupils "play the teacher" was supplemented by that of providing experience in observing and teaching the students in the model school which soon became a part of most normal schools. There was some early controversy about the relative merits of model school experience as contrasted with that of having pupils "play the teacher" and submit to criticism from the regular teacher and the other students.[91] However, as the period drew to a close the work of Edward A. Sheldon at Oswego, New York, systematized the practice school routine and made it potentially the heart of the professional sequence.

Summary of Teacher Education Theory
in the Formative Years

The rationale of early teacher education, like that of many operations in America, is seen partly only in retrospect. While each teacher educator may have had in mind a total vision of the ideal toward which he tried to bend his practice, he was more concerned with the day-by-day resolution of a great number of minor problems. The problems of a curricular nature tended to be solved in the light of his concept of (1) the general educational needs of prospective teachers, (2) the way to relate the meeting of these needs with the demands for professional education, and (3) the relative emphasis to be placed on the liberal as opposed to the technical function in the professional sequence. Running through all three of these was the basic question of how closely education should be related to the performance of specific tasks or the solution of specific problems. The present chapter has tried to organize, in these three dimensions, the thinking of the early makers of teacher education.

[90] See Norton, *The First Normal School in America*, p. 90.
[91] Letters from Dana P. Colburn, and "Proceedings of the First Meeting of the Association of Normal School Instructors, held in Springfield, Mass., August 21, 1856," in the *Second Annual Report of the Board of Trustees of the New Jersey State Normal School, 1857*, pp. 150–153, 182–188.

To reduce three dimensions to one, and to classify in a few categories a great number of educators, each of whose pattern of thought was somewhat unique and ever-changing, obviously does violence to precision. The fine distinctions in each dimension were most important in creating lingering habits of thought. However, to provide reference lines from one period to another it is sometimes useful, if due caution be taken, to construct intellectual categories. It seems generally reasonable to envision four groups among early thinkers on teacher education. In one group might be placed those members of the conservative colleges who stressed the need of maintaining an academic curriculum largely devoid of immediate practical objectives and organized in terms of well-established fields of learning. This group might be called the "academic purists." In the early period they tended to consider professional instruction of any kind hostile to their concept of liberal education, and to deny that there was justification for a professional sequence, as such, for teachers. They were apt to argue that when the college or academy had provided thorough instruction in the subjects to be taught and an example of good teaching methods the teacher was adequately prepared. A subgroup holding essentially this position, although desiring a more modern general education program and being willing to include occasional practical suggestions for teaching, was found among normal school people. This subgroup was represented by such men as Tillinghast.

A second position, not necessarily mutually exclusive of the first, might well be called that of the "professional purists." As represented by such people as Phelps, this group was reluctant to contend with general education in the professional school beyond the necessary brief review of the elementary branches. They considered instruction in academic branches disruptive. During the early period this group tended to emphasize a philosophical approach to the professional sequence.

A third position represented in the early period by such men as Wayland in the colleges and Crosby in the normal schools might be called that of the "harmonizers." This group was usually unwilling to support a teacher education program having too exclusively a professional slant. On the other hand, they were willing that the collegiate or normal school program be designed with the vocational objectives of the student clearly in mind and did not conceive the distinction between general and professional education as one of liberality or lack of it. From their point of view a curriculum could be functionally oriented to a significant degree and still be liberalizing. They tended, in the early period, to conceive of the professional sequences as being largely philosophical in nature. They looked with some disinterest on instruction of a technical nature.

A final general position might be seen as that of the "integrators." These were the men like Stowe, Peirce, and, perhaps, Page, who favored a reasonably extensive general education program, instruction in mental philosophy or science of education, and instruction and practice in the art of teaching. They insisted that all these segments should be intermingled and organized from the professional point of view. As Peirce suggested, the "art of teaching" was to be the core of organization. The total curriculum proposed by these three was as extensive as that usually suggested by the harmonizers. However, the theory was most rigidly followed in the earliest normal schools which were constantly urged to emphasize the lower branches (the elementary subjects) of the common schools. Moreover, these particular schools were under frequent attack in the legislature, and, therefore, had a precarious existence. They, especially, were forced quickly to produce demonstrable results in terms of teaching technique and to prove their difference from other types of schools with which they were accused of competing unnecessarily. Very shortly people holding this position became aggressive defenders of general education made up of professionally treated lower branches intermingled with professional instruction of a technical and ultrapractical nature.

Within each of these four positions, as well as in the intellectual and other social currents of the time, were forces tending to modify the complex pattern of teacher education thought which prevailed at the end of the Civil War. However, some patterns were already firmly entrenched in institutions and in the philosophies of American educators. While tremendous change has been made, the molds of the old American college, academy, and normal school continue to influence the direction of the change. The ensuing chapters will partly follow these influences.

chapter THREE

The "Strictly Professional" Ideal

and the University Study of

Education, 1865–1895

THE PRECEDING CHAPTER DESCRIBED THE SIGNIFICANT BEGINNINGS made in American teacher education before the Civil War and noted that some still lingering attitudes and tendencies were then institutionalized. However, the broad expansion of the normal school movement did not come until after 1865. In the ensuing thirty years both the normal school and the university department of education gained a secure place in the educational picture. The number of state normal schools grew from fifteen in 1865 to 103 in 1890.[1] Moreover, though the resistance to university departments of education was strong, a number of

---

[1] Benjamin Frazier, "History of the Professional Education of Teachers in the United States," *National Survey of the Education of Teachers*, U.S. Office of Education, Bulletin, 1933, No. 10, Vol. V, Part 1 (Washington, D.C.: Government Printing Office, 1935), pp. 12, 52.

influential private universities and most of the newly founded state universities had such a department by 1895.[2]

General Forces Influencing
Educational Thought

Changes in university and normal school education were, as always, related to the general patterns of intellectual development and to basic changes in economic, religious, political, and other institutions in the American culture. A brief glimpse at some ideas and developments which were rather closely connected with the evolution of teacher education thought might be useful.

INTELLECTUAL CROSSCURRENTS

As in the previous period, Americans continued to lean heavily on European thinkers for many creative ideas. This was particularly noticeable in respect to philosophy, psychology, and pedagogy. For basic educational theory the ideas of Pestalozzi, Froebel, Herbart, Wundt, J. K. F. Rosenkranz, Thomas T. Tate, and Alexander Bain were widely studied. Many of the leading educators were deeply influenced by the idealist philosophy of Hegel. In history of education, which became one of the most popular professional courses during this period, the writings of Gabriel Compayré, S. S. Laurie, and Robert H. Quick were studied extensively. In arguments for expanded instruction in pedagogy European practice was invariably used as supporting evidence. The establishment of chairs of pedagogy in the Scottish universities gave added weight to the long-cited German precedence.

Nor was the influence of European ideas restricted to philosophy, psychology, and pedagogy. The influence of British evolutionary thought, in the area of both the natural sciences and the social sciences, was overwhelming. It is doubtful if any thinkers had greater impact on American intellectual life than did Charles Darwin and Herbert Spencer.

[2] These included Columbia, Harvard, Johns Hopkins, Pennsylvania, Leland Stanford, New York University, Clark, and several others. In the Midwest, the Far West, and in some of the southern states the new universities concerned themselves to some extent, perhaps only in the form of normal or preparatory departments, with the training of teachers almost from the date of their founding. See Otto Walton Snarr, *The Education of Teachers in the Middle States: An Historical Study of the Professional Education of Public School Teachers as a State Function* (Chicago: The University of Chicago Press, 1945), pp. 43–95.

Richard Hofstadter, for example, has suggested that "It was impossible to be active in any field of intellectual work in the three decades after the Civil War without mastering Spencer." [3]

Moreover, the pattern of American university life, with its emphasis on research, specialization, and election, was profoundly influenced by the efforts of American students who had studied abroad, particularly in Germany. As a matter of fact, there were few areas in which America was not a debtor to Europe in the commerce of ideas. In philosophy, economics, physical sciences, and history the current of thought flowed essentially westward across the Atlantic.

Yet if America leaned heavily on Europe for ideas, she was not passive in receiving them. The spark of scientific interest from Franklin's kitestring burned through the pages of Benjamin Silliman's *American Journal of Science* and found explosive fuel in Louis Agassiz's Harvard laboratory. The continuing American interest in science became almost a national obsession after the publication of Darwin's *Origin of Species*.

The attempt to reconcile the new science with old religious dogma received attention from nearly every major figure in American religious, scientific, and philosophical circles. Agassiz, James Dwight Dana, John Fiske, Asa Gray, and Lyman Abbott were particularly concerned to harmonize the two.

Largely under the influence of Spencer such American scholars as William Graham Sumner turned their efforts to creating a rationale for the newly arising "Captains of Industry," and the titans themselves, particularly Andrew Carnegie, were quick to see justification in Spencer's social application of the "survival of the fittest" idea. Other scholars such as James McCosh and Noah Porter, though they appealed to the Puritan "gospel of wealth" rather than to evolution, were as vigorous as Sumner in rationalizing the harshly exploitive practices of the new industry.[4]

On the other hand, the forces of protest were also aroused and inspired by these new ideas. Under the joint stimuli of Spencer and Comte, Lester Frank Ward created his *Dynamic Sociology* which, though belatedly accepted, opposed some of the major commitments of Spencer and of Sumner and inspired a generation of social reformers

[3] Richard Hofstadter, *Social Darwinism in American Thought* (Philadelphia: University of Pennsylvania Press, 1945), p. 20.

[4] See Ralph Henry Gabriel, on the "Gospel of Wealth," *The Course of American Democratic Thought* (New York: Ronald Press Company, 1940), pp. 143–160.

and educational thinkers. Furthermore, the basic implications of evolution in the nature of humanity and in scientific principles—in truth itself as it were—were deeply pondered in the Metaphysical Club at Harvard. Out of these discussions of Darwinism, Charles Sanders Peirce, William James, and others were fashioning the pattern of thought which, through the medium of John Dewey, was to guide much American educational activity in the ensuing decades.

SOCIAL AND TECHNOLOGICAL CHANGE

Intellectual protest in academic circles was matched by the incessant efforts of agrarian reformers and industrial laborers to reform the social order. In the mine fields, the rail yards, and the steel mills the process of unionization proceeded, sometimes with violence and murder, in the face of management deeply committed to preventing, by force if necessary, any move for collective bargaining. In rural areas the Granges and the Farmers' Alliances organized and campaigned for a new economic order. Occasionally, labor and agrarian groups combined in political action and succeeded in capturing isolated states. More often, defeat, temporary periods of prosperity, or dissension among the protesting groups dissipated their efforts. Nevertheless, this era of protest set the pattern of reform which was to receive greater support in the following half-century. Regulation of public utilities, attempts to control monopolistic practices in business, income taxation, widespread unionization, banking and currency reform, and such political devices as the initiative and referendum were either achieved or forecast by the reformers of the period under discussion.

Moreover, new technological advances and improved techniques of finance capitalism laid the base for the second industrial revolution. This was the era in which, in the words of Louis Hacker, "American industry reached man's estate. . . ." [5]

With the new technology naturally came increased urbanization and increased specialization. While the United States remained essentially agrarian, the impending end of that status was quite apparent to the more discerning scholars. Thus, the important aspect of Frederick Jackson Turner's paper on "The Significance of the Frontier in American History" was its explicit recognition of the end of an era whose passing

[5] Louis Hacker, *The Shaping of the American Tradition* (New York: Columbia University Press, 1947), p. 688.

demanded that Americans take new stock of their experience and of their institutions. Americans spread themselves thinly over the vast areas settled between the end of the Civil War and the turn of the century, and the isolated, nearly self-sufficient family and neighborhood group continued to exist in some areas. Nevertheless, the cities were being filled, and their inhabitants, by 1900, constituted one-third of the American nation.[6] Even in the rural areas families became increasingly dependent on other agencies for essential materials and services.

The increasing number of school children alone was enough to demand much attention from a nation already largely committed to the ideal of universal elementary education. In the course of the period from 1865 to 1895 that ideal was extended in many states to include the opportunity for secondary education. The American public high school had had a slow but steady growth in the decades just before the Civil War. Its continued expansion after the war, in the face of heavy opposition from some taxpaying groups, brought the issue to a head. In Michigan, Illinois, and other states judicial decisions, of which the Kalamazoo Case is commonly cited, firmly established the legal status of tax-supported high schools. By 1890 the movement, which was to sweep the nation, was well under way.

Even at the elementary level, the number of years of attendance continued to grow as students had time or opportunity for schooling and as their parents became more convinced of the necessity for such attendance. According to the Commissioner of Education, based partly on estimate, the average length of schooling of Americans increased from 3.32 years in 1870 to 4.84 years in 1895. The per cent of children of school age who were enrolled in public elementary and secondary schools increased in the same period from 61.45 to 68.93.

The greater percentage of attendance, the longer stay in school, and the growing population raised the total number of children being educated in the public schools from 7,561,583 in 1870 to 14,379,078 in 1895. With this increased load came an increase in the number of teachers from 220,225 to 400,325.[7]

Finally, the need for citizens and workers to understand the increasingly complicated patterns of American life and to utilize the mush-

[6] *Ibid.*, p. 685.
[7] *Report of the Commissioner of Education for the Year 1895–96*, Vol. I (Washington, D.C.: Government Printing Office, 1897), pp. x–xiv.

rooming bodies of new knowledge forced every segment of education to review and expand its curriculum. This problem was particularly acute in the colleges which were attempting to retain the old unity and wholeness of liberal education while turning out leaders in the new highly specialized areas of life.

The problem of expanding schools, of expanding curriculums, and of an expanding demand for teachers did, of course, hold the attention of the professional teacher educators. Moreover, the intellectual turmoil which raged in academic circles was forming the thought of educators who were to play major roles in vast new programs for the preparation of teachers. Yet the most striking thing about the meetings of the professional teacher educators is the comparative lack of attention which was given to the major issues and changes tearing American society. The problem of how to change a program designed to prepare teachers for a pastoral civilization to one suited for a complex industrial society seems to have been largely ignored while the professional teacher educators debated the precise meaning of "the teacher's knowledge of subject matter."

However, as the end of the century approached, voices of men representing new methods of investigations, and of those more sensitive to new social realities were heard with increasing frequency. These were the years in which such leaders of teacher education as James E. Russell, Charles de Garmo, Charles H. Judd, Edward L. Thorndike, Charles A. and Frank M. McMurry, and John Dewey were building their philosophies.

The Concept of General Education

In his Annual Report for 1856 Chancellor Henry Tappan, of the University of Michigan, enunciated what was sometimes called "Tappan's Law" for the education of teachers. He argued that teachers at any level of the school system should be graduates of the unit just higher. Thus elementary school teachers should be graduates of secondary school, including normal schools; the secondary school teachers, including normal school instructors, should be college graduates; and college instructors should have a doctoral degree.[8] This principle seems to have been largely accepted throughout the period from its enunciation

[8] Quoted by William H. Payne, *Contributions to the Science of Education* (New York: Harper and Brothers, 1887), pp. 261–262.

until 1895. In the latter year, for example, the Committee of Fifteen of the Department of Superintendence of the National Education Association recommended essentially the same rule, although they were more specific, urging that every teacher should have a minimum of four years' education beyond the level at which he taught.[9]

GENERAL EDUCATION IN THE NORMAL SCHOOLS

In the 1870's, before the movement for university instruction in education took root, there was a great deal of agitation for the establishment of a series of graded normal schools based on this concept. Under the leadership of Phelps, then Chairman of the Committee on Normal Schools, the National Educational Association, in 1872, passed a resolution calling for such a system of professional schools.[10]

Except for those who advocated the professional treatment of academic materials, the normal school leaders seemed somewhat uncomfortable in respect to the question of general education. Their inclination, as we shall see, was to defend the normal school as a strictly professional institution, and to argue that, ideally, general education was not its function. Nevertheless, the quality of the student's pre-normal education was such that the need for including nonprofessional subjects seemed apparent. Moreover, there was apparently a demand on the part of students for the subjects usually offered in the secondary school. Consequently, though the normal schools insisted that they were professional and did not compete with general academic institutions, they nevertheless provided much the same general program as did the academies and high schools. Thus the Massachusetts Board of Education, to maintain a strictly professional school, had in 1866 restricted the normal curriculum to the common branches plus the professional sequence.[11] By 1880 most of the secondary subjects were offered. The Board's policy statement had been changed by adding a statement permitting the inclusion of subjects needed for "right mental training." [12]

Nor could the normal schools completely resist the temptation to at-

[9] H. S. Tarbell, chm., "Report of the Sub-Committee on the Training of Teachers," National Education Association, *Proceedings, 1895*, p. 238.

[10] National Education Association, *Proceedings, 1872*, pp. 37, 108.

[11] Resolution of July 9, 1866, quoted by Albert G. Boyden in *History and Alumni Record of the State Normal School, Bridgewater, Massachusetts* (Boston: Noyes and Snow, 1876), pp. 18–19.

[12] Westfield, Massachusetts, State Normal School, *Catalogue and Circular, 1880–81*, p. 12.

tract nonprofessional students by stressing the useful as well as the liberal value of their courses. For example, the catalogue of the St. Cloud, Minnesota, Normal School promised that:

In science the most advanced methods are pursued with all of the advantages of a fine laboratory and excellent apparatus. In mathematics and in English the practical value of the work is kept constantly in view. When there is added to the more strictly academic studies the liberal training in mental philosophy and other pedagogical subjects included in the course of study the student has a substantial preparation for any vocation. So that the young man or woman, who may not desire to make teaching a life work, will find himself possessed of a thorough education when he has finished the two years of teaching required by the state for the free tuition offered at the Normal School—a thoroughness of discipline and command of all his powers that will enable him to compete successfully in any business for the prizes of life.[13]

It is of passing interest to note that the professional sequence was the one cited for its liberalizing value. The terminology of the traditional liberal arts advocates was apparent in the promise that the total program would serve to provide "a thoroughness of discipline and command of . . . powers." Here, as elsewhere, general education, as then defined in terms of mental discipline, seems to have been "bootlegged" into the curriculum.

It was to be expected that practice would be chaotic in an agency trying initially to define its role in a period of rapid social change. Most of the schools offered a number of distinct courses varying in length and content. Some programs were designed to meet the needs of students having a bare knowledge of the common branches, and others to meet those of college graduates wanting only brief instruction in the art of teaching. Within the same school students often had the option of electing a one-, two-, three-, or four-year course. By 1895, a number of normal schools ostensibly required a high school diploma as a prerequisite to admittance, but there were many provisions for exception.[14] In addition to general education courses and a professional se-

[13] St. Cloud State Normal School, *Annual Catalogue of the State Normal School at St. Cloud, Minnesota, for the School Year Ending June 1, 1888,* p. 21. Interestingly enough, President Thomas Gray of this school was one of those who argued most vigorously for a strictly professional normal school.

[14] This variation in courses and the rather strained efforts to provide for students with vast differences of background are apparent, for example, in the 1895 catalogues of the Terre Haute, Indiana, Normal School and of the Westfield, Massachusetts, Normal. Both of these were highly respected schools.

quence it was possible by 1890 to find, in some normal schools, a smattering of subjects conceived of as pre-law, pre-engineering, pre-medical, and commerical.[15]

Because of the very wide variation, any generalizations are misleading in respect to specific schools. However, in their report to the National Council on Education the Committee on Normal Education did generalize in 1892 that the normal school course of study was still based on that of the common school and that a student qualified to enter high school was admitted as a rule without question.[16]

However, it was in the colleges and universities that the issues of general education on the level applicable to modern teacher preparation were being defined. Here a growing stress on functionalism and on the research ideal was shaking the foundations of the traditional program of higher education and preparing the way for an extended professional sequence in the colleges and universities and for a closer correlation of the general with the professional.

FUNCTIONAL CONCEPTS OF COLLEGIATE
GENERAL EDUCATION

As the nineteenth century drew to a close the new empirical study of psychology and the new psychology–philosophy of the Herbartians, who stressed interest as the essential condition of effective learning, began to force the believers in formal discipline and faculty psychology to retreat a bit. Throughout most of the period here discussed, however, the old theories prevailed even among the reformers, just as they had with such progressives as Wayland in the previous generation.

In arguing for his new education Charles W. Eliot couched his defense of the modern languages, sciences, and social sciences in terms of developing the powers of the mind.[17] Yet while using the terminology of the old educational thought, Eliot, Andrew Dickson White, Daniel Coit Gilman, and others thoroughly undermined the old collegiate system. Naturally, in so doing they were responding to forces deeply rooted in the American tradition and in the conditions of American life, as well as to the impact of European thought.

---

[15] See Frazier, "History of the Professional Preparation of Teachers," p. 29.

[16] National Education Association, *Proceedings, 1892*, pp. 781–788.

[17] Charles W. Eliot, "What is a Liberal Education?," *The Century,* June, 1884, reprinted in Eliot's *Educational Reform, Essays and Addresses* (New York: The Century Company, 1898), pp. 89–122.

By the time these forces, through the instrumentality of such men, had run a brief course, the theory of American higher education was profoundly changed in at least three ways, each of which has had major influence on the development of teacher education. First, the idea that functionally oriented instruction was hostile to, and could not be harmonized with, liberal education was profoundly challenged, and modifications of the general education program in the interest of professional goals were made more widely acceptable. Second, the old habit of equating liberal education with the traditionally prescribed curriculum had been shaken, and new subjects—modern languages, social sciences, exact sciences, and in some circles even education—began to gain recognition as potentially liberating studies. Finally, the emphasis on the university research ideal, based on the old liberal love of knowledge for its own sake, brought a new spirit into the college. The research ideal not only made it easier for modern subjects to enter the curriculum, it also introduced a new contender in the battle for the loyalties of the faculty and the students. Where the college had previously been torn by the conflict between general education and education for the old professions, it now had to contend with a new kind of specialism—that of the profession of advanced research.

These three trends were intimately related and affected probably every American institution of higher education. They can be nicely symbolized, however, by looking at the development of Cornell University in respect to the first trend, at Harvard in respect to the second, and at Johns Hopkins in respect to the third.

Harmonizing the utilitarian and liberal education traditions.—The formation of academies and of specialized scientific and technical schools was the early nineteenth-century response to public pressure for useful knowledge. In the older eastern states a number of ill-defined, practical "people's colleges" were established to give instruction in agriculture, engineering, and mechanical subjects. Some of these were of a very high order, such as Rensselaer Polytechnic Institute, while others were very elementary trade schools.

In the newer states of the West the belief that higher instruction should be provided in the useful as well as the traditional liberal arts found expression in the state universities which were often conceived as crowning the entire state educational system. They were designed as places where all things could be taught to all people rather than as institutions devoted exclusively to language arts. The historians of the University of Wisconsin illustrate the prevailing attitude with an editorial comment from the *Southport Telegraph* which pointed out that "if the people of Wisconsin intend to foster a hotbed of literary aristocracy . . . we have entirely mistaken their character, and have lived amongst them ten years to no purpose." [18]

Of prime importance in encouraging the states to implement their desire for useful knowledge was the passage in 1862 of the Morrill Act. To utilize the educational resources made available by that act state after state either established colleges of agriculture and mechanical arts or opened departments in existing state universities where those subjects could be taught.

The combination of forces which led to the growth of Cornell University is typical, and nicely illustrative of trends throughout the nation. In New York, as elsewhere, the interest in useful studies had led to the formation of technical schools of various sorts. Two of these are of passing interest here: The People's College which grew out of the activities of the Mechanics Mutual Protection Society, and the New York State Agricultural College which grew out of the efforts of the various agricultural societies in the state. Both of these were chartered in 1853; neither ever operated with success.[19]

These two colleges were competitors for Morrill Act funds in the early 1860's. Out of this competition came the establishment of Cornell University. The original colleges are of significance because they represented the growing popular interest in higher learning of a useful nature and because they enlisted the support of such men of affairs as Ezra Cornell.

Cornell, whose success with Western Union enabled him in 1857 to turn his major attention to the experimental agriculture which he loved, was in great measure a symbol of American activism and of the American faith in education. Having succeeded in the rough-and-

[18] *Southport* [Wisconsin] *Telegraph,* February 15, 1850, cited by Merle Curti and Vernon Carstensen in *The University of Wisconsin, A History, 1848–1925* (Madison, Wisc.: University of Wisconsin Press, 1949), Vol. I, p. 22.

[19] Ernest W. Huffcut, "Cornell University, An Historical Sketch of Its First Thirty Years, 1868–98," in Sidney Sherwood, *The University of the State of New York: History of Higher Education in the State of New York,* Contributions to American Educational History, No. 28, Herbert B. Adams, ed., U.S. Bureau of Education, Circular of Information, 1900, No. 3 (Washington, D.C.: Government Printing Office, 1900), pp. 320–328.

tumble of the marketplace, he offered, in 1865, a grant of a half-million dollars to found a school which would ". . . fit the youth of our country for the professions, the farms, the mines, the manufactures, for the investigations of science, and for mastering all the practical questions of life with success and honor." [20]

The nice distinctions between useful and liberal studies, of which the educational philosophers loved to speak, probably seemed like nonsense to Cornell. At least there was obviously no feeling on his part that fitting students for success on the farms and in the factories was incompatible with fitting them for the more purely intellectual activities of the professions and the investigations of science. In this he was characteristically American. Nevertheless, Cornell represented but one of the streams of thought which determined the pattern of the new university. Others were represented by the first president of the university, Andrew Dickson White.

White had missed the first act in the drama of reforming the pattern of higher education. However, Jefferson's work at Virginia and Ticknor's experimentation with election at Harvard, during a prior generation, had left their influence as American colleges continued to seek patterns of reconciling the ideal of a liberal education with the growth of new knowledge and the desire for new research. As White grew to intellectual maturity he contacted a number of the sources of reform.

In his *Autobiography* several of these sources are cited as contributing to the "Cornell Idea." He pointed to his reading about life in the English universities as providing the germ of the new idea, and went on to describe his resentment at the rigid, classical pattern of Yale, which he found dominated by a spirit of sectarianism and lacking instruction in modern literature. He mentioned having noted but having failed to respond favorably to the activities of the newly developing Sheffield Scientific School, although he later recognized that the experimentation and research which Silliman was there carrying on represented one of the most significant factors tending to force university reform.

After leaving Yale, White went to Europe on an educational pilgrimage as did so many American educators of the period. There, in

[20] Ezra Cornell, "Founder's Address," delivered at the Inaugural Exercises, October 7, 1868, reprinted by Alonzo B. Cornell, *"True and Firm." Biography of Ezra Cornell, Founder of the Cornell University: A Filial Tribute* (New York: A. S. Barnes and Company, 1884), p. 199.

England, at the Sorbonne, and finally at the University of Berlin, White's ideal of a university was enriched. Of Berlin he says, "There I saw my ideal of a university not only realized but extended and glorified—with renowned professors, with ample lecture-halls, with everything possible in the way of illustrative materials, with laboratories, museum, and a concourse of youth from all parts of the world." [21]

Shortly after his return from Europe, White received an appointment at the University of Michigan where Tappan was building what was, in some respects, the first real university in America. Like White and others, Tappan had studied in Europe and had been most impressed by the Prussian school system and, particularly, by the German university.[22]

At Michigan White saw his ideal complete except for the lack of technological education and for the failure to admit women. When he joined forces with Ezra Cornell they added technological instruction and shortly thereafter provided for the attendance of women. The movement which culminated in the program at Cornell—and it is only illustrative of developments going on throughout the nation—points up one significant effect of the university ideal on the concept of liberal education: namely, the insistence that a way must be found to harmonize the technical with the liberal function. In his inaugural address White listed as his first "Foundation Idea" the principle that there must be a ". . . close union of liberal and practical instruction."

The elective system in the new university.—As reform developed in colleges and universities a cluster of ideas was to be seen emerging in many places. Elements of each were apparent in Tappan's University of Michigan, in White's Cornell University, and in a number of others. However, special credit must be given to Eliot at Harvard for the most successful promotion of one of these—the elective system and the principle that all university subjects are, or can be, significantly liberalizing.

When Eliot came to Harvard in 1869 he assumed leadership of a school which had already proved its willingness to experiment with curriculum reform. Although conservative leadership had ended Ticknor's early program of election, Eliot's immediate predecessor, Thomas Hill,

[21] Andrew Dickson White, *The Autobiography of Andrew Dickson White* (New York: The Century Company, 1907), Vol. I, p. 291.
[22] For a summary of Tappan's reforms at Michigan see R. Freeman Butts, *The College Charts Its Course: Historic Conceptions and Current Proposals* (New York: McGraw-Hill Book Company, Inc., 1939), pp. 150–155.

had persuaded the faculty in 1865 and 1867 to restore free choice among a number of studies. Under Eliot's administration the doctrine of free election among all the studies offered by the university received its greatest extension.

Eliot rested his proposals largely on the belief that new social conditions required the cultivation of the new fields of knowledge with the vigor previously reserved for the older disciplines. His experience as a student of science at Harvard and as a professor of chemistry at Massachusetts Institute of Technology had made him sensitive to the fabulous new developments in every area. He realized that the addition of more subjects to the already overcrowded curriculum prescribed for undergraduates could result only in superficiality. Moreover, he recognized differences in the tastes and abilities of students and believed that the greatest development of the talents of each would result if he were free to follow his special interests.

In defending his thesis Eliot critically challenged the concept of liberal education which justified only the traditional subjects. In his essay on "What Is a Liberal Education?" Eliot argued for the extension of instruction in modern languages, English literature, history, political economy, and natural science. Eliot's argument was couched in terms of developing "powers," and he specifically disclaimed advocacy of "utilitarian" ends for liberal education. Yet in most cases the reasons advanced were based directly on the needs of the society or of the student involved. For example, French and German were needed because "Without a knowledge of these two languages it is impossible to get at the experience of the world upon any modern industrial, social, or financial question, or to master any profession which depends upon the applications of modern science." [23]

A more extended treatment of history was advocated for its value in broadening the interests of students, in extending their appreciation of the extent of the human community, and in being "useful" to the legislator, administrator, journalist, publicist, philanthropist, and philosopher. Consideration of the newly developing political economy, from which most of the current social studies emerged, was urged because of the seriousness of the "industrial, social, and political problems with which the next generations must grapple." Finally, Eliot proposed that more attention be given the natural sciences because of their unique

[23] Eliot, *Educational Reform*, p. 103.

value in teaching students to use a new type of intellectual tool which had vastly extended the powers and resources of civilization.[24] The defense of these subjects for their direct and intrinsic value in solving the problems of modern civilization was a significant departure from arguments relying solely on formal discipline.

It should be emphasized, however, that Eliot did not completely abandon the older concept. He did consider formal discipline important. Yet he argued, as had some of the leaders of the normal school movement, that there was nothing unique in the traditional subjects as agents for disciplining such faculties as observation, memory, and reason. When discussing means to develop the faculty of observation, for example, he argued, in a later article, "If the method be right, it does not matter, among the numerous subjects well fitted to develop this important faculty, which he [the student] chooses, or which be chosen for him." [25]

The continued allegiance to the idea of formal discipline is seen in the report of the Committee of Ten of which Eliot was chairman.[26] This was to be expected in 1892 when leading educationists such as William T. Harris and William H. Payne also continued to hold this psychological concept. The Herbartians were just beginning to organize their attack on the idea.[27]

The research ideal in the universities.—Basic to Eliot's advocacy of free election was his conception of the university as a center for advanced research and experimentation in all areas of human knowledge. Under his administration at Harvard this conception was thoroughly applied. Yet in extending the graduate school ideal he shared leadership with several others, the most notable of whom was, perhaps, Daniel Coit Gilman.[28]

---

[24] *Ibid.,* pp. 103–111.

[25] Charles W. Eliot, "Wherein Popular Education Has Failed," *The Forum,* 14:411–428 (December, 1892), p. 418.

[26] *Report of the Committee on Secondary School Subjects Appointed at the Meeting of the National Educational Association, July 9, 1892, with the Reports of the Conferences Arranged by This Committee and Held December 28–30, 1892* (Washington, D.C.: Government Printing Office, 1893), p. 53.

[27] Charles De Garmo commented on the Committee's statement in this respect, charging that it "seeks to correct an erroneous theory by making it universal." "Report of the Committee of Ten," *Educational Review,* 7:275–280 (March, 1894), p. 278.

[28] The very close relationship of Gilman and Eliot in ideas, in personal friendship, and in mutual assistance is thoroughly and interestingly documented from

Gilman had the advantage of opening a university relatively free from the confining influences of narrow function and partisan or sectarian control. Moreover, he started Johns Hopkins when the tradition of Jefferson, Ticknor, Tappan, and Wayland had matured in the hands of Eliot, White, and others.[29] The university which he developed came to have much in common with others throughout the land. Yet Johns Hopkins under Gilman symbolized nicely the ideal of free research. In 1885 Gilman emphasized this function for the university as follows:

It is the business of a university to advance knowledge; every professor must be a student. No history is so remote that it may be neglected; no law of mathematics is so hidden that it may not be sought out; no problem in respect to physics is so difficult that it must be shunned. No love of ease, no dread of labor, no fear of consequences, no desire for wealth, will divert a band of well-chosen professors from uniting their forces in the prosecution of study.[30]

Gilman went on to point out that research was not to be restricted to the physical sciences, but that the university scholars should investigate, as well, ". . . all that pertains to the nature of man, the growth of society, the study of language, and the establishment of the principles of intellectual and moral conduct." [31]

For Gilman, as for Eliot, the university proper was composed of the graduate and professional schools. Nevertheless, the ideal which they saw did have its implications for the undergraduate program, and the spirit of the university did pervade the college, leading to specialization as well as to breadth of offering. Years later Charles A. Beard characterized these developments in the following manner:

The original sin was committed, perhaps, when the university, in the German sense of the term, was placed in the midst of the college, and undergraduates from the provinces of life were brought into contact with a burning passion for universal knowledge. However that may be, we cannot retrace our steps.[32]

---

their correspondence by Willis Rudy, "Eliot and Gilman: The History of an Academic Friendship," *Teachers College Record,* 54:307–318 (March, 1953).

[29] Gilman summarized the assets, both material and intellectual, of the new university in his 1876 Inaugural Address, "The Johns Hopkins University in Its Beginning," *University Problems in the United States* (New York: The Century Company, 1898), pp. 1–41.

[30] *Ibid.,* pp. 55–56.

[31] *Ibid.*

[32] Charles A. Beard, "The Quest for Academic Power," *Bulletin of the American Association of University Professors,* 19:18–22 (January, 1933), p. 20.

The idea that the university should probe the frontiers of knowledge in every field seems to have been one of the greatest stimuli for adding chairs of education to university faculties. The process of bringing the graduate school of education and the primitive American normal school together defines a central problem which was to occupy professional teacher educators for a long time to come. It was complicated by the equally difficult problem of attempting to maintain the liberal ideal of unity and wholeness in the collegiate program—an ideal deeply challenged by both the university and the normal school traditions as they developed.

THE DEFENSE OF THE CONSERVATIVE
COLLEGE VIEW

Leadership in defending the conservative college and in supporting a prescribed general education curriculum relatively free from utilitarianism fell as before to Yale and Princeton. The most influential spokesmen included Noah Porter and James McCosh.[33] Their position was not essentially different from that contained in the report of the Yale faculty in 1828.

The conservatives granted that an occasional review of the curriculum was necessary, and that a place needed to be found for new subjects which had proved their value for disciplining the faculties. Moreover, the desirability of limited election to permit the exploration of special interest areas and the development of advanced scholarship in the traditional subjects was sometimes admitted.[34] Nevertheless, the carefully prescribed curriculum was vigorously insisted upon, and the claims that all subjects were "disciplinary" was answered by pointing out that all were not equally so and that the most effective were logically to be preferred and prescribed. Needless to say, those considered most effective were usually the classical languages.

Interestingly enough the man widely credited with organizing the first real university department of education, William H. Payne of Michigan,[35] strongly supported the conservative view in many respects.

[33] See Noah Porter, *The American Colleges and the American Public* (New York: Charles Scribner and Sons, 1878), and James McCosh, *The New Departure in College Education, Reply to President Eliot's Defense of It in New York, February 24, 1885* (New York: Charles Scribner's Sons, 1885).

[34] McCosh, *ibid.*, pp. 15–17.

[35] The Chair of Didactics, established at the University of Iowa in 1873, is usually cited as the first continuing university-level chair of education. Yet in

In creating his introspective science of education he arrived at a series of premises about educational values. One of these which he frequently repeated in one form or another, and which became the basis of his rather elaborate formulation of educational values, was that "the immediate practical value of a subject and its disciplinary value are usually in an inverse ratio to each other." [36] While neither Porter nor McCosh went quite this far, the idea that subjects having the greatest disciplinary result might not be immediately useful was frequently stressed.[37]

The argument about the value of directly useful subjects in disciplining the mental faculties was partly brought to a head by the famous debate in England between Herbert Spencer and Matthew Arnold about "What Knowledge Is of Most Worth?" [38] In his original essay on the subject Spencer had suggested that the acquisition of every type of learning has two values—value as *knowledge* (i.e., its use for guidance in conduct) and value for *discipline* (its use for "mental exercise"). Spencer, having made this rather common distinction, had gone on to prove, as he thought, that in the final analysis the learning of natural and social science which was best for guidance was also best for discipline—intellectual, moral, and religious. It was in opposition to this conclusion, and in favor of the traditional curriculum that such people as Payne and Porter insisted on the distinction between disciplinary and useful studies.

One more element in the conservative defense of the traditional collegiate general education curriculum should be noted. This was the stress on the necessity of providing a base of common learning experiences for all members of the educated class, regardless of their specialty. Porter especially emphasized this factor. He granted that the college had frequently combined professional training for the ministry with its general education function, but insisted that the curriculum had not

terms of patterns of organization and the ideals permeating the program Payne's University of Michigan department is frequently given precedence. See Luckey, *The Training of Secondary Teachers*, p. 105; and Frazier, "History of the Professional Education of Teachers," p. 33.

[36] William H. Payne, *Contributions to the Science of Education*, p. 50.

[37] Porter, *op. cit.*, pp. 69–70.

[38] Spencer's essay was first published in the *Westminster Review* for July, 1859, and subsequently became the first chapter of his book, *Education: Intellectual, Moral, and Physical*, which was issued in 1860. The edition here used is that published by A. L. Burt Company, New York (n.d.) in *The Home Library* series.

been organized on the basis of professional demands, as such. He explained that

The theory of education, after which a curriculum of study has been prescribed, has been, that certain studies (among which the classics and mathematics are prominent) are best fitted to prepare a man for the most efficient and successful discharge of public duty. By "public duty" we do not mean merely professional duty, but duty in that relatively commanding position, which a thoroughly cultured man is fitted to occupy.[39]

Later, in discussing the class system in colleges, Porter argued that

We assume that it is of the greatest service that the men of culture and education, in any country, pre-eminently in a country like ours, should have common convictions and common sympathies. Common convictions must have as their basis common studies. Common sympathies must grow out of congenial tastes. Unless the men of highest education have common thoughts and common sympathies among themselves, they can neither form a community of their own nor exert a strong and united influence upon the community without. Unless the students of our schools of liberal learning are held together in the same class by a curriculum of common studies, they will be divided into separate cliques or factions. If the devotees of science and culture desire and expect to exert that influence in the commonwealth which it is their duty and privilege to employ, they must be united by common bonds of thought and feeling.[40]

The rather obvious conclusion of this line of thought was that free election, or early specialization, would destroy the communication which ought to unite the educated people in all professions.

The Relationship of the General to the Professional Sequence

The changing concepts of higher education described in the preceding section were generally in the direction of (1) making the total program more flexible, and (2) of relating instruction in technology and the specialized areas of knowledge more harmoniously to general education in the liberal arts. So far as the professional sequence in teacher education was concerned, however, the implications of these developments were not widely explored in the nineteenth century. Most of those who

[39] Porter, *op. cit.*, pp. 92–93.
[40] *Ibid.*, pp. 328–329.

granted the necessity of professional instruction, as such, either proposed that it be rigidly separated from academic instruction of a general nature or else advocated the professional treatment position by which all the higher pre-service education was integrated around the professional objective. The three previously described positions about how to relate the sequences to each other continued to have their advocates, but differences within each position were often more significant than those between.

THE GENERAL AND THE PROFESSIONAL
AS DISCRETE SEQUENCES

Sentiment for a "strictly professional" normal school.—The desire to justify their existence and to elevate the public concept of the teacher's role made the word "professional" hallowed to the normal schools of the late nineteenth century. Nothing was more widely accepted in their circles than that the normal school should be "strictly professional." However, as is frequently the case with clichés, this term meant many things to many people. The only commonly held idea was that the normal school should not duplicate or compete with the secondary schools designed exclusively for general education purposes.

Granted this common idea, there were two conflicting views as to what a strictly professional school ought to do. One was the view of the "integrators" (see above, page 69) who favored the professional treatment of academic subjects and the integration of the entire curriculum of higher pre-service teacher education around the professional task. This view will be discussed later.

The other view held that an adequate general education should precede the professional program and that the normal school should not assume responsibility for academic subjects or general education as such. It is in this second sense that the term is here used. Of those holding this view,[41] William F. Phelps was one who continued to look with the

[41] Some of this group, including William T. Harris and Thomas Gray of the St. Cloud Normal School, believed that a brief *review* of the elementary subjects from a professional standpoint was essential in the normal school curriculum, and all granted the need to provide occasional subject-matter content to illustrate methodology. Such instruction was solely for professional ends, however. These men vigorously denied that the normal school should pretend to provide adequate "culture," "discipline," or whatever other objectives were conceived for general education. See W. T. Harris, Letter to the Normal Department, National Education Association, *Proceedings, 1888,* pp. 494–496.

greatest enthusiasm for the day when the normal school would receive students who had already finished an adequate general program. His argument usually hinged on the claim that academic instruction so consumed the time and energy of the professional school, and so diffused the attention of the students and faculty, that effective professional training was impossible.[42]

C. C. Rounds of Farmington, Maine, was also convinced that the burden of academic work prevented the normal schools from accomplishing the needed professional training. Arguing that time must be gained by cutting out the nonprofessional work, Rounds insisted that the attempt to provide all that the best secondary schools provided and also to add pedagogical instruction was fruitless. "Yet at best," he maintained, "we are likely to get scholars rather than teachers, at worst, cram instead of culture." [43]

Some of the normal school people were quite as concerned over the quality of the general as of the professional instruction. These included John Ogden and Larkin Dunton, both of whom felt that the mixing of general and professional lowered the quality of each.[44]

The case for the strictly professional school was summarized by Thomas J. Morgan, Rhode Island State Normal, in 1885. In commenting on academic work in the normal curriculum, Morgan argued:

A large part of the strength of normal schools is spent in giving their pupils the rudiments of the common-school studies. They do academic instead of professional work. Against this policy it may be urged that it is a waste of resources. The normal school faculties are required to do what the faculties in the high school should do. It creates rivalry and jealousy between the normal and high schools. It degrades the normal from a professional to a secondary school, thus helping it to defeat its own ends—the creating of a professional spirit. It fatally lowers the standard of attainment that should be required of every teacher. It overcrowds the course of study, and, by attempting to teach both matter and method, does neither with thoroughness. It attempts the

[42] William F. Phelps, "Normal Schools—Their Organization and Course of Study," National Education Association, *Proceedings, 1866*, pp. 131–139; and "Report on a System of Normal Schools Best Adapted to the Wants of Our People," pp. 28–41.

[43] C. C. Rounds, "Attacks on the Normal Schools," National Education Association, *Proceedings, 1877*, p. 164.

[44] John Ogden, "What Constitutes a Consistent Course of Study for Normal Schools?," National Education Association, *Proceedings, 1874*, pp. 216–229; Larkin Dunton, "What Must Be the Special Work of Normal Schools to Entitle Them to Be Called Professional?," *ibid.*, pp. 234–244.

impossible. Students need more culture and discipline than are now required upon entering normal schools, and the separation of matter and method before they can fully grasp the significance of methodology.[45]

The attitude of collegiate professors of pedagogy.—Many college professors of pedagogy also insisted that professional instruction should follow the completion of most of general education. This insistence was usually based on the assumption that such matured scholarship was needed if one were to profit from professional study. "The attempt to teach professional studies to callow minds," said Walter L. Hervey of the New York College for the Training of Teachers (later Teachers College, Columbia University), "disgusts the minds and discredits the studies. There exists no more fruitful source of complaint against professional training than this unfortunate blunder." [46]

Much the same concern was expressed by Burke A. Hinsdale in speaking to the National Education Association in 1891:

Academical preparation must precede professional. This arises from the nature of the case. The *rationale* of no subject can be taught before the subject is measurably mastered. Neither special methods nor general methods can be taught successfully until the pupil has a good academic education. The *what* must come before the *how*. Hence the effort to superinduce a professional education for teaching upon an unorganized or ill-informed mind must end in ignominious failure.[47]

The attitude of the liberal arts college.—In 1888 President Charles Kendall Adams of Cornell University told the New England Association of Colleges and Preparatory Schools that the colleges had a responsibility to provide professional training as well as liberal education for teachers.[48] Adams was not specific about the timing of his proposed program, which consisted of four pedagogical courses in addition to special instruction by subject professors in methods of teaching each of

[45] Thomas J. Morgan, *What Is the True Function of a Normal School?* Prize Essay, Award of the American Institute of Instruction (Boston: Willard Small, 1886), pp. 27–28.

[46] Walter L. Hervey, "The Function of a Teachers' Training College," National Education Association, *Proceedings, 1891,* p. 736.

[47] Burke A. Hinsdale, "The Teacher's Academical and Professional Preparation," National Education Association, *Proceedings, 1891,* p. 717.

[48] Charles K. Adams, "The Teaching of Pedagogy in Colleges and Universities," New England Association of Colleges and Preparatory Schools, *Addresses and Proceedings of the Third Annual Meeting, 1888,* pp. 17–29.

the secondary branches. At his own university such a course, open to juniors, seniors, and graduates, had been started the previous year.[49]

At the meeting of the Association the following year, J. B. Sewall gave voice to the liberal college answer.[50] Sewall granted the basic point that both a liberal education and professional training were needed by the teacher. He also endorsed the sequence of professional education recommended by President Adams: a sequence including the history of education, the philosophy of education, methods in the schoolroom, and a seminar for discussing pedagogical questions. No argument was needed, according to Sewall, to convince the intelligent person of the necessity for this training.

However, Sewall continued to argue, the real *sine qua non* of the secondary school teacher was an abundant background in liberal studies. It was the peculiar function of the college to provide this liberal education. To Sewall, any attention given to professional education could only dilute the student's interest in knowledge for its own sake. The college could help to prepare good teachers by providing the liberal background and in addition an example of teaching techniques.

One interesting twist in Sewall's argument was his claim that even the poor teaching which, he admitted, was characteristic of many college instructors would prove advantageous to the prospective teacher. He suggested that "As the good teacher is a permanent object lesson, so is the poor. Men, remembering their own difficulties and needs and how their teachers failed to see them . . . have successfully studied to be to their own pupils what their teachers were not to them." [51]

If the liberal college had no time for professional instruction, according to Sewall, the obvious answer was to turn to the university professional schools. He made a strong plea for the universities to set up graduate professional schools of education and noted the growing trend in that direction.[52]

[49] *Cornell University Register, 1886–87* (Ithaca, N. Y.: The University, 1886), pp. 70, 164.

[50] J. B. Sewall, "The Duty of the Colleges to Make Provision for the Training of Teachers for Secondary Schools," New England Association of Colleges and Preparatory Schools, *Addresses and Proceedings, 1889,* pp. 22–27.

[51] *Ibid.,* p. 25.

[52] Although Sewall's position was basically that of the conservative liberal college, he appeared more sympathetic to instruction in pedagogy than did Eliot who, with President Dwight of Yale, responded in a skeptical manner (*ibid.,* pp. 32–33). Within a year Eliot recommended to his faculty at Harvard the establishment of some courses in pedagogy; see "Minutes of the Harvard Faculty

THE GENERAL AND THE PROFESSIONAL AS
PARALLEL AND HARMONIZED SEQUENCES

There seems to have been no significant group between 1865 and 1895 who explicitly argued that the professional sequence be made parallel to the general with neither being completely dominant. Perhaps the very nature of teacher training institutions at the time accounts for the fact. The normal school was by definition professional, and, in many states, had not yet gained enough security to come into open competition with other institutions as "people's colleges." Political pressure to concentrate absolutely on their professional role was strong in a number of states.[53] As we have noted, the conservative liberal arts college was anxious to maintain its liberal purity, and the professors of education in the universities generally shared the feeling that a thorough general education should precede entirely the professional sequence. Only a few strands of thought and practice kept alive the idea of a well-blended program of parallel general and professional education.

For example, a philosophical advance guard action was fought against the idea that professional instruction in pedagogy was logically of a different kind and incompatible with the liberal instruction of the general sequence. In 1864 Thomas Hill, who preceded Eliot as president of Harvard, argued in effect that instruction in didactics was liberalizing in the same sense as was instruction in general education subjects.[54] In

---

Meeting of October 7, 1890," cited by Paul Hanus, *Adventuring in Education* (Cambridge, Mass.: Harvard University Press, 1937), p. 111. Eliot's action was, however, apparently in response to pressures in the state legislature for a university-level normal school.

[53] See Wellford Addis, "The Inception and the Progress of the American Normal School Curriculum to 1880," *Report of the Commissioner of Education for the Year 1888-89*, Vol. I (Washington, D.C.: Government Printing Office, 1891), pp. 295-299. Of particular interest is the fact that the New York Superintendent of Schools in 1877 conducted a determined campaign to free the normal schools from their efforts at general education. The same determination on the part of the Missouri Board of Regents is indicated in William S. Learned, William C. Bagley, *et al., The Professional Preparation of Teachers for American Public Schools,* Bulletin No. 14, The Carnegie Foundation for the Advancement of Teaching (New York: The Foundation, 1920), p. 71.

[54] Thomas Hill, "Remarks on the Study of Didactics in Colleges," National Teachers' Association, *Proceedings and Lectures, 1864,* pp. 177-179. Hill did *not* propose a parallel course. On the contrary, he held the four collegiate years were well filled with courses having value for all professions and should not be shortened for special instruction, however liberal it might be. He did propose a

1896 Burke A. Hinsdale, of the University of Michigan, again argued that general and specialized education were alike in terms of their psychological or philosophical results, differing only in that the specialized program was extended in one dimension.[55] The effect of the Hill–Hinsdale emphasis was to attack, with explicit reference to pedagogical training, the principle held by William H. Payne and others that the "disciplinary" or "cultural" value of a subject was necessarily in inverse ratio to its value for professional guidance.

There were occasional voices raised to protest the theories that the professional and liberal sequences should be separated or that the entire curriculum should be dominated by the professional goal. Thus in 1880 Grace C. Bibb, of the Normal Department of the Missouri State University, argued that elementary school teachers needed, during their professional training, to be close to the liberalizing influence of the university's general education program.[56] Much the same position was taken by Irwin Shepard of Minnesota in the 1888 meeting of the National Education Association's Normal Department.[57] Shepard insisted that the general and professional offerings should coincide in point of time. In this he was essentially in agreement with Lucy M. Washburne of San Jose, California.[58] Each of these people, as might be expected, was concerned with normal school programs offered under the sponsorship of colleges or universities. Bibb and Washburne were among the earliest normal school leaders to challenge the general assumption that secondary school teachers required a higher level of general education than did those in the elementary school.

The people who advocated parallel programs, though they seem clearly to have been a small minority of the more vocal teachers of

---

graduate-level normal school. The distinction that Hill made between the general education of the undergraduate school and the specialized program of the professional school was quite largely that used here, viz., that the two sequences are not different in kind but that the first is relevant alike to all professions while the second is peculiar to each.

[55] Burke A. Hinsdale, "The Dogma of Formal Discipline," a paper read to the National Council on Education, 1894, *Studies in Education, Science, Art, and History* (Chicago: Werner School Book Co., 1896), p. 56.

[56] Grace C. Bibb, "Normal Departments in State Universities," National Education Association, *Proceedings, 1880*, pp. 51–59.

[57] National Education Association, *Proceedings, 1888*, p. 479.

[58] Lucy M. Washburne, "The Subject-Matter that Properly Belongs to the Normal School Curriculum," National Education Association, *Proceedings, 1888*, pp. 485–494.

education, nevertheless appear to have defended the most common practice. While many leaders tended to apologize for the fact, there was a general agreement that most of the normal schools differed little from academies or high schools with a few courses in pedagogy.[59] Those who did not apologize for the normal school's concern with the subject matter of general education usually justified it on the grounds that such material was being professionally treated so that the normal student received a "teacher's knowledge of subject matter." Such knowledge was considered essentially different from that received in schools organized primarily for general education. To define this difference was a prime concern of many normal school leaders.

THE PROFESSIONAL TREATMENT POSITION

In 1889 the "Chicago Committee" of the National Education Association's Normal Department asked the principals of American normal schools to define what they meant by the term "teacher's knowledge of subject matter." The results were, according to the committee chairman, Thomas Gray, too diverse to permit of any generalization.[60]

Yet, if normal school leaders could not agree on a precise definition of the difference between the teacher's and the scholar's knowledge, they felt strongly that the future of the normal school depended on a distinction being established. The year before the Chicago Committee report, S. S. Parr, in a presidential address, had warned the Normal Department that

The distinction between academic knowledge of subjects, and teaching knowledge of them, is vital. If it does not exist, there is no reason why the preparation of teachers should not be turned over to colleges and their chairs of didactics.[61]

In presenting the Chicago Committee report, Gray also expressed the belief that the case for the normal schools could not be made save in

[59] Both the fact, and the tendency to apologize, can be documented by a casual scrutiny of the deliberations of the National Education Association's Normal Department between 1870 and 1895. For some specific evidences from a number of states see Wellford Addis, "The Inception and the Progress of the American Normal School Curriculum," pp. 295–299.

[60] Thomas Gray, "Report of the 'Chicago Committee' on Methods of Instruction and Courses of Study in Normal Schools," National Education Association, *Proceedings, 1889*, p. 581.

[61] S. S. Parr, "The Normal School Problems," National Education Association, *Proceedings, 1888*, p. 469.

terms of the concept of the teacher's knowledge.[62] Gray abstracted a number of responses to his questionnaire to indicate the general pattern of thought of those who found this concept meaningful. The more commonly noted aspects included the professional needs for the teacher (1) to see the subject in proper relationship to others in the curriculum, (2) to understand the psychologically sound order in which it might be presented to youngsters, (3) to have a closer insight into the logic of its organization, and (4) to be sensitive to the processes by which the student came to understand the subject.

However, Gray was not a supporter of professional treatment in its broadest sense.[63] A far more consistent advocate was William W. Parsons, president of the Terre Haute, Indiana, Normal School. In addressing the Normal Department of the National Education Association in 1890,[64] Parsons stressed the importance of focusing the normal school curriculum sharply on the professional function. He noted, as had the St. Cloud catalogue previously cited, that the normal schools might do their work in such a manner as to provide valuable general training but he insisted that this must not be the controlling aim.

Parsons granted that high schools, academies, and normal schools all taught many of the same branches. The difference, he insisted, was found in the fact that while the academic institutions aimed at "general culture" of the student, the normal school added to this the "teacher's knowledge." This "something more" included such items as (1) more attention to the "inherent logical order" of the subject, (2) an opportunity for the teacher to illustrate the principles taught in the education classes, (3) the shared motivation of students and teacher with a single goal in mind, (4) the opportunity for the student to assume the mental attitude of the teacher in looking at the subject, and (5) an opportunity for the student to analyze through introspection the process by which he came to understand the material.

Parsons agreed that the normal school could accomplish these pro-

---

[62] Gray, "Report of the 'Chicago Committee'," p. 581.

[63] Gray, who supported the "strictly professional" position, was concerned with only a professionalized *review* of material previously studied.

[64] William W. Parsons, "The Normal School Curriculum," National Education Association, *Proceedings, 1890*, pp. 718–724. Men holding this position usually insisted that they were defending a "strictly professional" normal school. Their position differed significantly from that of those who wanted the normal school to teach only classes in pedagogical subjects and to leave the responsibility for general education to other types of school (also see above, pp. 89–90).

fessional tasks by reviewing subjects previously studied, but he argued that such a procedure wasted time. Given the hypothetical case of the high school graduate with five years to complete a higher liberal education and also prepare for teaching, Parsons insisted that a five-year normal school course covering the general work of the college, professionally treated, was clearly superior in terms of both liberal and professional education to a four-year liberal arts course followed by a one-year professional course.

It is important to note two very significant differences between the professional treatment theory as advanced by Parsons and that previously developed by Cyrus Peirce. The latter had provided in practice for the professionalizing of subjects most of which would be retaught in the common school. Parsons, on the other hand, was suggesting that the higher subjects taught in the secondary school and even in the college be given such treatment. There was a clear implication that the entire pre-service program should be organized around the professional goal and made to serve professional purposes.

This extension of professional treatment to include secondary school and collegiate subjects was explicit in the catalogue of the Terre Haute Normal School for 1894. The discussion of the work in such departments as German, Latin, zoology, and history cited the liberal value of these subjects while also pointing to the stress placed on their professional utility.[65]

One other significant difference in the situation which prompted Parsons to advocate professional treatment from that which prevailed in the days of Cyrus Peirce should be noted. In the intervening years the tendency to provide special courses in the methods of teaching various subjects had grown. Largely under the influence of the Oswego movement the belief that one could become an expert in techniques of teaching with a minimum of work in the subject itself had apparently gained currency. Parsons' enthusiasm for professional treatment of subject matter was in opposition to this tendency toward excessive stress on methods by themselves.

The position held by Parsons had the support of a number of the

[65] *Twenty-Fifth Annual Catalogue of the Indiana State Normal School, 1893–94, Terre Haute, Indiana* (Indianapolis, Ind.: W. B. Burford, 1894), pp. 59–61, 66. By this time the Indiana Normal School had become essentially a post-high school institution. It continued to offer instruction in the elementary school subjects, but many of its courses might well have been on a collegiate level.

most influential normal school people during the period from 1870 to 1895. These included, at one time or another, E. C. Hewitt, Richard Edwards, C. Gilchrist, F. Louis Soldan, and others.[66]

If one judges from the deliberations of the Normal School Department of the National Education Association the professional treatment theory was not stressed as such until after 1870. Between 1870 and 1890 it received its greatest support. It represented the best rationale for a single-purpose teachers college which wanted to provide both general and professional education in competition with other types of institutions. However, the forces tending to create parallel general and professional programs which were distinct from each other, and those operating to create a "strictly professional" program to follow the general were to prove more powerful in the following period.

The Liberal and the Technical Functions Within the Professional Sequence

As the new social sciences developed in this period, more searching attention was given to the functioning of our social institutions. As the responsibility of the teacher was redefined a number of teacher educators more vigorously asserted their dissatisfaction with the technical emphasis of the traditional professional sequence.

BROADENING CONCEPTS OF THE ROLE
OF THE SCHOOL AND OF THE TEACHER

The school's function as an instrument of social policy.—We have noted the characteristic American faith in education as the instrument for solving social and individual problems. When the growth of nationalism, the extension of democracy, the rise of industrialism, and the influx of immigration from diverse political and religious backgrounds threatened the traditional political and religious values we have seen how Americans turned to the common school as an instrument for

[66] See Edgar Randolph, *The Professional Treatment of Subject Matter* (Baltimore: Warwick & York, Inc., 1924), pp. 65–93, for an extensive analysis of this point of view in the period under discussion. The present author believes a careful analysis would justify the thesis that the professional treatment position was most strongly defended by the midwestern normal schools which from the beginning aspired to prepare secondary as well as elementary school teachers and which tended more to assume a "community college" function.

their preservation. The assumption has always been widely held that the school should be close to the whole life of our people and highly functional in that life.

Yet with notable exceptions, particularly in the Enlightenment period,[67] educational thinkers had considered the role of the school to be that of transmitting cultural values defined elsewhere. The values which the school should transmit, and the guiding purposes for which the curriculum was organized, were found in the tradition of Christianity and democracy. It was assumed that instruction in the tool subjects and in the elements of the tradition would automatically create loyal and pious citizens. It was not considered a function of the school or teacher to raise questions in these vital areas. The experience of the race on the earth was assumed to be unfolding according to a fixed plan of God and under natural laws divinely conceived. While human effort was required to seek out the laws of God and of nature, and to live in accordance with them, the direction of progress was thought to be pretty well fixed and inevitable.

The first flush of evolutionary thought, shocking though it was in some respects, did not challenge the basic concept of a universe and a society evolving according to an immutable, divine plan. Even prior to Darwin's *Origin of Species* Spencer had suggested in his *Social Statics* that society would achieve its destined equilibrium only after the state had stripped away the functions, including tax-supported schools, which interfered with natural social evolution.[68] In 1894 Spencer's American sociological disciple, William Graham Sumner, criticized "The Absurd Effort to Make the World Over" by reminding his readers that "Everyone of us is a child of his age and cannot get out of it. He is in the stream and is swept along with it. All his sciences and philosophy come to him out of it. Therefore the tide will not be changed by us. . . ." [69]

[67] The precise nature of the relationship of the school to other social institutions seems to have been more carefully considered and more optimistically viewed in the first two decades of our national period than in any of the ensuing decades of the nineteenth century. See Allen O. Hansen, *Liberalism and American Education in the Eighteenth Century* (New York: The Macmillan Company, 1926), for an analysis of late eighteenth-century thought.

[68] Herbert Spencer, *Social Statics, Abridged and Revised; together with Man Versus State* (New York: D. Appleton and Co., 1896), pp. 156–187.

[69] William G. Sumner, "The Absurd Effort to Make the World Over," quoted in Harvey Wish, *Society and Thought in Modern America,* Vol. II of *Society and Thought in America* (New York: Longmans, Green & Company, 1952), p. 321.

Thus in the minds of some of the earliest evolutionary sociologists, the schools were thought to have little power consciously to affect the direction of social change. Yet largely unnoticed at the time, Lester Frank Ward gave voice to a concept which had far-reaching implications for education and for the training of teachers. Ward wrote basically in opposition to the Spencer–Sumner influence.

In his *Dynamic Sociology,* written in 1883, Ward developed the concept of "anthropo-teleology," the idea that by the use of intelligence man can control the forces of nature and shape the processes of social evolution somewhat to his chosen ends. Obviously, the idea was not totally original with him. He wrote essentially in the Comtean tradition. In American thought, however, his influence was most important. For our purposes one of the highly significant things about Ward's thesis was his selection of education as the instrument for this control. He pointed out that "Education thus defined [as "scientific and popular"] is the available means of setting the progressive wheels of society in motion; it is, as it were, the lever to which the power must be applied." [70]

Ward's direct influence on professional educators was not too apparent in the period before 1895. In fact, the idea that sociology, as such, had anything to offer the professional education of teachers was only partly realized as the period ended. He was, nevertheless, profoundly influential on the thinking of such early sociologists as Albion W. Small, who, with his colleagues at Chicago and other places, helped to create modern American sociology.[71] W. T. Harris, a staunch advocate of educational sociology, was also influenced by Ward as the result of a close relationship which developed between the two.[72]

In 1896 Small addressed the National Education Association on the implications of sociology for education. The influence of the Ward pattern of thinking was clearly evident in Small's conclusions:

Sociology demands of educators, finally, that they shall not rate themselves as leaders of children, but as makers of society. Sociology knows no means for the amelioration or reform of society more radical than

[70] Lester Frank Ward, *Dynamic Sociology* (New York: D. Appleton and Company, 1924 [c1883]), Vol. I, p. 26.

[71] Small likened the position of *Dynamic Sociology* in sociology to that of the Tower in London. He testified that he was affected by Ward as by "a pillar of fire." *Origins of Sociology* (Chicago: University of Chicago Press, 1924), pp. 341–342.

[72] Elsa P. Kimball, *Sociology and Education, An Analysis of the Theories of Spencer and Ward* (New York: Columbia University Press, 1932).

those of which teachers hold the leverage. The teacher who realizes his social function will not be satisfied with passing children to the next grade. He will read his success only in the record of men and women who go from the school eager to explore wider and deeper these social relations, and zealous to do their part in making a better future. We are the dupes of faulty analysis if we imagine that schools can do much to promote social progress until they are motivated by this insight and temper.[73]

In the present century this social policy function was to receive great emphasis. Such men as George S. Counts, Ross Finney, and E. George Payne, careful students of sociology as well as of education, became sensitive to the implications for teacher education of this broader vision.

The need for professional training for educational leadership.—In the first period of teacher education professional training was primarily designed to produce the skilled craftsman—the teacher who, using a curriculum prescribed by the lay community to serve ends determined by political and religious orthodoxy, operated under the very close supervision of lay and religious leaders to produce the results demanded in terms of mastery of elementary skills and factual subject matter. The education of such a craftsman was logically viewed as technical training almost in the same sense as used in respect to mechanics or other skilled tradesmen. Educational leadership was essentially in the hands of the members of the community who were most successful economically and of those who had had the advantage of the higher education provided by the academies and the liberal colleges. The "unnatural divorce between educational science and educational influence, between didactic skill and high literary attainment," which Alpheus Crosby had bemoaned in 1860 (see above, page 53) was the rule.

Even in the normal schools themselves, as Parr pointed out as late as 1888, the presidents, principals, and professors tended to be former headmasters of academies, former college professors without specific professional training, or former superintendents, also, as a rule, with no professional training, as such.[74]

[73] Albion W. Small, "Demands of Sociology upon Pedagogy," National Education Association, *Proceedings, 1896,* p. 184.

[74] Parr, "The Normal School Problems," p. 473. Parr's statement was probably exaggerated. Particularly in the western normal schools there was almost a tendency to "inbreed" the normal tradition. Such notable leaders as Richard Edwards, William F. Phelps, William W. Parsons, the McMurrys, and Parr himself were normal school graduates, although some of them later received university training.

More often than not, outside of the larger cities, the lay board of education assumed leadership, not only in laying down basic policy, but also in administering that policy. The American local school superintendency evolved essentially from these lay boards rather than from the teaching body.[75]

As the colleges and universities developed professional programs they focused on training secondary school teachers and school administrators whose professional role was far more broadly conceived than that of the normal school graduates. The gap was, in fact, so great in the minds of some that it had a negative as well as a positive effect on the future development of teacher education. This was a period in which it was impossible to find teachers with a minimum of normal school training to fill most of the nation's classrooms, and the prestige and the salaries of the profession were low. It seemed unreasonable even to hope that standards considered ideal could be met in preparing all teachers. While Utopias could well be projected the facts seemed to demand a much less ambitious program.

The obvious way to meet the need for well-trained leadership under the limitations imposed by the practical situation was to continue, and to rationalize, the existing dual pattern—setting one program for leaders and a second for followers. In spite of frequent objections this practice had, of course, prevailed from the beginning. Especially among the university professors of pedagogy there was a strong feeling that they should train educational leaders while the normal schools prepared skilled craftsmen to follow this leadership.

One of the more outspoken exponents of this view was Payne of Michigan who, considering the professional education for the great mass of teachers, asked,

Shall they be expected to pursue a liberal course of study in college or university, and to become versed in educational history and science? It is folly to dream of such a consummation. The most that can be expected, with any show of reason, is that this preponderant body of teachers receive a good secondary education, and, in close connection with it, instruction in the most approved methods of doing school work. This I repeat, is the utmost that can be expected of the transient mem-

[75] See *The American School Superintendency,* Thirtieth Yearbook of the American Association of School Administrators (Washington, D.C.: The Association, 1952), pp. 49–53.

bers of the teacher's profession. Here lies, as it seems to me, the function of the normal school.[76]

In developing professional programs for training educational leaders the universities placed increasing emphasis on philosophy and educational research in a number of areas. They focused attention on questions of educational policy which were not located in the classroom, narrowly conceived. Ultimately, their program came to consider such things as the need to redefine educational aims, to reconstruct the curriculum in keeping with rapidly changing social realities, to provide emotional security for youngsters whose lives were no longer fulfilled in a well-integrated community and family life, and to examine the role of the professional educator in the ever more apparent struggle of competing power groups to manipulate the school and society to their own preferred ends. However, in 1895 all this was only potential in university professional sequences. It could not even become that in respect to elementary school teachers while they were conceived as artisan followers of the university-trained administrators and secondary school teachers.

Nevertheless, in response to the newly conceived social role of the school and the newly sensed responsibility for the professional training of educational leaders, new areas of educational theory were gradually developed, and the importance of the liberal function within the professional sequence was more acutely realized by leaders in the normal school and the university. By 1895 something approaching the modern concept of educational foundations was being expressed.

BROADENING THE THEORETICAL FOUNDATIONS OF EDUCATION

The introspective approach to the science of education.—It has been noted that from the beginning the teachers of education had stressed the importance of the study of mental philosophy, or the "science of the mind." Until nearly the end of the nineteenth century this introspective study of how learning occurs, combined with some moral philosophy and some speculative rules to guide teaching method, constituted what was considered the science of education. It is the root from which both educational philosophy and educational psychology have largely grown.

[76] Payne, *Contributions to the Science of Education,* pp. 273–274.

In the post-Civil War period, the attempt to erect a science of education on the basis of introspective philosophy was greatly stimulated by such leaders as William F. Phelps, William H. Payne, and Thomas J. Gray. Gray, for example, deduced a series of "practical laws" to determine the course of study to which the would-be pedagogue should be exposed. These laws dictated an introspective study of mind in relation to the facts in "all the sciences and departments of learning." [77] Naturally, thought Gray, this would necessitate a mastery of Kant's thought—a rather substantial assignment to the average normal school student. Gray recognized, though deploring the fact, that the inadequate background of prospective teachers made his ideal unattainable at the moment. Yet, as a philosophical idealist, he was logically obligated to bring his practice as nearly into conformity with this ideal as possible.

Payne's approach to educational science was also of this highly philosophical variety. He was primarily concerned with the definition of a priori principles which could then be deductively applied to such educational questions as that of the proper relationship of liberal to technical education. While Payne argued that educational scientists were greatly dependent on such other disciplines as physiology, psychology, and sociology, he also suggested that there were certain areas in which the educationist had to develop his own science. He offered, as suggestive of these areas, his own thoughts about the educational value of the various subjects.[78] These thoughts exemplify the type of science contemplated by the introspective philosophers.

On rational and historical grounds Payne asserted that subjects could be defended either because of their *practical* value or because of their *disciplinary* value.[79] The former he saw as divisible into those having *direct* as opposed to those having *indirect* practical use. The latter he thought of as having *specific* (cultivating a distinct faculty such as reason) or *tonic* value (i.e., affecting the mind as a whole). With these definitions and a series of a priori assumptions,[80] Payne constructed a

[77] Thomas J. Gray, "The Normal School Idea as Embodied in the Normal School at St. Cloud," in J. P. Gordy, *Rise and Growth of the Normal School Idea*, United States Bureau of Education, Circular of Information, 1891, No. 8 (Washington, D.C.: Government Printing Office, 1891), p. 93.

[78] Payne, *Contributions to the Science of Education*, pp. 15–17, 23–68.

[79] *Ibid.*, p. 50. Payne insisted as a first principle that these types of values were usually found in inverse ratio.

[80] *Ibid.*, p. 65. Here Payne listed but a few of the types which appeared through-

table rating the common subjects as having "high," "medium," or "low" value of each kind.[81] He also offered a chart analyzing further which faculty was stimulated by which subject, and to what degree.[82]

The remainder of Payne's *Contributions* was largely given over to a discussion of mental philosophy, to a refutation of some currently popular educational theories (including those of Spencer, Eliot, and the Pestalozzians), to some discussion of historical issues such as the secularization of the school, and to a general apology for a professional sequence of a highly philosophical nature in which the direct concern with technical methodology was given little sympathy.

Not every rationalistic approach to educational philosophy was so clearly divorced from practical considerations. Some who wrote on the science of education, so-called, were positively sceptical of approaches such as Payne's. For example, Emerson D. White, whose *Elements of Pedagogy* seems to have been a widely used text, maintained that

It is feared that even the more thoughtful teachers are confused, rather than helped, by the mass of subtle facts and speculations, which are sometimes given under the name of psychology; and the author confesses his inability to see the practical bearing of much of the so-called philosophy now so often presented as the basis of educational methods.[83]

In respect to the amount of speculation about philosophical issues, White's book did differ a great deal from Payne's. However, both shared with other books used in general educational theory courses the common practice of reducing their speculation to a series of rules which they thought should undergird educational practice. It seems doubtful that normal school, or even university, students would be led to consider the broadest social and psychological implications of their educational decisions as the result of memorizing and discussing either Payne's charts or White's rules.

History of education as a liberal–professional offering.—Closely re-

---

out the book. For example, he suggested that direct and indirect practical values were apt to be in inverse ratio, and that no subject was apt to have a high tonic value and also a high specific discipline value.

[81] *Ibid.*, p. 64. For example, reading was rated high in direct-practical value, low in indirect-practical, and of low disciplinary value. History, on the other hand, rated high for tonic-disciplinary value and low in every other category.

[82] *Ibid.*, p. 65.

[83] Emerson D. White, *Elements of Pedagogy* (New York: American Book Company, 1886), pp. 10–11.

lated to instruction in the philosophy of education were the courses in the history of education. Such courses had been introduced in the normal school before the Civil War to a limited extent. After the war, and particularly when the colleges turned to instruction in education, they gained an unchallenged place in the professional curriculum. Their function was conceived clearly as liberal. Educational history tended to be essentially a study of comparative educational philosophy: that is, it dwelt largely on the theories of the classical thinkers.

Both the ideal content and the rationale for offering history of education were emphasized by F. A. P. Barnard when he proposed that Columbia College provide such instruction in 1881. Quoting indirectly from Robert H. Quick, Barnard argued:

If we can once get the teacher thoroughly interested in the thoughts of the greatest thinkers about education, and at all conscious of the infinite field of observation and varied activity which he may find in the school room, we have done both him and his pupils the greatest possible service. We have entirely changed the nature of his employment. He no longer thinks of it as a fixed course of routine work, and the dulness [sic] of routine at once disappears to the immense relief both of himself and his pupils.[84]

Essentially the same conception of the role and content of the educational history, which he maintained must be included in the ideal normal school, was expressed by Thomas J. Morgan in his American Institute of Instruction Prize Essay. He wrote:

Much is to be learned as to both the philosophy of education and methods of teaching by studying the systems of education that have been formulated, the theories that have been promulgated, and the methods recommended and followed by those who have wrought on this great question in past ages. Nothing, perhaps, so liberalizes the mind of the teacher as the intelligent study of the words and ways of such men as Locke, Ascham, Rousseau, Comenius, Pestalozzi, Froebel, and Spencer.[85]

In much the same spirit the Committee of Fifteen of the Department of Superintendence of the National Education Association, in the *Proceedings* for 1895, urged that prospective teachers should have a course in the history of education to give breadth of mind, inspiration, and caution against excess.

[84] F. A. P. Barnard, *Annual Report of the President of Columbia College, Made to the Board of Trustees, June 6, 1881* (New York: Printed for the College, 1881), p. 55.
[85] Morgan, *What Is the True Function of a Normal School?*, p. 14.

There were, of course, dissenters from the popular view of history of education. Eliot is reported to have told the New England Association of Colleges and Preparatory Schools in 1889:

I think, too, that we may offer another apology for not attempting to teach the history of education. It is the most terrible history in the world, and it is the most depressing for any human being, because there is no good history of teaching and no history of good teaching. There are no more discouraging biographies than those of men and women who give an account of their education.[86]

The most commonly used texts for courses in history of education continued to be those written by foreign scholars and dealing essentially with the theories of notable educational thinkers. Among the more popular of such texts were Compayré's *History of Pedagogy* and Quick's *Essays on Educational Reformers*. Such primary sources as the works of Rousseau, Pestalozzi, Plato, Froebel, and Spencer were frequently cited for reference.

So far as the universities were concerned, American historical scholarship was just emerging from the amateur stage in the latter part of the century. American students were working in Europe under the new "scientific" historians, and such scholars as Frederick Jackson Turner and Woodrow Wilson were being trained in Herbert Baxter Adams' seminar at Johns Hopkins.

Judged by present standards, or even by those achieved within the first decade of this century, there were no American scholars sufficiently interested and well enough qualified in educational history to produce thoroughly creditable work before 1895. The one possible exception was Richard G. Boone whose *Education in the United States* [87] was described by W. T. Harris as the first notable treatment by an American of educational history. Boone's account was strictly narrative with little attempt being made to relate it to the problems which were then most perplexing.

The child study movement and the growth of empirical psychology.— The philosophically minded students of education sought to broaden

[86] New England Association of Colleges and Preparatory Schools, *Addresses and Proceedings, 1889*, p. 32. Eliot was perhaps being facetious since within a year of this occasion he was persuading his faculty to authorize such instruction at Harvard.
[87] Richard G. Boone, *Education in the United States, Its History from the Earliest Settlement* (New York: D. Appleton and Co., 1889).

the teacher's vision by bringing the tools of logical analysis and historical perspective to bear on the problems of education. Growing originally out of the philosophical interest, as did most of the new disciplines, was the child study movement which sought specifically to help the teacher understand more fully the implications of her work upon the emotional development of the child. No subject, or area of concern, has found so congenial an atmosphere in professional teacher education as has this one.

So far as professional schools were concerned, the movement started at the Worcester, Massachusetts, Normal School in 1885 under the encouragement of G. Stanley Hall and the direction of the principal, E. Harlow Russell. Russell explicitly disclaimed any pretense that his students were capable of advanced scientific study, or that they hoped to deduce any absolute law. Nevertheless, he felt, as did Hall, that more mature workers might ultimately turn their findings to scientific use.

Russell explained the professional purpose in a manner which indicates that he hoped to bring an essentially new dimension to their work —a dimension which was not to be narrowly technical. He said:

Now the training which such young people [normal students] need is of quite another sort from that which they seek or even dream of. The very first step in the "professional" part of it should place them in a wholly different relation to children, a relation which combines two very dissimilar elements, namely, the maternal interest and the scientific interest. This change cannot be effected by precepts or lecturing, or by the study of systematic psychology.[88]

The "scientific" interest was picked up and highly stimulated by the developmental and educational psychologists, from Hall and William James through J. McKeen Cattell, J. Mark Baldwin, Edward L. Thorndike, and on through the ever-growing list of contributors.

A factor which perhaps represents the "maternal" interest cited by Russell needs to be seen in longer historical perspective. This was the emotionalized interest in children which developed through the romantic and mystic tradition of Comenius, Rousseau, Pestalozzi, and Froebel. This interest, among those which made child study so congenial to the normal school, was anti-intellectual in its emphasis on the irrational elements of experience. In a sense the depth psychologies,

---

[88] E. Harlow Russell, "The Study of Children at the State Normal School, Worcester, Mass.," *Pedagogical Seminary*, 2:343–357 (1892), p. 353.

with their emphasis on subconscious motivational and irrational tendencies of humanity, continue this tradition. It is interesting that of the leading American psychologists Hall, the guiding light of the child study movement, was apparently most receptive to Freud. Abraham A. Roback suggests the possibility that Freud might never have come to this country except for Hall's interest.[89]

In 1891 Hall started publication of *The Pedagogical Seminary,* a journal devoted largely to the comparative study of education and to the publication of findings in philosophy ("as literature rather than as dogma") and in "the natural history of the child and youth."

In his opening editorial Hall attacked the prevailing rationalist philosophies of education. He argued that there was an undue prevalence of dogma in both philosophy and methods of education and that its problems were discussed and settled far too abstractly. He was bitterly critical of philosophical "systems" of education, complaining that

There is no philosophy or science yet developed that is large enough to cover education. To rely on any one or all of these is a sign of that precocity that marks sterility in a student, and of unpedagogic methods in teaching education—the worst taught of all subjects—on the part of its professors.[90]

In a sense, then, the child study movement and the empirical study of psychology were born in an anti-rationalist revolt. Besides embracing the romanticism of Rousseau, Pestalozzi, and Froebel, it fell heir to the anti-rationalist bias of Renaissance empirical science. Alfred North Whitehead pointed out the latter in describing Galileo's disagreement with the Scholastics. He said:

It is a great mistake to conceive this historical revolt as an appeal to reason. On the contrary, it was through and through an anti-intellectualist movement. It was the return to the contemplation of brute fact; and it was based on a recoil from the inflexible rationality of medieval thought.[91]

When one compares the excessive rationalism, almost Scholasticism, of William H. Payne with the rigid empiricism of Hall and William

[89] Abraham A. Roback, *History of American Psychology* (New York: Library Publishers, 1952), p. 158.

[90] G. Stanley Hall, Editorial, *Pedagogical Seminary,* 1:(1)iii–viii (January, 1891), p. iv.

[91] Alfred North Whitehead, *Science and the Modern World* (New York: The Macmillan Company, 1927), p. 12.

James, and when, moreover, one notes the aura of "maternal" interest with which E. Harlow Russell hoped to infuse the child study movement, it is apparent that the stage was early set for later quarrels between the educational scientists and the educational philosophers of the rationalistic variety.

The increased emphasis on comparative education.—Besides his interest in the child study movement, Hall was also instrumental in stimulating the growing emphasis on comparative education as an element in the teacher's preparation. Such a study was one of the things which he hoped to stimulate through his *Pedagogical Seminary*.

There was nothing new in this emphasis. From the very beginning of teacher education in America the citing of foreign examples had been constant. Courses in the theory and art of teaching, in principles of education, and in history of education had contained something of the comparative emphasis. Moreover, the periodicals, especially Henry Barnard's *American Journal of Education,* had been filled with descriptions of foreign practices and systems. However, their systematic study, and the establishment of courses in comparative education, had awaited the university study of education. By 1890 such courses were being offered in some of the universities. These courses were conceived essentially as part of the preparation of secondary school teachers and educational leaders, but presumably their content would have bearing on the pre-service education of elementary school teachers.

Instruction in history of education, philosophy of education, child study, and comparative education was obviously "education." In respect to other disciplines, not obviously such, there developed in the years before 1895 the roots of a new concept which provides the base for what is now called the "foundations of education."

The "foundations of education" concept.—Certain materials and techniques from other university disciplines, while not actually part of the study of educational practices or systems, have peculiar and essential bearing on what the proper role of the teacher and the school should be. The specialized professional implications of these techniques and understandings are spread over so wide an area that it is not possible for the classroom teacher to contact them all adequately as part of his general education program. Consequently, arrangements must be made within the professional sequence for such contact. This realization came early in relation to such subjects as sociology, anthropology, physiology, and various branches of philosophy. It was extended to modify existing concepts of the place of psychology, history, and philosophy in professional education.

Obviously, to say when a concept is first described is difficult since ideas are constantly evolving, and are subject to such divergent definitions. The problem of bringing those foundational studies into the most productive relationship with the rest of pre-service education still needs a great deal of attention. However, a number of teacher educators clearly realized before 1895 that such materials do have an important liberal function in the professional sequence.

In 1874, for example, John Ogden pointed out that the most fruitful source of error in the entire normal school program was its failure to give an adequate understanding of man, viewed psychologically, physically, socially, and historically.[92] While Ogden did not mention sociology—indeed, that discipline as such scarcely existed in the universities—his emphasis on seeing man in "all his possible relations in life" almost suggests a sociological approach.

A dozen years later, in 1886, Thomas J. Morgan proposed that certain "anthropological" studies, including physiology, psychology, ethics, and logic, be considered essential parts of the professional curriculum even though they were not part of the study of "pedagogy," in which he included philosophy, history, and principles of education.[93] Moreover, Morgan suggested that there also be advanced "anthropological" instruction in "ethnology and sociology."

Morgan readily recognized that instruction in such subjects might be included in the pre-professional program as part of what is now general education, and rather hoped that such could be the case. Nevertheless, he indicated that they needed an additional treatment as part of the professional sequence so that they could more specifically be brought to bear in the work of education.

During the same year the annotator of J. K. F. Rosenkranz's *Philosophy of Education,* presumably William T. Harris who edited the vol-

---

[92] Ogden, "What Constitutes a Consistent Course of Study for Normal Schools?," National Education Association, *Proceedings, 1874,* p. 225. To a surprising extent Calvin Stowe seems to have anticipated the modern concept even as early as 1839 in his *Common Schools and Teachers Seminaries* (Boston: Marsh, Capen, Lyon and Webb, 1839).

[93] Morgan, *What Is the True Function of the Normal School?* pp. 9–14.

ume, also called attention to the dependence of pedagogy on othe1 disciplines. He maintained:

The science of education is not a complete, independent science by itself. It borrows the results of other sciences, e.g., it presupposes psychology, physiology, aesthetics, and the science of rights (teaching of the institutions of the family and civil society, as well as of the state); it presupposes also the science of anthropology, in which is treated the relation of the human mind to nature. . . . Now it is clear that the science of education treats of the process of development by and through which man, as a mere animal, becomes spirit, or self-conscious mind; hence it presupposes all the sciences named, and will be defective if it ignores nature or mind, or any stage or process of either, especially anthropology, phenomenology, psychology, ethics, rights, aesthetics, religion, or philosophy.[94]

Six years later Harris stated a thesis, sometimes cited as the first call for educational sociology as such:

But no philosophy of education is fundamental until it is based on sociology—not on physiology, not even on psychology, but on sociology. The evolution of civilization is the key to education in all its varieties and phases. . . .[95]

The idea implicit in the foundations approach was described by Edward Shaw of New York University in this manner:

There is a large body of knowledge searched out by investigation in different realms, printed in the reports of the various societies, and laid aside, which becomes lost for want of application; for the want of some middleman, so to speak, to put it in order, to point out its direct application, so that teachers may make use of it. . . . We need, therefore, a middleman. The university should supply this—should fulfill this office—should gather up all that is discovered in the different realms, order it as a body of pedagogical doctrine, so that those going into teaching can have all that has been discovered put at their command for use.[96]

Shaw went on to specify medicine, aesthetics, ethics, history, physiology, philosophy, psychology, and comparative education as the fields having important contributions to make. He was, of course, discussing the work of the university, and specifically disclaimed any idea that

---

[94] J. K. F. Rosenkranz, *The Philosophy of Education*, trans. by Anna C. Brackett (New York: D. Appleton and Company, 1886), pp. 1–2.

[95] William T. Harris, "Review of H. Courthope Brown's *Froebel and Education by Self-Activity*," *Educational Review*, VI:84 (June, 1893).

[96] National Education Association, *Proceedings, 1894*, p. 563.

normal school students were capable of doing advanced research in these various areas. Nevertheless, the clear implication of his idea was that the materials thus uncovered and sifted for their educational implication should become part of the teacher's equipment.

At New York University, whose School of Pedagogy Shaw came to head, courses in "Aesthetics in Relation to Education," in "The Relation of Medicine to Pedagogy," and in "Sociology in Relation to Education" appeared in the early 1890's.[97]

The Herbartians were also active in promoting the idea that a careful study of the social sciences, beyond that usually required to teach them in the common schools, was an essential part of the prospective teacher's professional equipment. They suggested a concentration of studies around a central core, of which history, broadly defined to include literature, was the most popular. The concept of "culture epochs," the idea that the child "recapitulated" the experience and development of the race and that therefore the progressive study of whole cultures, from the primitive to the complex, would provide the most meaningful core for curricular organization, predisposed them to favor anthropological studies. One of the best statements of this aspect of the Herbartian position was made in 1894 by Richard G. Boone, a man not always identified with the Herbartians, but one who here revealed their influence.

In addressing the National Education Association's Normal Department Boone described the culture-epoch theory as a most meaningful guide to education. He insisted that a rich background in anthropology, literature, and history was essential for all teachers, and concluded:

It is not enough that pedagogy be rooted in psychology; it sustains, of necessity, vital relations with ethics, physiology, anthropology and logic, in addition to the almost equally helpful ones of sociology and philosophy. Indeed, the one thing that most distinguishes the current study of educational questions is, perhaps, this vitalizing of our notions and our interpretations of them, through a better insight into and employment of these collateral relations. No one can be thought an expert in such matters who only knows the school.[98]

[97] See University of the City of New York, *Catalogue for 1893–1894; ibid., 1895–1896.* Similar courses drawing from sociology, anthropology, aesthetics, history, philosophy, and physiology appeared during the same period in several universities.

[98] Richard G. Boone, "The Teacher as an Expert," National Education Association, *Proceedings, 1894,* p. 867.

Boone was more akin to Harris and the Hegelians than to the Herbartians in some respects, but when he based his argument for anthropology, sociology, history, and literature on the culture-epoch approach and concentration of studies, he bore clear evidence of the Herbartian influence.

One element of the foundations approach in its embryonic nineteenth-century form was a recognition that such subjects might not necessarily yield direct rules for classroom technique. This element was clear in the thinking of Josiah Royce, who, though extremely skeptical of all study of "education," as such, and positively hostile to the pretensions of systematized "sciences" of education, was instrumental in the early organization of the department of education at Harvard.[99]

Royce's denial that a "science of education" existed [100] has, of course, made him anathema to some educationists. He opposed much that educationists have held dear. There was, however, a positive side to his criticism which they have tended to ignore. To begin with, the educationists themselves have now turned against the particular systematized "sciences" which he denounced—the mechanical rules of object teaching, the formal steps of the Herbartians, and the abstract classifications of values and rules of such idealist educational philosophers as William H. Payne. Royce did not deny that teachers need special training. What he emphasized was that "scientific" rules must be tempered by a broad individual sympathy for children, and a sensitivity to social and cultural forces and values.

William James was even more emphatic in pointing out that the foundational subjects of education, in his case psychology, must not be seen as directly providing rules for classroom practice. In his *Talks to Teachers,* an 1899 revision of the lectures delivered to Harvard students of education in 1892, James insisted:

I say moreover that you make a great, a very great mistake, if you think that psychology, being the science of the mind's laws, is something from which you can deduce definite programmes and schemes and methods of instruction for immediate schoolroom use.[101]

[99] See Paul Hanus, *Adventuring in Education* (Cambridge, Mass.: Harvard University Press, 1937), pp. 117–121.

[100] Josiah Royce, "Is There a Science of Education?," *Educational Review,* 1: 15–25 (January, 1891).

[101] William James, *Talks to Teachers on Psychology: And to Students on Some of Life's Ideals* (New York: Henry Holt & Company, Inc., 1923), p. 7.

INSTRUCTION IN TECHNICAL THEORY AND
DIRECT-EXPERIENCE PROGRAMS

We have noted that foundational theory was just beginning to receive systematic attention in the closing decades of the nineteenth century. In contrast to this late development, theories of technical method, growing from early instruction in the modes of teaching, were becoming very elaborate. Most of the writers of textbooks in pedagogy or the science of education included a list of principles to guide the actual teaching practice of students.[102] These principles were, presumably, deduced from the philosophy of mind which the author held. For example, Emerson D. White, having discussed the intellectual processes of man, turned to their implication for teaching and developed seven principles, among which were the following:

1. Teaching, both in matter and method, must be adapted to the capability of the taught.
2. There is a natural order in which the powers of the mind should be exercised, and the corresponding kinds of knowledge taught.
3. A true course of instruction for elementary schools cuts off a section of presentative, representative, and thought knowledge each year.
4. Knowledge can be taught only by occasioning the appropriate activity of the learner's mind.
5. The primary concepts and ideas in every branch of knowledge must be taught objectively in all grades of school.[103]

Under the definition of science which seems to have been most widely held by educationists (i.e., that science consists of an orderly arrangement of things based on a uniformity of relationships, and that its method is synthetic),[104] there was a continuing emphasis on the need to systematize the rules and thus make teaching "scientific." As a result, the period was one of system builders. It opened with the work of Edward A. Sheldon at Oswego who tried to erect a complete system of philosophy and method based on Pestalozzi. His great hope for such a system was apparent as early as 1861 when he said:

[102] See Alexander Bain, *Education as a Science,* International Education Series, Vol. 25 (New York: D. Appleton, 1887), Chapters 8 and 9; Emerson D. White, *Elements of Pedagogy,* pp. 100–130; and Francis B. Palmer, *The Science of Education* (New York: Van Antwerp, Bragg and Co., 1887). Palmer's treatment is throughout a series of deductive "laws," "proofs," and derived rules.

[103] White, *Elements of Pedagogy,* pp. 100–130. Each law is followed in the text by an extended discussion of application.

[104] See Palmer, *The Science of Education,* pp. 22–23.

If we mistake not, we are on the eve of a great revolution in our methods of teaching in this country. We say methods, for we have hitherto had nothing that is worthy of being called a national system of education. We have been teaching too much at random; with no intelligent views of the true character of the human mind in its early development, and the proper adaptation of studies to such development.[105]

As the program at Oswego was perfected, Sheldon came very near to accomplishing his revolution. Starting with Pestalozzi's sense realism and his ideal of the harmonious cultivation of the moral and mental faculties, the Oswego people developed a series of general rules for teaching, organized classes in which the special rules for teaching each subject were studied, and, to cap the system, developed a thoroughgoing training school program.

The training school emphasis had existed before the foundation of the Oswego school, but the thorough organization of teacher education around the training class, and the systematic organization of method were essentially outgrowths of the Oswego influence. Both Ned H. Dearborn and Andrew P. Hollis emphasized this point in evaluating the Oswego contribution.[106] Hollis particularly stressed the fact that the pre-Oswego normal school lacked the systematic set of organized rules around which the entire program of teacher education could be organized.

With the general rules provided by the Pestalozzian theory, as conceived at Oswego, the problem of creating set procedures for teaching each subject became comparatively easy. It was a small step to the assumption, clearly feared by Sheldon himself,[107] that anyone with a good grasp of technique could teach anything.

[105] Edward A. Sheldon, "Annual Report of the Board of Education for the Year Ending March 31, 1861," *Historical Sketches Relating to the First Quarter Century of the State Normal and Training School at Oswego, N. Y.* (Oswego, N. Y.: R. J. Oliphant, 1888), p. 18.

[106] Ned H. Dearborn, *The Oswego Movement in American Education* (New York: Bureau of Publications, Teachers College, Columbia University, 1925), pp. 106–108; and Andrew P. Hollis, *The Contribution of the Oswego Normal School to Educational Progress in the United States* (Boston: D. C. Heath & Company, 1898), pp. 37–38, 9–15.

[107] In an 1863 address to the National Education Association, Sheldon decried the tendency of teachers to study methods without proper regard to underlying principles. Even he, however, stressed the technical aspects of professional edu-

Moreover, the Oswego movement involved a revolt against the reliance upon textbooks. This revolt developed into a tendency to suspect the printed word in any context.

Systematized object teaching apparently dominated normal school practice to a significant extent until near the close of the period here discussed. When it gave way it was largely to a second systematized theory of method, that of the Herbartians. In 1893 Frank McMurry suggested that pedagogy had remained dull and ineffective primarily because it had not been thoroughly systematized.[108] He argued the need to adopt in detail a systematized method of teaching logically related to a clearly stated educational goal. Such a system he found already developed by the disciples of Herbart in Germany. In the years that followed, the technical theory described by him, his brother Charles A. McMurry, Charles De Garmo, and others, was to become highly influential.

But while some of the normal school people were developing, probably to an excess, the area of technical theory and of direct-practice teaching experience, some of the university people were vigorously denying that technical concerns had any important place in the professional sequence. As might be expected, William H. Payne exemplified the type. He argued:

In the matter of normal-school instruction, the case, under the foregoing hypotheses, will stand thus: in proportion as the technical element is brought into prominence, the course of study will lose its culture value, and by so much will diminish the real teaching power of the pupil.[109]

Much the same attitude was expressed by B. A. Hinsdale when he repeated the popular cliché that the teacher firmly grounded in theory would stagger a bit at first but would soon regain his balance and rapidly improve, while the one trained in method but with an inadequate theoretical background would be strong at first but fail thereafter to show improvement.[110]

cation and evidently thought of theory as being technical in its application. See Edward A. Sheldon, "Object Teaching," National Education Association, *Proceedings, 1863,* pp. 93–102.

[108] Frank McMurry, "Value of Herbartian Pedagogy for Normal Schools," National Education Association, *Proceedings, 1892,* pp. 421–433.

[109] Payne, *Contributions to the Science of Education,* p. 294.

[110] Hinsdale, "The Teacher's Academical and Professional Preparation," National Education Association, *Proceedings, 1891,* p. 718.

THE FUSION OF THE LIBERAL AND
THE TECHNICAL FUNCTIONS

Prior to 1895 two tendencies in professional teacher education were clearly evident: one which focused on the need to view educational problems and decisions in the light of extensive general knowledge and with the aid of newly developing disciplines of investigation, the other which took its clue from the need for teachers who had technical mastery of a high sort. In a very real sense these two tendencies were in direct opposition in 1895, and current biases on each side must be understood in the light of that opposition.

To assume that everyone was partisan to one or the other tendency is distortion. On the contrary, most of the educationists claimed to recognize the need for good technique as well as for a liberal approach to professional decision making. The opposition was and is usually implicit, not explicit. In many cases it was not apparent even to those who in practice denied the importance of one function or the other. However, the sincere, intelligent, and continued concern of many that the professional sequence give adequate attention both to the broad implications of the educative task and to its techniques should be noted.

We have noted the concern of such professional treatment advocates as William W. Parsons over the excessive technical emphasis. They were not alone among the normal school people. Thomas J. Morgan and Thomas Gray were equally concerned that the normal-school graduate conceive his job broadly in addition to becoming technically skilled. So was E. Harlow Russell who started the child study movement at Worcester, and the list could be extended at great length, including George P. Beard, John Ogden, Lucy M. Washburne, H. B. Buckham, and a host of others who rose in the meetings of the National Education Association to protest against those who denied either the need for good technique or the need for a liberal view of the professional program. However, before 1895, in spite of their good intentions, the normal schools were simply faced with an impossible task if they attempted to bring their students up to par in their knowledge of the subjects to be taught, give them an adequate general education program, teach them to view the child and educational practice in the broadest possible light, and also train skilled craftsmen.

Moreover, it was only as the period ended that men well trained in the developing social sciences, education, psychology, and philosophy were available to turn their attention to the task of teacher education. The normal schools emphasized training in methods, the universities which established schools of education sought to train leaders. While it does violence by oversimplifying, it is useful to look at teacher education in 1895 as torn between the new graduate school of pedagogy at New York University, with its courses in sociology, aesthetics, physiology, philosophy, and history applied to education on the one hand, and the Oswego Normal School with its well-organized training school and systematized courses in methods for teaching each subject on the other— one designed to train the educational architect, the other the carpenter.

In some respects the synthesis of the technical and the liberal was best symbolized by the developing program at Teachers College, Columbia University. Here belief in the importance of industrial training, of collegiate preparation for teachers, and of the graduate study of educational problems came together. An institution seeking the approval of such a university as Columbia and such a philanthropic organization as the Industrial Education Association had to make room for both technical training and university research in education and its related subjects.[111]

The College was founded ostensibly to train teachers for the Industrial Education Association in 1887. By 1895 standards had been raised to the extent that a Teachers College diploma meant essentially four years of training in addition to high school graduation. A reasonably satisfactory working arrangement with the undergraduate colleges of the University was in operation, but the College did not become part of the university system until 1898. Although appearing fairly late among university departments of education the College had sufficient financial independence to develop, under the leadership of Nicholas Murray Butler, Walter L. Hervey, and James Earl Russell, into the type of university-level, strictly professional school for preparing teachers which had long been cited as ideal. As will be seen, the problem of balancing the claims of the liberal and technical subjects within the College has been difficult, but the question of whether or not the College would be concerned with both was settled when the academician, Nicholas Mur-

111 See Walter L. Hervey, "Historical Sketch of Teachers College from Its Foundation to 1897," *Teachers College Record*, 1:12–34 (January, 1900); and James Earl Russell, *Founding Teachers College* (New York: Bureau of Publications, Teachers College, Columbia University, 1937).

ray Butler, joined the Industrial Education Association to set up their teacher training program.

Summary

As the twentieth century approached, the issues, the potentialities, and the responsibilities of American teacher education were more dramatically seen than they had been thirty years before. The advocates of special education for teachers had established their beachhead in the curriculum of the colleges and universities, and the normal schools were entrenched in many states. While the opposition would continue, sometimes furiously, the opponents of professional instruction would be fighting a containing action with little hope, and generally little desire, to eliminate it completely.

The general positions sketched in the conclusion of the last chapter (see above, pages 67 to 69) continued to be distinguishable, although the axis—from "purist" to "harmonizer"—along which they were defined had become less adequate for distinguishing significant differences of emphasis.

The "academic purist" of the conservative liberal college continued to hold essentially the old position, though with increasing opposition within the college from those attracted by the research ideal and the desire to expand their specialized academic knowledge. The threat of specialization seemed to make the traditional value of a common learning experience for all collegiate trained people both more important and more difficult to maintain.

The "professional purists," those who wanted a sequence in which the claims of the professional task were uncomplicated by the need to provide general education, more nearly dominated the thought of the educationists than at any other period in the history of American teacher education. By stressing a vigorous singleness of purpose the normal school had won at least a temporary victory over the academy as the proper climate for the professional sequence, and the new collegiate professors of education were still too insecure in their position on the university faculties to do other than accept the idea that the professional must logically follow the general sequence, even if they had been inclined to do so. Current proposals, which seem generally to receive their greatest support from the academicians, for a concentrated fifth-year professional sequence would probably have been enthusiastically received by the professional purists of the second half of the nineteenth century.

But to understand the professional purists of the period here summarized, a second axis needs to be drawn. This axis would terminate at one end in the vigorously and systematically technical emphasis of the Oswego type normal school. At the other end would be the kind of graduate school of philosophy which seemed to constitute the ideal of such people as William H. Payne and Thomas Gray. At one extreme, reduced to absurdity, might be seen the prospective teacher thoroughly mastering the philosophy of Kant and introspectively applying this philosophy to all branches of learning. At the other, similarly exaggerated, could be seen the student, with his set of memorized steps for object teaching, completely occupied with perfecting his technique by drilling before the training school class. Closer to the balance point of this axis were those who were insisting (1) that the prospective teacher, through a study of the newly developing disciplines of social science and psychology, learn to see more completely the forces at work in an educational situation and the ramifications of educational decisions, (2) that he give attention to the psychological and philosophical implications of teaching techniques, and (3) that he also receive some direct experience under careful supervision in building his technical skill.

In many respects the "integrators," those who argued that the general and specialized sequences should be completely oriented toward the professional goal—that general education should be professionally treated—occupied the middle ground. They shared with all types of purists the assumption that a single focus was needed around which to organize any educational program; they partly shared with the philosophical–professional purists a rejection of the developing cult of method; with the technical–professional purists they opposed the excessive rationalism and some of the foundational theory of the philosophers; and they agreed with the "harmonizers" that general and professional education could be largely alike in kind and ought to be pursued in conscious relation to each other. However, the general education level of teachers and of the general public had moved upward, and the normal schools were offering some secondary school and collegiate instruction. While it was clear what professional treatment meant in respect to academic materials designed to be retaught on the elementary level, the normal school concept of the professional task did not adequately demand the type of material needed in collegiate-level general education.

We have noted that the "harmonizers," who favored partially parallel sequences, were a minority of the outspoken educationists. It was often politically necessary for the normal school leaders to disclaim any ambition to operate a school for general education, and the university professors were too busy holding their small beachhead to argue vigorously for a revision of the entire university curriculum. Yet the battle for specialized sequences which paralleled the general and were harmonized with it was being effectively fought. In the front lines were those interested in the specialism of the graduate disciplines and of applied sciences such as engineering and agriculture. These new specialties represented forces at work in the intellectual, social, political, and economic scenes. Had these forces, through the new universities, not broken down the cloistered walls of the old college it seems probable that the educationists would have found their continuing struggle to secure and hold a place on the undergraduate faculties even more difficult.

The revolution in educational thought brought about by the new education of Francis Parker, the new philosophy of John Dewey, the new psychology of Edward L. Thorndike, the new methodology of the Herbartians, and the new statistical science of Joseph M. Rice, had clearly threatened before 1895. Its treatment has here been held back for the next chapter when its overwhelming impact can be more clearly seen.

chapter FOUR

New Educational Doctrines and Collegiate

Teacher Education, 1895–1930

The period from 1900 to 1930 is in full swing, and gee-whacky! how it is going! It will break its damn neck long before it gets through if it tries to keep up the speed.[1]

HENRY ADAMS NEVER FOUND THE "LAWS OF HISTORY" WHICH HE LONG sought. But the search for them did make him a most perceptive observer of social trends and developments. He was quite correct in the above prognosis of the early decades of our century. Civilization did suffer two catastrophies in the period—World War I and the Great Depression—and though there has not been a sufficient period of stability to permit an anatomical examination of the "neck" it is clear that the period did try to keep up the speed.

[1] *Letters of Henry Adams, 1892–1918,* Worthington Chauncey Ford, ed. (Cambridge, Mass.: Harvard University Press, 1938), Vol. II, p. 301.

General Forces Influencing
Educational Thought

It is trite to elaborate on the rapidity of social change between 1895 and 1930. One need but try to subtract the effects of the automobile and electricity from contemporary life to sense the tremendous difference. These developments, and others which occurred during the period, served cumulatively to increase the smothering—but vastly rewarding—interdependence of individuals and groups upon each other.

In varying forms most of the acute problems which arose during this period involved a conflict of interests of individuals and social groups to which the old cultural patterns responded sluggishly. New techniques of production, communication, corporate structure, and research brought greater potentiality for controlling physical and social forces than any other period had dared to dream possible. These techniques were largely an outgrowth of the application of science, as controlled and validated experimentation, to industry, commerce, and the social sciences, as well as to the natural and physical sciences.

SOCIAL TRENDS

Only a few trends having more or less direct bearing on teacher education need to be specifically cited here. These included (1) the increased awareness of social issues coming in the wake of America's unparalleled material progress, (2) the greater involvement of the United States in world affairs, (3) the apparent loss of coherence and unity in the life patterns of individuals, (4) the continuing urbanization, and (5) the growth of new ethical, social, and political philosophies.

The agrarian and labor unrest of the late nineteenth century came to a head in the 1893–97 depression, and social issues were in clear focus as the new century opened. Prodded by such critics as Lincoln Steffens, Henry Demarest Lloyd, Thorstein Veblen, Upton Sinclair, and Jane Addams, both of the major parties turned to reform—cautious to be sure, but nevertheless reform. In the states, laws regulating public utilities, providing workmen's compensation, controlling the labor of children, establishing minimum salaries, providing for old-age pensions, and reforming the agencies of government were passed in the early decades.

In the federal government Theodore Roosevelt, reversing his maxim for handling international affairs, carried a small stick but spoke loudly of the abuses of big business. Though the actual social reform accomplished during his administration was slight—the passage of the Pure Food Act and the Meat Inspection Act, some extensions of employers' liability, and some control of hours for trainmen—he nevertheless popularized demands for the effective control of business malpractice and for the amelioration of social ills. His successor, William H. Taft, followed generally similar policies.

Under Woodrow Wilson's "New Freedom" the tempo of reform increased. Tariff revision, the Federal Reserve Act, progressive income taxation, farm relief, and increased regulation of child labor were among the achievement of the new administration which, with the LaFollette wing of the Republican Party, had inherited the mantle of the old Populist movement.

So far as educational theory was concerned these developments were significant for at least two reasons: (1) they focused attention on social sciences and social issues from which educational philosophy drew its inspiration, and (2) the humanitarian concern in which the reform was rooted not only led to the prohibition of child labor, and the consequent freeing of older children for school, but it also made people more conscious of some of the problems which young people faced in an urban society already turning to slums.

It was probably not coincidental that the "Chicago School" of sociologists, social psychologists, anthropologists, and social philosophers did some of their most productive thinking and received widespread attention during this period. Thorstein Veblen's clear vision of social issues was shared by Albion Small, John Dewey, George Herbart Mead, William I. Thomas, and others. The social emphasis within the circles of the New Education was clearly rooted in the spirit of the times, and reflected the thinking of this group.

During this, as during previous periods, the core of American aspiration was to wring from reluctant nature, by the application of knowledge and industry, the material base for the good life. And the "good" was defined by the majority will of a nation proud of, but not tightly bound to, its traditions. These were a people fond of experimentation and habituated to seeing the results of their efforts. Thus, regardless of the beliefs which they verbalized, the philosophy by which they acted was pragmatism. It was, however, the pragmatism of William James, whose roots in New England had sensitized him to the power of religious experience, and of John Dewey, whose humanitarianism was deeply rooted in the same tradition.

The pragmatic synthesis of applied science and humanitarianism was a tenuous one. Randolph Bourne, speaking out of disillusion because of Dewey's support of World War I, called attention to the preoccupation of Dewey's disciples with the technical rather than the humane side of life. He granted that a clear concern with values marked Dewey's own thought and practice, and recognized the Deweyan emphasis on vision as well as techniques. He argued, however, that pragmatic philosophy had led the new intellectuals to sacrifice the former to the latter.[2] Bourne joined Van Wyck Brooks in the complaint that pragmatic Americans lacked the "poetic vision" needed to create more than immediate and minor goals.

That such poetic vision was lacking in much of American life, and that an obsession with technical competence frequently obscured humane ends, seem beyond question. This emphasis on techniques largely divorced from vision was pronounced in the study of education, where from 1897 until 1930 the attempt to engineer the educative process by the use of quantitative techniques gained increasing popularity. As we shall see, the educational followers of Dewey were among those consistently advocating the use of the scientific experimental approach to problems. But they also emphasized the necessity of grounding this approach firmly on social values.

A more bitter criticism of the American public because of its emphasis on applied science and social reform came from literary figures who felt that the times were running against the spirit of Classical Humanism and of the belles lettres. Nowhere was their protest more clearly focused than in their opposition to new trends in collegiate education.

As the attention of the American people turned to war and then to "normalcy" both social protest and social reform ebbed—the activities of the I. W. W. and other radical groups notwithstanding. Needless to say, the post-war administrations of Harding, Coolidge, and Hoover were not particularly noted for reform.

As the nation turned away from social issues in the immediate pre-

---

[2] Randolph Bourne, "Twilight of Idols," *Untimely Papers,* James Oppenheim, ed. (New York: B. W. Huebsch, 1919), p. 13.

war and post-war years, those educators most concerned with this emphasis were thrown on the defensive against the advance of individualist–behaviorist psychology and the statistical, as opposed to the sociophilosophical, approach to curriculum making. Only as the period ended in the great depression did people begin to emphasize once more the importance of the social sciences in the education of teachers.

It is one of the paradoxes of American history that as the nation began to develop greater intellectual independence from Europe she became politically more involved in Old-World affairs. Naturally the currents of thought continued to flow both ways in the early twentieth century. American scholars continued to study in Europe, and to draw from there most fruitful leads. Nevertheless, in the exact sciences and the social sciences, indigenous thought seems more nearly to have dominated the domestic market than at any previous time.

The frontier, in addition to draining off some economic tension, had also consumed much of the creative energy of the American public. With it closed, and with the development of machine power to free more people from the necessity of purely physical labor, American interests turned elsewhere. The exploitation of foreign markets for goods and the exploitation of knowledge in the universities were both results of the growing ability to produce a surplus of material wealth.

The whole series of foreign adventures which marked American policy from the War with Spain in 1898 to the Nicaraguan Affair in 1927 clearly indicated that the desire, perhaps the necessity, for economic expansion had destroyed United States' isolation. At some point along the line Americans lost a real share of their sovereignty in international affairs—not by surrendering it to another power, national or world, but by becoming inextricably involved in world events which dictated policy. That knowledge which teachers must pass on if their students were to participate effectively in the life of the national community was vastly expanded by this development.

The strains of disillusioning wars, of models (whether automobiles or social custom) which quickly became obsolescent, of commercialized recreation, of the small family unit with homes no longer so firmly tied together by economic or religious sanctions, of increased geographical mobility, of "keeping up with the Joneses," and of intoxicating mass media were most severe. To live serenely and intelligently in the midst of these conditions was hard enough. To assume active responsibility for them through political and social action was even more demanding. To prepare youth for such a world obviously complicated the educative task.

In no small part the discontinuities which marked the life of so many Americans grew out of the continuing urbanization. By 1930 almost half (49 per cent) of the people lived in cities of eight thousand or more. This was in contrast to the one-third so living in 1900. Such larger metropolitan centers as New York, Detroit, and Los Angeles continued to draw in vast numbers of young people seeking opportunities.

The farm, which had provided opportunities for large families to remain together, and the necessity for older children to spend a good share of their time working, by 1930 occupied only one-fifth of the gainfully employed workers. Many of these were migratory. With mechanization, which hit agriculture with force especially in the 1920's, the amount of manpower needed to cultivate the land steadily decreased, so that even farm families lost the continuity of experience which they had previously maintained. Here again increasing leisure and the greater complexity of life provided both the necessity and the opportunity for longer schooling.

EDUCATIONAL TRENDS

As communication facilities were improved and the density of population increased the growth of public elementary education was steady and imposing. Between 1900 and 1930 the number of children enrolled in the lower grades increased around 13 or 14 per cent each decade.[3] Moreover, such students were in school for an average of 143 days per year in 1930 compared to 99 in 1900. Finally, they required a total of over 640,000 elementary school teachers whereas slightly fewer than 403,000 were adequate in 1900.

Yet the more phenomenal increase occurred in secondary school enrollment. This increase was particularly significant because it put a premium on college trained teachers and because it brought into the high schools a greater proportion of less easily interested students. While the total number of children of school age was increasing by about 50 per cent, the enrollment of young people in public high schools in-

[3] Statistics in this section are based on the United States Office of Education, *Biennial Survey of Education, 1928–1930*, Bulletin, 1931, No. 20 (Washington, D.C.: Government Printing Office, 1932), pp. 5, 8, 40, and 338.

creased eightfold. Compared to approximately 500,000 in 1900 the total reached about 4,500,000 in 1930. The number of teachers needed to handle the influx of students increased from approximately 20,000 in 1900 to over 200,000 in 1930. Although collegiate enrollment also increased rapidly (about sevenfold in this same period) it failed to keep pace with the need for secondary school teachers. Consequently, an increasing percentage of the college educated people were needed to man the high school classrooms. As standards of certification and hiring were raised, the demand that teachers be actual college graduates became more general. Moreover, as the period drew to a close, collegiate study was also increasingly expected of elementary school teachers.

The period between 1895 and 1930, and particularly the decade from 1920 to 1930, is generally described as that in which the normal schools became teachers colleges. The mythical typical elementary school teacher in 1895 had received less than the equivalent of a high school education. In 1922, this was still true of perhaps one-fourth of all elementary school teachers, while over half of them had less than two years of college. By 1933, however, the average was estimated at somewhere between two and three college years, although tremendous regional variation was reported.[4]

There was a less marked increase in the level of training of secondary school teachers. As early as 1904 it was estimated that perhaps 60 per cent had completed a college course. By 1930 this majority had grown, and the tendency to encourage graduate study as part of the pre-service program existed in some scattered localities.

This consistent improvement in the length of teacher education reflected a similar increase in material wealth, in leisure, and in the complexity of social–economic life. It was also the result of the demand of the general public for higher standards enforced by certification laws and more rigorous hiring practices. The task of molding a climate of opinion favorable to higher qualifications was largely the work of the profession itself, particularly in its organized form.

Among those most active in raising standards was the American As-

---

[4] This statistical information, and that on secondary school teachers which follows, is derived from a number of studies summarized by Benjamin W. Frazier. "History of the Professional Education of Teachers in the United States," *National Survey of the Education of Teachers,* United States Office of Education, Bulletin, 1933, No. 10 (Washington, D.C.: Government Printing Office, 1935), Vol. V, Part I, pp. 42–59.

sociation of Teachers Colleges which grew out of previous organizations of normal school leaders. Although neither this body nor its predecessors engaged in actual accreditation until 1927, they did provide forums for discussing such standards and for making recommendations. The various departments of the National Education Association issued pronouncements from time to time which served as guides and stimuli.[5]

Other influential agencies which encouraged the exchange of ideas and the systematic study of teacher education problems were the National Society for the Study of Education, the National Society of College Teachers of Education, and the Supervisors of Student Teaching. The list, of course, could be extended.

The time gained when the curriculum was extended was largely given over to "academic" subjects in one form or another. The new entrance standards required completion of the high school curriculum, and as the normal schools sought collegiate status the general practice was to expand their academic programs in the fashion of the liberal arts colleges. Often the expansion of academic areas was so rapid that standards were pathetically low, and ill-prepared teachers were the result. Nevertheless, the common exaggeration that the "pedagogical locusts ate up the harvest" of added time when the conversion was made from normal school to teachers college is denied by careful studies of the transition.[6] On the contrary, the trend seems to have been to lean over backwards in adding courses of the kind which other colleges would approve.

The Concept of General Education

R. Freeman Butts has pointed out that during the period before 1910 the elective system won its victory in controversies over the college curriculum.[7] As that year approached, the continuing conflicts took the

[5] "Report of the Committee on Normal Schools," National Education Association, *Proceedings, 1899,* pp. 836–903; "Report of the Committee of Seventeen on Professional Preparation of High School Teachers," *ibid., 1907,* pp. 523–668.

[6] Arthur Bestor, in "Liberal Education and a Liberal Nation," *The American Scholar,* 21:139–149 (Spring, 1952), p. 143, is one of the last to stress this myth. See Jessie M. Pangburn, *The Evolution of the American Teachers College* (New York: Bureau of Publications, Teachers College, Columbia University, 1932), and Walter S. Monroe, *Teaching–Learning Theory and Teacher Education, 1890–1950* (Urbana, Ill.: University of Illinois Press, 1952), pp. 301–306, for summaries of evidence to the contrary.

[7] R. Freeman Butts, *The College Charts Its Course: Historic Conceptions and Current Proposals* (New York: McGraw-Hill Book Company, Inc., 1939), p. 239.

form of trying to work out acceptable compromises which, by major–minor systems, group systems, or partial election, balanced the work taken in different departments and in different courses. After about 1910, however, other basic questions, challenging the whole concept of discrete courses with their emphasis on narrow bodies of knowledge, came into the foreground.[8]

The new controversies can be seen as having revolved around four persistent problems: (1) the nature of the skills to be sought, (2) the need to ensure breadth of exposure and interests while sharpening the student's realization of the relatedness of all knowledge, (3) the effect of the growing vocational emphasis on the liberalizing quality of the program, and (4) the need to provide a common background among the members of society.

THE CONSERVATIVE POINT OF VIEW

On these issues, the position of the ultra-conservatives, the Classical Humanists, remained much what it had been in previous periods. As represented by such thinkers as Charles Eliot Norton, Irving Babbitt, Paul Shorey, and Paul Elmer More, the twentieth-century Classical Humanist found much to criticize about all of American life, and especially about education. The obsession with material goods, the sometimes grotesque behavior of the American citizen in his political life, the obvious lack of genteel standards of taste, the attempt to make secondary and collegiate education nearly universal, the abandonment of classical languages in the curriculum, the obsession with scientific studies, and the insistence on utilitarian standards of value were all revolting to these men.

In respect to the important liberal function of bringing students to identify with the human community in its centuries-old search for the examined life this group has always been most consistent. Its early twentieth-century representatives were no exception. Yet while their time concept, as applied to this community, was broad, the area of their sympathies was narrow. Babbitt, for example, placed great emphasis on the difference between Humanism and Humanitarianism and rejected the latter precisely because of its failure adequately to temper broad sympathy for the whole of the race with discipline and selectivity. He stressed the need to counterbalance the excess of democracy and lib-

[8] *Ibid.*, pp. 247–248.

erty with aristocracy and restraint.[9] This narrowed sympathy led the Classical Humanist to oppose social meliorism in the larger scene. It also led him to oppose movements aimed at providing higher education for more than the intellectual elite.

The Classical Humanists insisted most firmly that liberal education must not be presented as a disorganized, unrelated mass of miscellaneous knowledge. Because of their failure to concentrate on a comparatively small number of subjects well taught, Babbitt insisted that the colleges and preparatory schools had fallen into the "encyclopaedic smattering and miscellaneous experiment" which even Plato had found harmful to the training of the young.[10]

The obvious answer from the Humanist point of view was to free the college from the influence of the university research ideal, provide greater prescription, and center the curriculum around the humane studies. Babbitt was willing to accept a modified group system which would allow student choice so long as studies were distributed over a satisfactory number of broad fields and so long as adequate concentration in one field was provided. Babbitt's qualification to this acceptance was the proviso that such a program must be directed by men whose loyalty was to the traditional American college rather than to the German university.

Yet in spite of his emphasis on developing the "well-rounded" man, on providing an integrated curriculum, on maintaining contact with the humane community historically, and on providing sufficient leisure that the student could ponder the implications of his academic experiences, Babbitt was still writing in defense of the Classics and in opposition to the sciences, both natural and social. His biases against democracy, naturalism, science, and humanitarianism were not in keeping with the spirit or demands of the times. His concept of the intellect remained narrow and unrelated to much of life.

The conservatives among the college educators continued to defend their favored curriculum on the basis of formal discipline and faculty psychology. Paul Shorey, in his 1917 defense of Humanism, repeated the usual claims that Latin aids the study of English and that, being hard, it was good for providing discipline. He also very forcefully

---

[9] Irving Babbitt, *Literature and the American College: Essays in Defense of the Humanities* (Boston: Houghton Mifflin Company, 1908).

[10] *Ibid.*, p. 84.

argued that the opponents of the classical languages, in concentrating their fire against these psychological theories, had largely ignored what he considered the real liberal goals of humanistic studies. Shorey defined the main issue in this manner:

It is the survival or the total suppression, in the comparatively small class of educated leaders who graduate from high schools and colleges, of the very conception of linguistic, literary, and critical discipline; of culture, taste, and standards; of the historic sense itself; of some trained faculty of appreciation and enjoyment of our rich heritage from the civilized past; of some counterbalancing familiarity with the actual evolution of the human man, to soften the rigidities of physical science, and to check and control by the touchstones of humor and common sense the *a priori* deductions of pseudo-science from conjectural reconstructions of the evolution of the physical and animal man.[11]

Here again Shorey used the phraseology of formal discipline and faculty psychology. He had previously insisted that the psychological evidence on this subject was as yet inconclusive. Moreover, he argued that the literal fact of the existence of different faculties, as such, was comparatively unimportant since these or similar conceptual tools had to be used even by the educationists to express their meanings. He considered it an obvious fallacy to take a literary figure of speech into the laboratory for an analysis of its physiological accuracy.

That the ultraconservative was opposed to vocational specialization of any kind within the liberal or, for our present purposes, general education program is obvious from his basic position. The liberal arts were still to him the arts befitting a free man—a man of leisure.

However, the Classical Humanists, the ultraconservatives, were by no means the sole representatives of the idea that the liberal college should resist all specialism—whether directly vocational or simply that reaching down from graduate school research in academic disciplines. Although some of the others avoided such terms as faculties and discipline, which brought down the wrath of the educational testers, they still defined the goals of liberal education in terms of intellectual habits or attitudes.

Perhaps one of the best series of statements defining a conservative position, compared to which that of the Classical Humanists must be considered reactionary, was gathered from the writings of President

[11] Paul Shorey, *The Assault on Humanism* (Boston: The Atlantic Monthly Co., 1917), pp. 73–74.

Alexander Meiklejohn of Amherst in 1920.[12] It might be noted that R. Freeman Butts placed Meiklejohn on the side of reform and the progressives.[13] That Meiklejohn was interested in reform, that he denied the old concept of intellect as a separate faculty to be cultivated in isolation from the rest of the student's ongoing life, and that he wanted the liberal college to organize a program consistent with the realities in modern American life are true. In the present context, however, where the defining issue is the relationship of vocational or professional education to general education, Meiklejohn was conservative in the best sense of the term. While he was quite willing to experiment with the curriculum and to break away from the traditional subject-matter classifications and content, he was nevertheless primarily interested in conserving the basic values which, as he saw it, had always provided the commanding goals of liberal education.

Meiklejohn saw the role of the college as completely nonspecialized and nonprofessional. Its area of concern was with those activities common to all men. In a sense he identified "liberal" with what is here called "general" education. He argued that all higher education is governed by the belief that "activity guided by ideas is on the whole more successful than the same activity without the control of ideas." He then distinguished between the liberal and the professional school on this basis:

Every professional school selects one special group of activities carried on by the members of one special trade or occupation and brings to the furtherance of these the full light of intellectual understanding and guidance. The liberal school, on the other hand, takes as its content those activities which all men carry on, those deeds which a man must do in virtue of the fact that he is a man; and within this field it seeks to achieve the same enlightenment and insight.[14]

Meiklejohn had previously made a similar distinction in his 1912 Inaugural Address at Amherst. On that occasion he had also made the distinction between a technical and a professional school on the grounds that whereas the former was concerned with skill in carrying on specific operations under direction the latter operated within the realm of ideas

---

[12] Alexander Meiklejohn, *The Liberal College* (Boston: Marshall Jones Co., 1920). These essays were written between 1912 and 1918.

[13] Butts, *The College Charts Its Course*, pp. 304–308.

[14] Meiklejohn, *The Liberal College*, p. 26. Obviously Meiklejohn thought the professional school should be "liberal" as the term is used in this survey.

and principles. In the professional school, he pointed out, the selection and relating of materials and ideas was governed by a specific human interest.

The concern of the liberal college was different, as he saw it:

But the college is called liberal as against both of these because the instruction is dominated by no special interest, is limited to no single human task, but is intended to take human activity as a whole, to understand human endeavors not in their isolation but in the relations to one another and to the total experience which we call the life of our people.[15]

Meiklejohn was emphatic that the college should be primarily concerned with intellectual development. He did not posit the Intellect as a faculty capable of formation in isolation from real problems, nor did he view its development as opposed to a concern for utility and practicality. "The issue," he said, "is not between practical and intellectual aims but between the immediate and the remote aim, between the hasty and the measured procedure, between the demand for results at once and the willingness to wait for the best results." [16]

Butts noted that on this very crucial issue of intellectualism versus intelligence Meiklejohn was clearly on the side of the progressives who saw intelligence as definable only in terms of a way of meeting problems.[17]

Meiklejohn was also conservative on the question of election versus prescription. The idea that it made no difference what fields of knowledge a student explored as long as they were studied thoroughly was, he thought, heretical. Though he was highly sensitive to the demands of the growing bodies of knowledge, he insisted that the college had a responsibility to help the student see these bodies of knowledge in some sort of unity. In 1914 he suggested a tentative curriculum, largely prescribed for the first two years and partially prescribed throughout, which he conceived as forming "one continuous intellectual inquiry." [18]

The difference between his position and that of the Classical Humanists is seen in the clear focus of Meiklejohn's program on problems in contemporary life, in the far broader social philosophy, in a different

[15] *Ibid.,* p. 38.
[16] *Ibid.,* p. 39.
[17] Butts, *The College Charts Its Course,* p. 305.
[18] Meiklejohn, *The Liberal College,* pp. 138–148.

concept of intelligence, and in the comparatively minor attention given to classical languages and belles lettres.

REFORM IN COLLEGIATE GENERAL EDUCATION

The elective system and the university research ideal led inexorably to the compartmentalization of the general education program in the interests of the graduate disciplines. No one was more bitingly critical of this trend than were the Classical Humanists who, as noted above, constantly demanded a return to the traditional curriculum. Their desire to break down the stress on isolated disciplines was shared by college leaders of many different philosophies. In the period following 1910 the colleges experimented increasingly with schemes to reintegrate general education. By 1926 Frederick J. Kelly noted that a new demand for a critical re-examination of the whole program of collegiate education had replaced the general feeling of satisfaction of earlier years.[19]

Such experimentation took many forms. One was that of the orientation course based on a general, integrated study of man and his institutions. Illustrative of this type of course was Columbia College's offering in Contemporary Civilization. A second type of reform involved broad fields courses which surveyed the offerings of whole divisions such as the social sciences and the humanities. Other colleges introduced systems of individualized instruction (based on honors courses or specialized individual guidance), or extended such devices as the major–minor system. The cumulative effect of all these reforms was more completely to prescribe the program of the first two years, which came to be largely devoted to ensuring breadth, while leaving greater freedom for the student to concentrate on a specialized interest in the last two college years.

As the period drew to a close far more ambitious and far-reaching reforms, aimed largely at eliminating the system of isolated courses, were under way. Examples of these included Meiklejohn's Experimental College at the University of Wisconsin, the direct-experience pro-

---

[19] Frederick J. Kelly, "Curriculum-Reconstruction in the College," *The Foundations and Technique of Curriculum-Construction,* Part I, Twenty-Fifth Yearbook of the National Society for the Study of Education (Bloomington, Ill.: Public School Publishing Company, 1926), p. 383.

gram at Antioch and Whittier Colleges, and the use of achievement tests and other substitutes for course credit at the University of Chicago.

When the American Association of University Women made their extensive study of college education in 1930 [20] they uncovered overwhelming evidence, not only that the colleges were sensitive to the problems, but that a great deal was being accomplished. Their report constitutes an excellent summation of the state of liberal arts education in the United States at the end of the period here discussed.

Opposition to overcompartmentalization had come essentially from two sources. One was the old liberal arts tradition with its emphasis on the "well-rounded man." In its narrower sense it was characterized by the position of the Classical Humanists. In its broader sense perhaps Meiklejohn was representative. The second source of opposition grew up, in a way, from the concern held by such men as Francis Parker for the personality and developmental patterns of child life. This new education, drawing from the findings of the child study movement, the new psychology, and the Herbartian emphasis on interest and motivation, focused attention on the way the material and experiences of instruction look from the student's frame of reference.

While his direct and immediate influence was not responsible for much of the reform in liberal college education, John Dewey, and the educational thinkers in his general orientation, provided the most systematic rationale for that reform. Essentially Dewey represented a synthesis of the two forces described above. His essay on *The Child and the Curriculum* nicely symbolizes and expresses that synthesis.

When Dewey wrote, the claims of the student for consideration were finding little sympathy in systematic thought. Currently, however, his association with the progressive education movement has almost blinded the public to another half of his doctrine. For present readers attention must be recalled to his view of the curriculum.

Dewey pointed out that the curriculum, with its logical organization of subject matter, represents the accumulated intellectual experience of the race. He maintained that by virtue of this organization such experience was made most readily available for use. He insisted that the processes of memory, observation, and reason were aided by such logi-

[20] National Society for the Study of Education, *Changes and Experiments in Liberal-Arts Education,* Part II, Thirty-First Yearbook (Bloomington, Ill.: Public School Publishing Company, 1932).

cal organization. He emphasized the value of such organization in giving human experience "that net form which renders it most available and most significant, most fecund for future experience." [21]

Moreover, Dewey insisted that such formulated results were not opposed to the process of growth, but, rather, occupied a critical turning point in that process. At the point in life when the logically organized materials came to have psychological meaning they became, as he thought, essential instruments to further growth. Because they represented a mature potential for organizing experience they provided an end-in-view to be followed by the teacher in guiding the growth of the pupil. If, however, these logically organized disciplines were made the starting point of the educative process, their premature forcing would destroy precisely that capacity for logical thought which they were designed to aid.

Dewey argued that the meaning which a student sees in any situation is completely dependent on the way it is related to his own past experience. To present logical subject matter to one ill prepared to appreciate the logic of its organization was to reduce it to mere stuff for memorization. In the meantime the interest which might ultimately have led the child to grow into the ability to use logically organized disciplines would be dissipated.

The Child and the Curriculum was obviously not written in reference to the problems of collegiate general education. However, when the position charted there and elsewhere in Dewey's writings was extended to collegiate level teacher education, as it tended to be, some implications became clear. For example, it was clear that, except for the specialist, Dewey did not see subject matter, the curriculum, or academic disciplines—however these terms are defined—as ends in themselves of education. Their usefulness was to be determined by the aid they gave the process of inquiry into meaningful problems. Moreover, he emphasized that at any stage of the student's development the instructional program must start with the student's frame of reference. On the other hand, he indicated that the teacher, presumably on any level, should consider the ability to use the organized disciplines and to see the logic of their organization as standards for guiding and measuring growth. He clearly believed that one of the marks of a mature mind, which

---

[21] John Dewey, *The Child and the Curriculum* (Chicago: University of Chicago Press, 1902), p. 28.

surely that of the college student should approach, was the capacity to use these organized disciplines effectively.

Presumably, then, the college in its general program ought not to consider the academic disciplines as ends in themselves, or as the sole centers around which instruction should be organized. On the other hand, it should be most concerned if its students were not approaching the point at which these very effective tools were readily available. Moreover, one of the reference points by which the college should direct its program should be that of progressive improvement in the students' use of these tools. The whole argument contained in *The Child and the Curriculum* assumed that teachers on every level have sufficient appreciation of the methodology and organization of the major disciplines to use them continually as a reference point in directing the growth of the child.

Dewey's followers were not all of one mind in respect to the amount of emphasis which should ultimately be placed, in organizing the curriculum, on the disciplines as such. William H. Kilpatrick, who became the prime advocate of the activity curriculum, finally, as we shall see, proposed that such an organization of study continue throughout the teacher's collegiate education. This trend of thought in the Dewey tradition is widely recognized. On the other hand Boyd H. Bode leaned in the other direction. He argued, in 1927, that

In the light of this long discussion we may conclude, then, that logical organization is a matter of supreme importance, not only for the scientific specialist but for education in general. The recognition of this importance is a protection against both undue narrowness in vocational education and the danger of diffuseness and superficiality in the types of education that take their cue from the doctrine of pupil interest and activity. The drift of things at present is towards substituting "activities" for "subjects" in curriculum construction, these activities in the one case being the activities of adult occupations and in the other case the spontaneous activities of childhood. In either case the substitution is fraught with danger. By stressing the importance of logical organization we restore to ourselves a sense of direction, and we achieve a new meaning for the old ideas of discipline and power. The discipline that comes as the result of such a program signifies, not the strengthening of mythical "faculties," but training in method. By organizing our knowledge as science has taught us to do we acquire both a keener sense of evidence and a better equipment for dealing with new problems. . . .

As was pointed out, however, this is only one side of the story.

Logical organization is indispensable, but it must be a final result and not a starting point. Psychological organization is equally necessary. This is the truth in the contention that activity must be encouraged as much as possible.[22]

The Relationship of the General
to the Professional Sequence

Differing concepts of general education and of the ideal professional sequence were most significant in the early decades of the twentieth century, as they had been in the closing years of the nineteenth. In many respects these concepts controlled the thinking of teacher educators concerning the question of how to relate the general education sequence to the professional one. This is most obvious if we consider the position of the academic purist. As noted above (see pages 130 to 136), the conservative liberal arts college people, even such forward-looking ones as Alexander Meiklejohn, insisted that the general education years should be largely free of specialism or of the pressure for immediate utility.

THE PURIST POSITION

This position was comparatively easy to maintain in the small liberal arts colleges. It was far more difficult in the larger universities where technological and professional schools and large graduate faculties were present. In these universities, as had been the case in the preceding period, the problem of relating general to specialized education became really acute.

In 1910 both the National Association of State Universities and the Association of American Universities discussed the relationship of the liberal arts course to that of the specialized schools. There were those who defended the conservative position. Woodrow Wilson, for example, insisted that the moment any professionalism enters learning, "it ceases to wear the broad and genial face of learning." [23] Wilson maintained that specialism was the greatest intellectual as well as economic danger

---

[22] Boyd H. Bode, *Modern Educational Theories* (New York: The Macmillan Company, 1927), pp. 64–65.
[23] Woodrow Wilson, "The Position and Importance of the Arts Course as Distinct from the Professional and Semi-Professional Courses," Association of American Universities, *Journal of Proceedings and Addresses, 1910*, p. 84.

of the times, and argued that one should not enter any specialized training until he had completed a liberal education.

At the meeting of the National Association of State Universities, President Thomas Franklin Kane insisted, in the same manner, that the unique and highly important function of liberal (general) education must be kept clearly in mind and that it must serve as the foundation for the technical and professional schools.[24]

In the previous period many normal school people were among the purists insisting that the academic work be completed before students entered the "strictly professional" normal school. In the early twentieth century, however, as normal schools aspired to longer curricula and higher status, this opinion largely disappeared. An occasional "practical" dissenter was heard in the early years. For example, James M. Green in 1903 protested against the belief that only people possessed of "accuracy as well as refinement" in their knowledge should teach. He granted that this was a nice ideal but was clearly impossible, and suggested that the normal schools should stick to their business of reteaching the common branches, the needed psychology, and some methods. If people wanted academic training, he thought, they should go to the colleges.[25]

The university educationists did not, as a rule, make sharp distinctions between general and professional teacher education though the tendency was to restrict the latter to the upper years. This was partly the result of the pressure from the arts faculties, but it also represented the continued feeling on the part of some educationists that the ideal was a strictly professional graduate school similar to those provided for law and medicine. Among those who, at an early period, expressed some preference for an independent college of education were Elwood P. Cubberley, Frederick E. Bolton, William H. Burnham, Charles F. Thwing, and Frank McMurry.[26]

---

[24] Thomas F. Kane, "The Maintenance of the College of Liberal Arts in a State University in Competition With the Professional and Technical Colleges in the Same Institution," *Transactions and Proceedings of the National Association of State Universities, 1910*, pp. 120–139.

[25] James M. Green, "To What Extent and in What Manner Can the Normal School Increase Its Scholarship?," National Education Association, *Proceedings, 1903*, pp. 582–593.

[26] See W. F. Sutton, "The Organization of the Department of Education in Relation to Other Departments in Colleges and Universities," *The Journal of Pedagogy*, 19:81–130 (December, 1906; March, 1907).

THE GENERAL AND THE PROFESSIONAL AS
PARALLEL AND HARMONIZED SEQUENCES

In the matter of relating specialized curricula to general education the case for parallelism continued to be made most effectively in behalf of the applied sciences and technology—of agriculture and engineering, for example. In direct response to Wilson's argument (see above, page 140), President Charles Van Hise of Wisconsin insisted that the liberal function of education was not a matter of the presence or lack of professional objectives, but inhered in the manner the material was taught. Professional studies, he maintained, could be taught in such a way as to have precisely the same intellectual effects as if offered in a general education program.[27]

President Kane's speech at the meeting of the National Association of State Universities drew much the same sort of criticism from President G. E. MacLean, of Iowa State University, who denied the alleged hostility between liberal and professional education, although he did indicate a feeling that the general program should largely precede and supplement the professional.[28] Others were less tolerant of Kane's position. President W. O. Thompson of Ohio State University, for example, maintained that the answer was not one of "foundation" at all, but was rather one of "parallelism." He frankly opposed the idea that everyone should have a general course divorced from his specialization, and broadly implied that the general course in the liberal arts college was actually inferior because of its lack of motivation.[29] President Baker of the University of Colorado was even stronger in his denial that the liberal arts course served uniquely the liberal function. He suggested that the only thing to do with the liberal arts course in the form it then took was to abolish it. He pointed out that the university and the high school had more than filled its place. He did suggest, however, that "preparatory" work ought to continue until about the age

[27] Association of American Universities, *Proceedings and Addresses, 1910*, p. 87.
[28] The term "general education" was not used in these discussions. The university presidents were usually speaking of "the liberal arts course." The present author has taken the liberty of trying to interpret their positions in terms of the definitions given to liberal, technical, general, and professional in the first chapter of this study.
[29] National Association of State Universities, *Transactions and Proceedings, 1910*, pp. 141–143.

of twenty and should be followed by the specialized education of the university.[30]

The argument of those who favored the mixing of general and professional education in the university centered as a rule on the belief that really effective professional education would properly emphasize the liberal aims of breadth and unity. This attitude was well supported by John Dewey in a paper read to the 1917 meeting of the Association of American Universities. Dewey located the problem in varying concepts of the vocational:

> I imagine that many of the most intense differences of judgment which exist regarding the proper solution of the problem . . . are due to great differences in the connotation of the vocational. These meanings vary from the bread-and-butter conception which identifies "vocational" with an immediate pecuniary aim to a conception of the calling of a man in fulfilling his moral and intellectual destiny. With the first idea it is not difficult to attack the growing trend toward the vocational as the source of all our educational woes; with the latter, it is easy to glorify this trend as a movement to bring back the ideal of a liberal and cultural education from formal and arid bypaths to a concrete human significance.[31]

While encouraging continued experimentation with the old-type liberal or general college, Dewey doubted that any significant adjustment could be achieved in that direction. Nor did he see any promise in a "mechanical and formal marking out of territories and boundaries, tempting as it is to seek some procedure by which the professional motive shall receive full recognition while at the same time a definite and free field is reserved for purely liberal study." [32]

However, to quote further, Dewey pointed out:

> Yet I am convinced that harm threatens the development of the free intellectual life of our country if our colleges become chiefly places of preparation for professional schools, and the graduate school of

---

[30] *Ibid.*, p. 147.

[31] John Dewey, "The Modern Trend Toward Vocational Education in Its Effect Upon the Professional and Non-Professional Studies of the University," Association of American Universities, *Journal of Proceedings and Addresses, 1917*, p. 27. A case could easily be made for placing Dewey in the camp of the integrators who advocated the professional treatment of all collegiate education. The question of placement depends on how broadly one defines "vocational." It is the opinion of this author that historically many of those advocating the professional treatment position have used "professional" in its more restricted and more common sense.

[32] *Ibid.*, p. 29.

arts and sciences becomes itself a professional school in all but the label.

With these three paths closed, I look to such a utilization of the vocational trend as will serve to make the professional school itself less narrowly professional—less technically professional. Such a transformation is not mere pious desire. The demand for it is found already in the changed relation which the professions bear to the conditions of modern society.[33]

The new relations which Dewey saw developing were such that, because of the major social issues involved in professional practice, the "professional interest and public concern" were beginning to coincide. He saw this new condition already developing in relation to the practice of engineering and medicine. He maintained that as the professions became more sensitive to the social implications of their work the dilemma might be solved by the liberalizing and the humanizing of professional education. To him it seemed that the only intelligent meaning of the adjective "liberal" was suggested by such considerations. He argued:

Is it possible that training in law, medicine, or engineering when informed by an adequate recognition of its human bearing and public purpose should not be genuinely liberal? Is it anything inherent in these careers that confers upon preparation for them that sense of narrowness and selfishness carried by the ordinary use of the words "professional" and "technical"? Or is this signification due to the frequent limitation imposed upon them because of exclusion or neglect of the public interest they contain? Assuredly there is lack of imagination implied in the current identification of the humanities with literary masterpieces; for the humanism of today can be adequately expressed only in a vision of the social possibilities of the intelligence and learning embodied in the great modern enterprises of business, law, medicine, education, farming, engineering, etc.[34]

Dewey concluded his argument by insisting that neglecting the real forces and motivations in contemporary society, in order to give students a leisurely exposure to the traditions of the past, simply dissipated the interests and efforts of the students. He insisted that an overemphasis on classical learning and an illiberal conception of professional education could result only in social reaction.

Dewey had, in other places, stressed the illiberal and dangerous re-

[33] *Ibid.*
[34] *Ibid.*, pp. 30–31.

sults of a too-narrow conception of the professional or vocational role. In his *Democracy and Education* [35] he had noted the tendency of every vocation to become too dominatingly and too exclusively absorbed in its technical method and skill. Moreover, he had insisted that it was the primary task of education to safeguard against this tendency.

In yet another place Dewey had attacked the concept that truly practical men were concerned only with immediate results. In *How We Think* he had cautioned:

Truly practical men give their minds free play about a subject without asking too closely at every point for the advantage to be gained; exclusive preoccupation with matters of use and application so narrows the horizon as in the long run to defeat itself. It does not pay to tether one's thought to the post of use with too short a rope. [36]

In 1923 Dewey repeated his suggestion that the most promising resolution of the conflict between "culture and professionalism" might lie in greater emphasis on the scientific spirit of inquiry and love of thinking within the professional program. Again he insisted that professional studies, pursued with ultimate application to practice in view, could nevertheless be focused on broadly social ends. "In the degree in which the broad human factor enters in," he maintained, "culture is a consequence."

Here again, however, Dewey cautioned against the usual professional tendency to neglect philosophy, history, and the social and natural sciences. He reminded his audience that

The more theoretical studies do not attain their highest development until they find some application in human life, contributing indirectly at least to human freedom and well-being, while the more practical studies cannot reach their highest practicality save as they are animated by a disinterested spirit of inquiry. [37]

The logical consequence of the Dewey position, then, would seem to have been the organization of a curriculum in which the total destiny and interest of the student provided the guiding objective. This

---

[35] John Dewey, *Democracy and Education: An Introduction to the Philosophy of Education* (New York: The Macmillan Company, 1916), p. 360.

[36] John Dewey, *How We Think* (Boston: D. C. Heath & Company, 1910), p. 139.

[37] John Dewey, "Culture and Professionalism in Education" (an address presented at Columbia University in 1923) in *Education Today*, Joseph Ratner, ed. (New York: G. P. Putnam's Sons, 1940), p. 183.

would have involved the planning of the entire collegiate pre-service course as a unit in which the objectives of general and professional education would be interrelated. While the vocational objective would have been utilized as motivation, no narrow concept of what the teacher needs to know for effective classroom behavior would have been permitted to blot out a concern with major social problems and ideas.

In practice, the educationists who favored something of a parallel sequence were restricted by the situation in which they found themselves. There were many of them who, especially in respect to the preparation of secondary school teachers, were most emphatic about the need for advanced general education to be closely related to the professional sequence. Frequently they included advanced study in the liberal arts as part of the "professional equipment" of the teacher. Thus, James Earl Russell, of Teachers College, Columbia University, insisted that "general knowledge," which he equated with "liberal education," was logically part of the professional program for secondary school teachers.[38]

In the same spirit the Committee of Seventeen prescribed, in addition to general background and subject specialization, certain extra academic courses strictly for their professional value. These included courses in the social sciences, philosophy, and psychology.[39]

Other early twentieth-century advocates of close relationships between the arts faculty and the education faculty included J. H. Tufts and Walter B. Jacobs.[40] These men were fearful that pedagogy would lose the spirit of high scholarship and break down from overorganization if it got too far away from the rest of the university.

Later, in 1931, the committee selected by the Department of Superintendence of the National Education Association to study the relationship of general to professional education of teachers also insisted that the total pre-service program should be planned as a unit. This committee maintained, as the first principle underlying the solution of the problem, that "Problems must be solved in the light of a total edu-

[38] James Earl Russell, "The Training of Teachers for Secondary Schools," National Education Association, *Proceedings, 1899,* p. 288.

[39] Reuben Post Halleck, chm., "Report of the Committee of Seventeen on Professional Preparation of High School Teachers," National Education Association, *Proceedings, 1907,* p. 536.

[40] W. F. Sutton, "The Organization of the Department of Education," pp. 114, 130.

cation program for teachers." [41] This total program was to include both professional and avocational education which they saw as overlapping and as mutually valuable. They did suggest, without explanation, that there was an advantage in making a separate classification of education designed with primary emphasis on preparation for life outside the teacher's professional role. It is of incidental interest here to note the objectives which, though cited also as goals of *professional education,* were to fall in this special avocational group. They included the development of intellectual interests, aesthetic appreciations, high ideals of conduct, habits of effective sharing in community activities, and habits of effective thinking. They constitute, of course, rather commonly listed objectives of general education.

As the century progressed the degree of autonomy actually granted the department or college of education varied a great deal. However, it is doubtful if differences of opinion among the educationists were primarily responsible for the variation. Walter S. Monroe, after long personal experience and a careful sudy of the evolution of such colleges, indicated that such factors as the strength of the old liberal arts tradition in the faculty, the attitude and interests of the university president, and the scholarship and personal ability of the head of the education department were by far the most determining factors. [42]

Where parallel sequences existed they were frequently the result of an arrangement which simply divided the student's time between the school of education and the rest of the college or university. Such an arrangement avoided the real issue of how best to relate the two. The implicit assumption was that there is no necessary relationship—that they are either unrelated or that the nature of their relationship is inconsequential. In practice, such a course more often than not probably resulted from the tacit agreement among the faculties to leave each other alone. When the general program is planned to have a deliberate and specific bearing on the specialized sequence an element of "pro-

[41] Department of Superintendence, "The Relation of General to Professional Education of Teachers," *Five Unifying Factors in American Education,* Ninth Yearbook of the Department of Superintendence (Washington, D.C.: The Department, 1931), p. 269. The committee was chaired by John W. Withers of New York University, and included President James Angell of Yale University, Ned Dearborn, Ben W. Frazier, and President Raymond A. Kent of the University of Louisville.

[42] Monroe, *Teaching–Learning Theory,* p. 321.

fessional" treatment enters into the picture. At this point the real issues start to arise.

THE PROFESSIONAL TREATMENT POSITION

When Dewey suggested that the entire collegiate program be organized around a very broadly conceived professional goal, his proposal was clearly related to the professional treatment position. So, too, was the approach of the Committee of Seventeen which addressed itself to the whole college program of the prospective teacher and suggested a fairly complete pattern of academic and professional studies, all pointed at the teaching job. These were not, however, what was usually meant by the term "professional treatment of subject matter" in the early decades of the century.

In this century the argument for professional treatment shifted its ground a bit. The old theory had been centered on the treatment of subject matter which would, in turn, be taught to younger children. As the nineteenth century ended we noted that William W. Parsons had somewhat extended the application to higher studies, though partly by implication alone. As the twentieth century opened, the advocates of this theory started with the insistence that the program of the whole normal school or teachers college must be organized around the work of the training school. The argument, as it developed, was in some respects quite different from the position which William C. Bagley was later to recommend. Its relation to the "pure" form seems clear, however.

The Herbartians were chiefly responsible for the twist which the theory took during the first decade of the 1900's. In discussing the difference between the teacher's knowledge and the scholar's knowledge, Frank M. McMurry pointed out that the scholar was interested in "fact as fact," while the teacher was interested in "fact as related to life." [43] The bearing of the "fact" on human interest was, according to McMurry, an important professional element added to the scholar's knowledge. In the light of this added element it was necessary to select the materials presented to the prospective teacher in terms of their usefulness in teaching. Here was discriminating selection of content, an important item in professional treatment. McMurry illustrated in this manner:

[43] National Education Association, *Proceedings, 1903*, p. 563.

For example, the student of literature in college may well, perhaps, attempt to acquaint himself with some of the best poetry, novels, essays, and speeches. And this suggests the common plan followed in such work. But the teacher should certainly make a careful study of fairy-tales and fables, of *Hiawatha*, the *Iliad* and *Odyssey*, and *Pilgrim's Progress.* . . .

The teacher also needs a different knowledge of history from that of the scholar. The latter often specializes in European history, or it may be in any phase of American history that happens to interest him. But the teacher of history in the grades should be well acquainted with pioneer history and throw special emphasis on the Revolutionary War.[44]

The clear implication was that the content of collegiate academic courses for teachers should be selected, not in terms of the dictates of the discipline itself, but largely in terms of its usefulness in the elementary or secondary school classroom. To the Herbartian, the standards of value were (1) the degree to which material fostered the development of moral character, and (2) the extent to which the material would challenge the interest of the student.

According to these criteria, the American Herbartians found history and literature of greatest importance, and urged that they be taught in close relationship to each other. In so doing, they were responsible for an increase in the attention which these subjects received in the elementary school.[45] However, in spite of their own statements that the materials taught as history must be factually true,[46] their devotion to Herbartian pedagogical theories sometimes led them to be careless in their judgment of what was good history. Dorothy McMurry made precisely this point in her analysis of their contribution:

The Herbartians, while they felt that the best and fullest materials should be used in teaching history, in the search for such materials did not always confine themselves to those which could meet the strictest demands of historical accuracy. Their interest in literature as related to history tended to make them place more value upon interest or literary form than upon historical accuracy.

. . . .

Some of the fundamental principles of Herbartianism led to a distortion of history. When history was treated from the literary point of

[44] *Ibid.*

[45] See Dorothy McMurry, *Herbartian Contributions to History Instruction in American Elementary Schools,* Contributions to Education, No. 920 (New York: Bureau of Publications, Teachers College, Columbia University, 1946), *passim.*

[46] See Charles A. McMurry, *Special Methods in History* (New York: The Macmillan Company, 1913; first edition, 1903), pp. 19–20.

view, there was danger that accuracy became of less importance: the imaginative reproduction of the poet or novelist was accepted as truth.[47]

In a paper discussed at the 1903 meeting of the National Society for the Scientific Study of Education, Charles A. McMurry exemplified this tendency when he suggested that "Often a masterpiece of literature is, for children, the best possible treatment of a topic in history, e.g., Cowper's *Battle of Blenheim*, Holme's *Grandmother's Story of Bunker Hill*, Plutarch's *Alexander the Great*, Shakespeare's *Julius Caesar*, etc." [48]

Henry Johnson, professor of history at Illinois Normal University and later at Teachers College, Columbia University, apparently in reference to Charles A. McMurry, reported that at the meeting which discussed the above statement, ". . . it was mildly suggested to a certain well-known normal-school man that certain materials which he had been exploiting did not seem to fit any known historian's conception of history." [49] The response was, according to Johnson, one of complete indifference. Johnson continued:

There is a zeal inspired by pedagogy which regards the subject-matter of instruction as something to be determined wholly by principles derived from sources outside of the subject-matter itself.

> "It was two by the village clock,
> When he came to the bridge at
> Concord town."

"This," says pedagogy to the child, "is history." "But," protests some big dull book, "he was stopped on the road by British soldiers and ———." "Objection overruled," retorts pedagogy, "the educational value of the story does not depend upon its literal accuracy." [50]

Johnson's example was obviously a caricature, but like most caricatures it might have contained that element of truth which made people suspicious of all advocacy of professional treatment.

The idea that the things to be taught were to be determined solely by

[47] Dorothy McMurry, *Herbartian Contributions*, p. 73.
[48] Charles A. McMurry, "Course of Study in History in the Grades," *The Course of Study in History in the Common Schools*, Part I, Second Yearbook of the National Society for the Scientific Study of Education (Chicago: University of Chicago Press, 1903), p. 18.
[49] Henry Johnson, "The Academic Side of Normal School Work," National Education Association, *Proceedings, 1903*, p. 579.
[50] *Ibid.*

their professional value to the teacher made one's concept of the professional role most crucial. That some of the Herbartians thought of this role almost solely in terms of technical classroom management was clear from Frank M. McMurry's discussion of the training school which appeared as part of the 1899 report on normal schools.[51]

Here, McMurry discussed his thesis that the entire work of the normal school should be centered around the training school and adjusted thereto. To illustrate the implications of this thesis he suggested that since the training school course required home geography, including excursions, that topic, including the excursions, should be part of the normal school course; and that since the training school required an abundance of imaginative literature, such as fairy tales, then that literature should be a major part of the normal school literature course. The basic consideration was, as Johnson had insisted, that the selection of content was to be determined by considerations outside of the logical organization of content. Moreover, these considerations had to do only with the teacher's technical role.

It should be noted that this discussion was going on precisely at the time Dewey wrote his *Child and the Curriculum* to break down the apparent dichotomy between subject matter on the one hand and the child's interest and experience on the other. As has been suggested, Dewey critized those who ignored the fact that the subject matter constitutes a distillation of valuable experience of the same type, though on a more mature level, as that which the child naturally has. He also criticized those who made subject-matter considerations the sole standard for organizing the educative program.

The insistence that everything in the pre-service program be organized around the actual teaching task in the training school will be considered later in a different context. The important point to note here is that, at least so far as McMurry was concerned, the professional treatment theory was intimately associated with a technical and limited view of the teacher's role.

When the theory received its next important emphasis something of a different philosophy was involved. Its leading advocate was, perhaps, William C. Bagley. The definitive statement of the position appeared in

---

[51] Z. X. Snyder, chm., "Report of the Committee on Normal Schools," National Education Association, *Proceedings, 1899*, p. 852.

1920 in a Carnegie study [52] for which Bagley wrote the curriculum sections. However, for a general view of Bagley's over-all attitude, in contrast to that of McMurry, a later article is revealing. To begin with, Bagley clearly placed his confidence in the academic subject matter and in the college specialists who taught such disciplines. He said:

Now one hope that I have had in urging a greater emphasis upon subjectmatter in the professional education of teachers is that the subjectmatter specialist, working as he does in a much more limited field than that of the educationist, and concerned as he is with much more definite and tangible materials, will counteract looseness and softness toward which, for some inexplicable reason, the educationist almost always tends. But the subjectmatter specialist cannot exert a corrective influence as long as he holds himself aloof from the lower schools and their problems.[53]

Bagley expressed great surprise that the professors in the academic departments had given him so little support in his campaign. Contrary to the position held by McMurry, Bagley apparently felt that considerations growing out of the logic of subject matter should have a determining influence.

In a second respect there was an important difference between the two positions. McMurry taught in effect that correct method, based on a sound psychology, and dominated by the clear goal of moral development, was the essential qualification for teachers. He was most active in turning out texts for special methods classes. Bagley, on the other hand, objected to the whole concept of special methods divorced from content. As long as this separation existed he insisted that "we may be certain that what ought to be the finest of all fine arts will remain very largely a trade, and that its technic, which ought to grow out of the substance with which teaching deals, will remain a mere bag of tricks." [54]

Returning to the Carnegie study it should be noted that its authors were guided by a concept of the teacher's role far broader than that of

[52] William S. Learned, William C. Bagley, et al., The Professional Preparation of Teachers for American Public Schools, A Study Based Upon an Examination of Tax-Supported Normal Schools in the State of Missouri, Bulletin No. 14, The Carnegie Foundation for the Advancement of Teaching (New York: The Foundation, 1920).

[53] William C. Bagley, "Twenty Years of Progress in the Professionalization of Subjectmatter for Normal Schools and Teachers Colleges," American Association of Teachers Colleges, Yearbook, 1928, p. 75.

[54] Ibid.

mere technic. They felt that the teachers, while not the sole instruments, were the most important instruments through which a people controls its own future.[55] As will be seen, they also stressed the need for teachers to participate in the making of administrative policy.

In their recommendations, the Carnegie group stressed the conviction that no professional curriculum should look exclusively toward the development of "skill" in teaching. The ability to participate in constructing large educational plans and policies was cited as an essential goal of all professional education. Professional courses were to be judged not only by the extent to which they increased technical teaching ability but also by the degree to which they contributed to broader professional intelligence and insight of the teacher.

The essence of their recommendations for professionalizing the curriculum was concisely stated in a few paragraphs of their conclusion. Some of its components included:

Curricula of collegiate grade that have for their purpose the preparation of teachers should be professionalized throughout in the sense that every course should be chosen with specific reference to the contribution that it makes to the teacher's equipment. This would, by definition, include courses of the "liberal" type.

. . . .

As far as possible, the distinction between courses in "special methods of teaching" and courses in the subjectmatter itself should be eliminated. Every professional curriculum should embody thorough courses of distinctly collegiate character in all of the subjectmatter that the student proposes to teach. In these courses the specific organization of materials for elementary or secondary teaching should be fully discussed, and the approved methods of teaching should be both exemplified and justified. All teachers of the so-called academic subjects should hold a direct and responsible relationship to the training school.

. . . .

The importance of the training school in the scheme of curriculum construction above outlined suggests . . . the employment of teachers of educational theory and teachers of "academic" subjects as supervisors of teaching under the general control of the director of training.[56]

In making these recommendations the authors argued that the common practice of adding a few courses in "education" to a "general college course" of patched-together electives was a travesty on the term

[55] Learned, et al., The Professional Preparation of Teachers, p. 7.
[56] Ibid., pp. 393-394.

"professional education." Moreover, they insisted, as had many others before them, that the sole justification of a single-purpose teacher preparing institution was that is could provide a carefully planned and unified program. Ten years later, when most normal schools had achieved teachers college status, Edward S. Evenden emphasized precisely this same point.[57]

These recommendations were made by leading educationists of the conservative group. At Teachers College, Columbia University, Bagley was popularly assumed to hold the role of a counterbalance to William H. Kilpatrick. Throughout his entire career he emphasized the traditional ideals of academic subject-matter specialists in opposition to the "child-centered" school. Moreover, the Carnegie study, based on a very careful analysis of statistical and historical evidence, stressed the importance of broad scholarship on the part of the teacher if he were to fill a broadly conceived social role. The recommendations were in line with the theory of many of the leading teacher educators throughout the history of the normal school, as we have noticed. Yet in 1929 Evenden noted that they had had very little effect on the actual practice of teachers colleges. The bitterness with which the Carnegie study had been received in academic circles was noted by Bagley himself in 1928.[58]

In reviewing the Missouri situation ten years after the Carnegie report, Clyde M. Hill reported that professionalization of courses had made little progress.[59] In proposing ways to achieve such progress he stressed the need for developing textbooks and syllabi from this point of view. By implication it would seem that he considered the lack of such materials a fundamental barrier. However, behind this lack was the refusal, noted by Bagley, of teachers of academic disciplines to accept the position. Perhaps one reason was the very close historical tie which the theory had with the idea that such courses must include a large

[57] Edward S. Evenden, "The Critic Teacher and the Professional Treatment of Subject-Matter: A Challenge," *Supervisors of Student Teaching,* Ninth Annual Session, Association for Student Teaching (Cleveland, Ohio: The Association, 1929), pp. 39–48.

[58] William C. Bagley, "Twenty Years of Progress in the Professionalization of Subjectmatter," p. 75.

[59] Clyde M. Hill, *A Decade of Progress in Teacher Training: Specific Administrative Modifications in Missouri Teachers College Which Have Taken Place During the First Decade Following the Carnegie Survey of Tax-Supported Normal Schools in Missouri* (New York: Bureau of Publications, Teachers College, Columbia University, 1927), p. 137.

amount of elementary school material. Moreover, it seems probable that academic professors were unwilling to determine what was significant in their discipline by standards derived from pedagogical theories outside the discipline itself. This was especially true where the educationists held a narrowly technical concept of the professional role.

One other point should be given more explicit emphasis before Bagley's definition of the professional treatment position is left. That is his conviction that an artificial separation, even in terminology, between the "academic" and the "professional" was most serious. The failure of academic and professional teachers in the college jointly to consider, plan, and administer the program seemed to him tragic. While he was very critical of the "professionals," he insisted that their failure was partly the fault of the professors in other departments who had failed to take a constructive and positive interest in teacher education as such.

In this connection Bagley raised the argument that an artificial separation of "culture" from "vocation" destroyed the value of both—giving the student the impression that "culture" was something of only dilettante interest rather than the most important part of the professional equipment.

Bagley was convinced that the total pre-service program should be so conceived that the student saw no dichotomy between his professional and nonprofessional life nor felt that the two aspects of his education were unrelated. In this attitude Bagley was joined by a number of teacher educators who did not go along with other aspects of his proposed "professional treatment." Basically, in a sense, this was the position of all those normal schools which maintained the academic department strictly independent from the professional, though offering both.

The Liberal and the Technical Functions
Within the Professional Sequence

These early decades of the twentieth century saw the normal school tradition of educating for professional craftsmanship and the university ideal of training for educational leadership come increasingly under the same roof. To design a professional sequence adequate to both these traditions was the central concern of the schools of education.

REDEFINING THE ROLE
OF THE TEACHER

The growing emphasis on education as an instrument of social policy.
—We have already noted Lester Frank Ward's basic thesis that intelligent control of the processes of social evolution was possible if education were effectively used, and his conviction that the school was the
point at which leverage should be applied. We have also noted that
his influence was important in the development of the "Chicago School"
of social philosophers—Albion Small, W. I. Thomas, John Dewey,
and George Herbert Mead. Small's suggestion that the teacher must
consider herself society's agent in bringing about progressive improvement in social life has been cited (see above, page 100).

Between 1895 and 1930 this position was consistently held and developed by leaders in educational sociology and educational philosophy.
Although the Herbartians tended to concentrate on method and to
exalt the claims of rather elementary subject matter, some of them,
especially Charles De Garmo, were highly sensitive to the school's social responsibilities. In 1897 De Garmo pointed out that with the passage of the frontier and the trend toward urbanization and industrialization the old nonsocial individualism would have to give way to a
new "social individualism." In bringing about this change De Garmo
gave the school a major role.[60]

In much the same spirit, Richard G. Boone, in 1900, pointed to the
rapidity of social change and to the confusion about the role of the
school in respect to other social agencies. He, too, insisted that, if the
school were adequately to fulfill its destiny in guiding this conflict of
forces, teachers must be infinitely better prepared than previously.
Boone saw the welfare of the school itself under serious threat if teachers, even with their intelligence, vigor, and broad understanding of society's problems, proved unable to compete with the demands of aggressive, selfish individuals and organizations.[61]

For a systematic and well-conceived defense of the school's social
policy role, however, it is necessary to turn to the educational sociol-

---

[60] Charles De Garmo, "Social Aspects of Moral Education," *Third Yearbook
of the National Herbart Society* (Chicago: University of Chicago Press, 1897),
pp. 35–56.
[61] Richard G. Boone, "General Culture as an Element in Professional Training,"
National Education Association, *Proceedings, 1900,* p. 356.

ogists, who were products of the Ward tradition. One who developed that tradition most fruitfully and who continues to be one of its greatest exponents is George S. Counts. Counts was educated at Chicago under the direct influence of such men as Albion Small and W. I. Thomas. The basic position which he espoused was clearly stated, in 1924, in this manner:

Viewed as a mode of social control and as the most powerful force for good or evil in the Great Society, it [education] becomes the most significant, and at the same time the most humanistic, of all the social sciences. In its education we see Society attempting to liberate itself from its own folkways, we see it seeking to become conscious of its own aims, we see it essaying to control the course of its own evolution, we see its genuine philosophy brought into the arena of action.[62]

Counts's emphasis on the social role of the school grew out of an acute sensitivity to the great social and economic changes which had occurred. He pointed out that as the result of industrialization and urbanization nonschool agencies of education were becoming ever less adequate, and that the school was being forced to fill the gap. Two factors—increased responsibility growing out of the greater complexity of American life, and the need for the school to assume leadership in the progressive reconstruction of that life—made the work of the teacher far more difficult and significant.[63]

Sometimes the educational sociologists were carried away with their sense of what the schools could accomplish. Extreme statements here, as in any area, tended to blind people to the real merit which lay in a more restrained and moderate view. One who was most optimistic was Ross L. Finney, who insisted that the task of making social evolution purposeful was that of the social scientists and the educators. As fast as social scientists found leads toward profitable social change he thought teachers should translate them into reality through the schools. It followed from his basic philosophy that all educators needed to be trained for social leadership. In a passage marked by overenthusaism,

---

[62] J. Crosby Chapman and George S. Counts, *Principles of Education* (New York: Houghton Mifflin Company, 1924), pp. xii–xiii. This specific quotation, appearing in the Author's Preface, could have been written by either Chapman or Counts. The division of labor involved in the text, however, placed responsibility for the social aspects on Counts and for the psychological aspects on Chapman. Passages here attributed to Counts are so attributed on the basis of this division, on style and emphasis, and on Counts's recollection in 1953.

[63] *Ibid.*, p. 45.

but nevertheless containing an element of the growing attitude toward teacher education, he said:

> If it were only the schools that they are running it might be excusable for them to study the Herbartian lesson plans, the psychology of the learning process, tests and measurements, statistical methods as applied to administrative problems, and such like subjects, with nothing much besides. But the school is the least thing they are running. They are running the world.[64]

The new view of the teacher as a participant in making educational policy.—The growing social responsibility of the school naturally complicated the task of the teacher. Even within the narrowest confines of his classroom, adjustments had to be made in the light of new problems facing his students and new attitudes toward school work. Moreover, if the school were to anticipate further social change and prepare its students for easy transition to new conditions, his job was again made more challenging. If building sound attitudes toward complex social issues were included, he needed a far better grounding in social affairs. If, in earlier periods, the school, as such, had assumed this broader role the classroom teacher himself would have been but slightly concerned. Basic decisions were made by administrative personnel or by the lay boards. However, as the twentieth century progressed there were increasing demands that the teacher be given a more important role in determining educational policy.

These demands came partly from leaders who were sensitive to the educational implications of universal participation in government. As early as 1903 John Dewey noted the inconsistency between basic democratic theory and the practice in the school.[65]

Dewey identified the ethical principle upon which democracy rests as the "responsibility and freedom of mind in discovery and truth." He pointed to democracy's method as being the substitution of the internal authority of truth known to reason for external authority. As he looked at the schools, however, he failed to see a single system wherein teachers had a regular and representative way to register effective judgment on questions of curriculum, discipline, textbooks, methods, or other edu-

---

[64] Ross L. Finney, *A Sociological Philosophy of Education* (New York: The Macmillan Company, 1928), p. 131.

[65] John Dewey, "Democracy in Education," *The Elementary School Teacher,* 4:193–204 (December, 1903).

cational issues, or in which absolute external authority did not prevail to a great extent.

Dewey hailed the then recent tendency to submit such educational decisions to the judgment of professional educators rather than leaving them solely in the hands of a lay body. He asserted that the principle of professional responsibility argued for the participation of teachers, who have a particularly good view of the educational situation. He faced the common argument that teachers were not capable of making such decisions by showing that such was always the argument against democracy. Moreover, he insisted that if it were true in this case then the remedy was to prepare the teachers better by giving them additional responsibility.

The directors of the Carnegie Foundation study of the professional preparation of teachers in 1920 expressed a similar concern. They insisted that

If the ideals of democracy are to be reflected in the educational system, the teachers themselves must be charged with some measure of responsibility for constructing, evaluating, and criticizing general educational proposals and programs; they must know the relation of education to other social forces; they must know the functions education has to discharge, what institutions and agencies are available, and under what limitations these institutions and agencies do their work. The process of teaching is, of course, the primary concern of every teacher, but education comprehends far more than this, and the teacher is a minister of education.[66]

The idea of teacher participation in school administration took root very slowly among administrators as might have been expected. The texts prepared on school administration before 1930 generally followed the same old line of placing responsibility on the superintendent for selecting texts, determining courses of study, preparing syllabi, and closely supervising his teachers, even to the point of prescribing method.

Some measure of the rate of progress among administrators can be seen in the revisions between 1916 and 1929 of Ellwood P. Cubberley's text.[67] The chapters on training and supervision of teachers were alike in most respects. Cubberley included in each a brief discussion of teachers' meetings which, he thought, would give the superintendent a good

[66] Learned, *et al.*, *The Professional Preparation of Teachers*, p. 181.
[67] *Public School Administration* (Boston: Houghton Mifflin Company, 1916 and 1929).

chance to inspire teachers to better work. In 1916 nothing was said of any teacher participation in solving problems of curriculum, discipline, or public relations. By 1929 Cubberley was ready to add a section on teacher participation in the work of the school system. Here Cubberley suggested that if the formation of teachers' councils were handled carefully they might be useful in providing increased interest in the school and in stimulating professional growth. He cautioned, however, that the teachers must be made to understand their limits clearly and to realize that final executive authority remained in the hands of the administrator. "The danger always lies in that teachers' councils may try to go too far," he solemnly advised.

The teachers themselves, especially in the larger cities where better salaries and higher standards resulted in a concentration of potential leadership, increasingly urged that they be given some participation in making educational decisions.[68] After the organization of the American Federation of Teachers as part of the American Federation of Labor in 1916, this group exerted leadership in demands which received the endorsement of the entire AF of L in 1917, 1918, and 1919.[69]

The editor of the *American School Board Journal,* a magazine catering to administrators and lay boards, noted in 1919 that one could hardly expect a nation, which had just finished a war to "make the world safe for democracy," not to turn attention inward on its own institutions.[70] In the same issue Lotus D. Coffman, dean of the College of Education at the University of Minnesota, granted the justice of teacher participation in making school policy, but expressed fear that the agitation was partly grounded, at least, on "unprofessional" motives.[71] In spite of his basically conservative position, however, Coffman did suggest reform.

Some superintendents were quite ready for teacher participation in making administrative decisions. For example, Frank V. Thompson, superintendent of schools at Boston, warmly urged such a policy on the

[68] See *The American School Board Journal* from 1918 through 1921, a period in which such articles frequently appeared, and *The American Teacher* which in its early volumes featured some such demand in almost every issue.

[69] Charles B. Stillman (president of the AF of T), "Democracy in the Management of the Schools," *American School Board Journal,* 60:39–41 (June, 1920).

[70] Editorial note, *American School Board Journal,* 59:(3)31 (September, 1919).

[71] Lotus D. Coffman, "The Need for the Substitution of a Cooperative Type of School Organization," *ibid.,* pp. 29–30.

basis of the social role of the school and its need to reflect the highest ideals of the society.[72]

In the early 1920's when the unity and enthusiasm of war had worn off, the old pressures for social reform began to be felt again throughout the country. In reaction to this threat against the *status quo,* the professional patriots also gathered force. Much suspicion, fear, and name-calling were directed at the schools. Charges of disloyalty and socialism were hurled with increasing frequency at teachers, and programs to ensure loyalty, such as New York State's Lusk Laws, were enacted.

In this period, as in the similar period of the early 1950's, the demand for political and social orthodoxy was accompanied by a demand for the return to religious orthodoxy. The latter demand was, of course, highly dramatized in Tennessee's Scopes Case which tested the law making the teaching of evolution illegal.

These pressures against teachers provided evidence that the public clearly recognized the strategic position held by teachers in respect to social issues. Though the implication of this might not have occurred to teachers generally, many recognized the fact that a broad understanding of these problems was the only defense a teacher had, and that this was essential if he were to educate his students adequately.

We have noted several factors, some widely recognized and some sensed by only a few leading thinkers, which logically demanded a vastly richer education for the teacher. These new factors included: (1) the increased complexity of life which not only created additional psychological problems for teachers to meet, but which also made the school responsible for educational tasks formerly performed by other social institutions; (2) the realization, first by educational thinkers and second, in a very negative fashion, by the professional patriots, that the teacher occupied the strategic position in determining the direction of social change; and (3) the development of new concepts of school administration which placed on the shoulders of the classroom teacher increasingly greater responsibility for making educational policy in such matters as curriculum, textbook selection, discipline, and the organization of classroom activities.

The cumulative effect of these changes demanded of teachers a

[72] Frank V. Thompson, "Democratization of School Administration," *ibid.,* 61:(1)42 (July, 1920).

thorough understanding of the American social and economic scene. It also required greater knowledge of the way the child would react to these new conditions and of ways to prepare him to meet them. Such understandings implied a qualitative as well as a quantitative adjustment of both general and professional education for teachers. Adjustment occurred, but generally it resulted from the vague feeling that, like everyone else, the teacher ought to be better educated, rather than from a careful analysis of the new situation. The period from 1907 to 1925 was rich in the development of differentiated curricula designed to prepare teachers for different professional roles, in the lengthening of the program and the quantitative raising of standards, and in the statistical study of educational problems. It was also one in which the purposes of teacher education were somewhat ignored. With the notable exception of the Carnegie Foundation study there was little serious effort to come to grips with the problems of determining objectives for teacher education.[73]

NEW APPROACHES TO EDUCATIONAL THOUGHT

In preparing teachers adequately to assume these increased responsibilities the pre-service program was modified in two ways. One, not as a rule directly oriented toward professional problems, was to reform general education in such a manner that the student became more conscious of the nature and interrelationship of social patterns and problems, including educational ones. The second was to broaden the scope and orientation of the professional sequence, to prepare teachers liberally to understand the relationship of the schools, and of educational practices, to nonschool forces.

In the period being discussed there were three lines of professional emphasis which, in varying degrees, tended to be crucial in determining the balance of attention given to the liberal function and that given to the technical function. These included (1) certain attempts to create educational sciences which, either on the basis of deductive logic or statistical evidence, would govern the practice of education by certain clearly demonstrable principles, (2) the "foundations" concept which, by reference to other disciplines, attempted to throw greater light on the practice of education, and (3) laboratory experiences which, though always properly concerned with the development of skill, have also at

[73] See Monroe, *Teaching–Learning Theory,* pp. 210–211.

times been so conceived as to combine this function with the liberal function.

The educational science of the Herbartians.—The science which predominated when this period opened was of the variety conceived in previous times by the intellectual philosophers. It was thought of as a body of first principles to be arrived at by deductive thought. Though based on a more adequate psychology and social orientation it was akin to the "sciences" of the Oswego movement and of such Idealist philosophers as William H. Payne. It was the Herbartianism of Charles De Garmo, the McMurrys, and Charles C. Van Liew. On its fringes in the very early years of the National Herbart Society were such men as John Dewey and Nicholas Murray Butler, who, however, broke significantly with the movement in several respects.

The enthusiasm with which Frank McMurry, in 1892, hailed the Herbartian system because of its unity and completeness of organiation has been noted. He had clearly felt that a "new day" in which educational problems could be authoritatively solved by careful deduction from the principles of Herbart had arrived. Two decades later his brother and collaborator, Charles, noted the failure of these high hopes. Tucked inconspicuously among other one-time panaceas Charles McMurry included his own young dream:

Reforms in education are usually disappointing to all concerned. They come in waves of fashion and subside while the old fashions return. In the last twenty-five years we have had a rapid succession of reform movements, such as the kindergarten, natural science and nature study, the elective system, physical geography, classical English literature, manual training, the Herbartian movement, child study, and more recently agriculture and vocational training. None of these propagandas have had any such success as their advocates at first expected.[74]

The Herbartians, if they accomplished nothing else, placed great emphasis on the necessity for the teacher to become technically competent. In their books, their speeches, and their teaching, they stresesd careful planning and systematic operation to the extent that Herbartian lesson plans became almost a mania. Moreover, they insistently demanded that theory be closely wedded to the actual practice of teaching. Their criticism of theorists and even of academic specialists who failed

[74] Charles A. McMurry, *Conflicting Principles in Teaching and How to Adjust to Them* (New York: Houghton Mifflin Company, 1914), p. 262.

to test the value of their assertions in the actual classroom was bitter. The following selection from Charles McMurry is typical:

The problem of training teachers in both normal schools and in universities involves, as one of its chief difficulties, the induction of the young or inexperienced teacher into the difficulties of actual practice. All pure theorists both in the normal schools and in universities persistently dodge this problem. Reasons, excuses and explanations are invented, manufactured and multiplied in order to escape from this problem. No coward ever invented more reasons for keeping out of battle, for hiding behind stumps, than the theoretical pedagogue will invent for escaping from the hardships of teaching. There must be deep down in the consciousness of the pure theorist the conviction that his theories will not stand the test, that they will dissipate like the mists in the presence of real difficulties. Whether he thinks so or not, everybody else does. Among the rank and file of good teachers, the theorist who declines the smoke of battle, who like Xerxes takes his safe position in some high tower where he can overlook the battle, is regarded with intermingled suspicion and distrust. Superintendents and supervisors who talk glibly and learnedly about philosophical theories, about psychology and method, but leave all the actual handling of children to others are not conscious how empty and farcical their work appears to real teachers.[75]

This insistence that theory be related to classroom practice was present in Charles McMurry's later work.[76] Though there were frequent notes that theory was most important, the implication was always that if it could not be directly translated into specific action in the classroom it was useless. Theory, to the Herbartians, was usually related to method of teaching, or it had, as they conceived it, no practical bearing and, by implication, no professional bearing.

The same belief that theory must have immediate, demonstrable bearing on classroom technique was expressed by Van Liew in 1905. He pointed out that the classroom teacher must have the general culture of the average citizen, "liberally, not meagerly, acquired." He also praised the growth in "professional culture" which he defined as "ideas belonging peculiarly to the teaching profession." When he came to evaluating

75 National Society for the Scientific Study of Education, *The Place of Vocational Subjects in the High School Curriculum*, Part II, Fourth Yearbook of the National Society for the Scientific Study of Education (Bloomington, Ill.: Pantagraph Printing and Stationery Company, 1905), p. 53.

76 Charles A. McMurry, *Conflicting Principles*, pp. 237–251.

these ideas, however, the test was whether or not they increased technical skill.[77]

Apparently when the Herbartians talked about educational theory they conceived it as theorizing about "how to teach." This being the case, they consistently insisted that such theories meet the actual test of being used in the classroom situation. Their criticism of theorizing of this nature showed a healthy disdain for ideas unrelated to realities.

The implication that educational theory can properly be concerned only with "how to teach" greatly restricted the liberal function in the professional program. Moreover, Herbartian pedagogy actually had a negative effect on the technical function. This was contrary to the intent of its supporters. However, in presenting a closed system of thought focused on a specifically described method, they made it easy for teachers, already inclined to grasp for the security of systematic, approved rules, to become mechanics. The Herbartian Five Formal Steps thus followed the path of "object-teaching," tending to reduce the teacher's technical skill to arid routine.

Some qualifications to this evaluation need to be made. The Herbartian emphasis on the humanistic core of history and literature, the natural science core, and the "economic" core made breadth in the general background of teachers much more important. Even though the selection of content was dictated by its inherent interest to children, it was thought to be important for the teacher to range over the broad field of human history. Moreover, the culture-epoch theory did sensitize teachers to some of the implications of what is now cultural anthropology.[78] Though modern scholarship rejects much of the culture-epoch concept and the use to which history was put, the Herbartian influence in stressing the humane and the cultural studies for teachers was important.

Occasional stress was placed on liberal–professional study, particularly by Charles De Garmo. His moving into university circles may have made him more sensitive to these considerations than were some of his colleagues in the Herbartian movement. On at least one occasion De Garmo insisted that extended study of the mental sciences, philos-

---

[77] Charles C. Van Liew, "A Statement of Issues Before the Department," Presidential Address of the Normal Department, National Education Association, *Proceedings, 1905*, p. 522.

[78] Charles De Garmo, *Herbart and the Herbartians* (New York: Charles Scribner's Sons, 1896), pp. 107–118, 228–256.

ophy and psychology, and of the social sciences rather than of general teaching method provided the most acceptable approach to educational theory.[79]

The Herbartian movement was the last notable systematic attempt of educationists to erect a "science" of education solely on the basis of a priori principles and deductive thought. It is true that the activity movement and the child-centered school, as conceived by some of its advocates and practiced by some teachers, also became a fad controlled by clichés, slogans, and routinized procedures. To the extent that it did so, however, it denied its own philosophy, if Dewey's Instrumentalism was such. The essence of the Instrumentalist philosophical position was the insistence that the system remain open and that empirical testing be demanded of all theories. When educationists began to make any methodology finished and universal they were in opposition to this principle.

The educational science of the empiricists.—Except where some religious and philosophical issues were concerned, the tenor of Amerian thought shifted, some time toward the end of the last century, from rationalism to empiricism of one form or another. It is not surprising, therefore, that the idea of educational science should undergo a similar shift. While Herbartianism, the last of the rationalistic sciences of education, was running its course the most vigorously empirical science was developing. The one in its descent crossed the other in its ascent somewhere around 1915.

It seems customary to designate Joseph M. Rice's study of "The Futility of the Spelling Grind" [80] as the beginning of the empirical study of the science of education. Actually this study followed some of the laboratory and testing activities of the early psychologists, such as G. Stanley Hall, William James, Francis Galton, and J. McKeen Cattell. Yet, though there is an intimate relationship which ought not be neglected, there is some justification for separating the scientific study of educational practice from the more general study of psychology. So far

[79] Charles De Garmo, "Relative Advantages and Limitations of Universities and Normal Schools in Preparing Secondary Teachers," *The Education and Training of Secondary Teachers,* Part I, Fourth Yearbook of the National Society for the Scientific Study of Education (Bloomington, Ill.: Pantagraph Printing and Stationery Co., 1905), pp. 89–90.

[80] Joseph M. Rice, "The Futility of the Spelling Grind," *The Forum,* 23:163–172, 409–419 (April, June, 1897). A report of tests showing lack of correlation between time spent in drill on spelling and empirically verifiable results.

as teacher education is concerned, this distinction found expression in courses in educational psychology as distinguished from general psychology. Frank N. Freeman made the point in 1919 that the "science of education" starts with an analysis of an actual pedagogical problem, whereas he conceived general psychology as more concerned with general principles aside from their immediate bearing.[81]

In the early years of the movement there was a tendency to identify scientific study with any method of controlled inquiry having respect for objectivity and giving attention to the verification of hypotheses. Such at least was the consensus of members of the National Society for the Scientific Study of Education in 1905.[82] While responses to the question of what constituted such a study varied broadly, there was no insistence either on quantitative measurement or on first principles. Moreover, of those who specified the sources of data for this science, the larger group referred to a broad base, including the social and natural sciences, while only three restricted the sources of data strictly to psychology or to statistical analyses of concrete school practices.[83]

As the period progressed, however, the tendency to emphasize quantitative studies gained popularity. Walter S. Monroe follows the judgment of Charles Judd in designating the year 1915 as the turning point.[84] In making the study of education quantitative the influence of Edward L. Thorndike was tremendous. He threw the weight of his great reputation behind the idea that measurement could ultimately provide every answer needed. In 1910, for example, he said:

Experts in education are becoming experimentalists and quantitative thinkers, and are seeking to verify or refute the established beliefs concerning the effects of educational forces upon human nature. Students of history, government, sociology, economics, ethics and religion are becoming, or will soon become, quantitative thinkers concerning the shares of the various physical and social forces in making individual

[81] Frank N. Freeman, "Courses in Educational Psychology in Colleges, Universities, and Normal Schools," *College Courses in Education*, Eighth Yearbook of the National Society of College Teachers of Education (Chicago: University of Chicago Press, 1920), pp. 43–61.

[82] *The Place of Vocational Subjects in the High School Curriculum*, Part II, Fourth Yearbook of the National Society for the Scientific Study of Education, pp. 66–78.

[83] *Ibid.* The ratio stated is based on the present author's analysis of the statements.

[84] Monroe, *Teaching–Learning Theory*, p. 63.

men differ in politics, crime, wealth, service, idealism or whatever trait concerns man's welfare.[85]

In justifying the testing movement against attacks which claimed that important values were in danger of being overlooked and destroyed by a too vigorous application of testing, Thorndike in 1922 restated his faith:

I have no time to present evidence, but I beg you to believe that the fear is groundless, based on a radically false psychology. Whatever exists, exists in some amount. To measure it, is simply to know its varying amounts. Man sees no less beauty in flowers now than before the day of quantitative botany. It does not reduce courage or endurance to measure them and trace their relations to the autonomic system. . . . If any virtue is worth seeking, we shall seek it more eagerly the more we know and measure it. It does not dignify man to make a mystery of him. Of science and measurement in education as elsewhere, we may safely accept the direct and practical benefits with no risk to idealism.[86]

The scientific study of education influenced the education of teachers in many ways. In so far as its findings became part of the teacher's understanding they were obviously liberal or technical depending on their focus. In giving the teachers more effective tools with which to check presuppositions and theories and to discover more adequate ways of meeting problems it filled both the liberal and technical function. In making teachers more sensitive to the developmental patterns of students and to the way young people act and feel in different kinds of situations, educational science functioned most liberally. In so far as it provided reliable information concerning the validity of different techniques an essential technical function was served. Perhaps when it failed to function in a wholesome manner it was bad science.

The limitations of this science and its contributions to education were debated in a series of papers growing out of a National Society of College Teachers of Education symposium on the sources of fundamental assumptions about education. These arguments involved Frank N.

[85] Edward L. Thorndike, *Educational Psychology*, revised ed. (New York: Bureau of Publications, Teachers College, Columbia University, 1910), p. 135.

[86] Edward L. Thorndike, "Measurement in Education," *Intelligence Tests and Their Use*, Twenty-First Yearbook of the National Society for the Study of Education (Bloomington, Ill.: Public School Publishing Co., 1922), p. 9.

Freeman, Boyd H. Bode, Edward H. Reisner, Charles C. Peters, E. M. Freeman, George S. Counts, and William H. Kilpatrick.[87]

The symposium revealed basic differences, especially in respect to the effectiveness of science in determining values and in relating its findings to each other and to their educational implications. Beyond these, the discussions revealed broad areas of agreement. There was no doubt that in certain areas scientific study had made notable contributions, nor did anyone challenge Freeman's thesis that it is preferable, whenever possible, to settle problems by scientific investigation instead of by plain philosophizing.[88] Moreover, Freeman himself was critical of much that had been done as being "bad" science, revealing a tendency to triviality, to negativeness, to lack of good controls. He pointed out the responsibility of the scientist to be philosophical in creating and testing new hypotheses.

The arguments of philosophy versus science, as such, are familiar, however, and are not of prime concern here. There were two specific tendencies of the educational scientists during this period which need attention because of their illiberal effects. One was the tendency to be overambitious in their claims and to be overconfident of their results. This tendency was typified by the Thorndike statement (see above, pages 167 and 168). This was a particularly dangerous tendency for science in the American culture since the American's naïve faith in scientific methods too easily leads him to accept uncritically anything that has an appearance of mathematical validity.

So far as the education of teachers was concerned, the idea that a specifically desired trait could be directly achieved by a conditioning process, and the sublime confidence in quantification seem to have been unfortunate. They led to an oversimplified assumption that every problem of teacher education could be solved simply by analyzing the traits considered essential to a good teacher, or the specific functions involved in the teacher's job, and, in a process almost akin to manufacturing, create teachers possessing precisely the proper traits and skills. There were many refinements of procedures for obtaining lists of the most important traits, problems, or job activities.[89]

---

[87] See *Educational Administration and Supervision*, 17:361-392 (September, 1928); and *School and Society*, 30:39-52, 103-112 (July 13, 27, 1929).

[88] Frank N. Freeman, "Contribution of Science to Education," *School and Society*, 30:107-112 (July 27, 1929), p. 109.

[89] See W. W. Charters and Douglas Waples, *The Commonwealth Teacher*

The positive faith that their techniques were authoritative in every area of professional concern came at a time when educational science was at best in its embryonic stage. The zeal of the educational statisticians tended to shut their science off from the corrective influence of other disciplines.

It might be noted that the tendency to overconfidence in their specific discipline was not restricted to educators in the psychological area. Some of the educational sociologists were sure that their discipline was largely sufficient. Charles A. Ellwood, for example, while granting that the science of psychology had some value in solving the technical problems of the classroom, pointed out that the major problems of education, the aims of education and the curriculum designed to meet those aims, were essentially problems of applied scientific sociology.[90]

A second tendency of some who conducted investigations under the banner and prestige of educational science was the failure to criticize adequately their own presuppositions about teacher education. The climate of opinion which prevailed in teacher education circles included a tendency to look upon professional education as essentially technical. The construction of some surveys inevitably "proved" that it should be so. An example of many studies of this type was that conducted by Leonard V. Koos and Clifford Woody in the state of Washington.[91] Woody and Koos recognized that in asking teachers for the rating of courses on the basis of their being "most helpful in teaching" they were prejudicing the results against any course whose function was primarily liberal. They noted, as expected, and indeed requested, that the teachers approved only courses which had to do with the technical aspects of teaching. There could be no quarrel with this procedure. They had set

Training Study (Chicago: University of Chicago Press, 1929); Wesley E. Peik, *The Professional Education of High School Teachers* (Minneapolis, Minn.: University of Minnesota Press, 1930); David Snedden, *Sociological Determination of Objectives in Education* (Philadelphia: J. B. Lippincott Company, 1921); and Charles C. Peters, *Objectives and Procedures in Civic Education* (New York: Longmans, Green & Company, 1930). For criticism of these approaches see Boyd H. Bode, *Modern Educational Theories;* and Ross L. Finney, *A Sociological Philosophy of Education,* pp. 533–556.

[90] Charles A. Ellwood, "The Sociological Basis of the Science of Education," *Education,* 32:133–140 (November, 1911), p. 135.

[91] Leonard V. Koos and Clifford Woody, "The Training of Teachers in the Accredited High Schools of Washington," *Professional Preparation of High School Teachers,* Part I, Eighteenth Yearbook of the National Society for the Scientific Study of Education (Bloomington, Ill.: Public School Publishing Company, 1919), pp. 213–257.

out to find whether or not courses designed to be technically helpful were actually so considered. The criticism comes in their use of such a study to argue that, on the basis of this "scientific" evidence, the curriculum should be made more consistently technical.

The trend toward programs in foundations of education.—In the preceding chapter attention was called to the tendency to stress, on professional grounds, the techniques and findings of certain academic disciplines. Though not directly concerned with education these disciplines were thought to provide valuable insights. As their role was conceived in the late nineteenth century they were organized to make available to teachers intellectual skills and understandings whose significance was not immediately apparent as one looked solely at the technical job of teaching. The "practicality" they presumed was not that which could be immediately translated into a rule of teaching method. They included psychology, anthropology, sociology, aesthetics, and philosophy, to mention a few.

At the turn of the century there were suggestions that educational history, which previously had tended to be either a study of comparative educational theory or a narrative historical description of educational events, adopt a broader scope more consistent with the "foundations" concept. For example, James Earl Russell, speaking in the spirit which came to be known as the New History, suggested:

Such a study of the history of education is more than a study of scholastic institutions, of didactic precepts, or the theories of educationists; it is *Kultur-Geschichte,* with special reference to educational needs and educational problems.[92]

In so far as history of education and philosophy of education took on this broader function of criticizing educational developments from the viewpoint of general scholarship they enlarged their foundational role.

However, none of the foundations disciplines save, in a sense, developmental psychology and sociology, were able, consistently, to occupy the critical mid-point between academic interest in advancing the disciplines as such and the technical problems of teaching. The tendency of some teacher educators was to insist that the sole responsibility for pro-

[92] James Earl Russell, "The Training of Teachers for Secondary Schools," National Education Association, *Proceedings, 1899,* p. 288. See also William H. Burnham, "The History of Education as a Professional Subject," *Proceedings of the National Society of College Teachers of Education, 1908* (New York: Bureau of Publications, Teachers College, Columbia University, 1908), pp. 12, 20–21.

viding the broad view belonged to general education which could not afford special attention to educational policy problems. Others, especially of the educationists, demanded that every offering called "professional" have either obvious practical bearing in helping the teacher to teach or demonstrable scientific promise in solving a recognized specific problem.

The problem of how to get at foundations concepts was neatly illustrated in the findings of the Committee of Seventeen on the professional preparation of high school teachers.[93] The committee recommended as part of the "academic" preparation the usual broad "culture" and adequate subject specialization. They also recommended, still as "academic," the study of one or more of the social studies to give the teacher "a proper outlook on the social aspects of education," and a course in psychology and one in philosophy to give a proper outlook upon education "as the development of the individual." [94] These courses were to be chosen from among the academic offerings, presumably drawing directly from the techniques and materials of the regular university disciplines, for their specific *professional* bearing. In addition to these professionally functioning "academic" courses, the committee suggested that attention be given to history of general and secondary education, principles of education, special methods of teaching, organization and administration of schools, school hygiene, and some form of induction into actual teaching.

An interesting conflict appeared in the papers of Charles H. Judd and that of the chairman, Reuben Post Halleck, in respect to the teaching of pyschology.[95] The significant issue, for purposes of this discussion, was that Halleck saw the possibility of treating psychological problems in such a way that they would be obviously relevant to education and also provide training in using the techniques of scientific study on other educational problems which might arise. Judd, on the other hand, felt that the development of the discipline of science must come through a study not directly concerned with education. He insisted that the student must learn to use the method of science in the general course,

---

[93] National Education Association, *Proceedings, 1907,* pp. 523–668. This committee was composed of professors of education, normal school presidents, and school administrators.

[94] *Ibid.,* p. 536. It is interesting to note, in this context, the current tendency to divide "foundational" courses into the "social" and the "personal development" emphases.

[95] *Ibid.,* pp. 525–529, 584–586.

not in one dealing with the facts of education. He also suggested that the school of education might properly provide a middle course in which the discipline was related more specifically to the peculiar problems of education.

One problem was that of how to keep the attention of the professor, who is thoroughly interested in an academic discipline, clearly focused on professional concerns. This problem was discussed by Dean James Earl Russell, of Teachers College, Columbia University, in 1924. Russell distinguished between "academic" and "professional" on the basis of one's attitude toward the study. He argued that people simply *are* academic- or professional-minded. If academic-minded, they are led by the fascination of the subject to constantly expand and broaden. "Such work well done," he said, "gives breadth to life and universality of interests." The professional, he suggested on the other hand, demanded the concentration of powers and of interests on a specific job.[96]

Russell argued that any subject taught in the professional school could be motivated by either the academic spirit or the professional.[97] If it were the former he cited the danger of pyramiding course on course, each designed, not for its value to the prospective teacher, but to further knowledge in that area. He called attention to the fact that such a development had occurred in history of education, as well as in educational administration, psychology, and in many others. He lauded the "academic" attitude as bringing an essential, broadening element to the professional school. He insisted, though, that academic-minded professors in a professional school must be willing to see the curriculum organized in a consistent and unified manner to serve professional ends. The extensive pursuit of knowledge for its own sake was, as he saw it, a graduate school function.

Of the foundations disciplines, educational philosophy and history of education started the period here discussed with great popularity, and were strongly endorsed by the Committee of Seventeen. In 1917 the reputation of the Committee of Seventeen still ran high. It served as a

[96] James E. Russell, "A Summary of Some of the Difficulties Connected with the Making of Teachers Colleges," American Association of Teachers Colleges, *Yearbook, 1924*, p. 23.

[97] See *Report of the Dean for the Year Ending June 30, 1927, Teachers College Bulletin* (November, 1927), pp. 6–22, for an extended discussion of the relationship of professional education which, Russell says, is concerned with ". . . what the student will do with the subject," as contrasted with liberal education in which the concern is ". . . what . . . the subject [will] do for the student," p. 9.

base for the Koos–Woody study previously mentioned. These authors, however, raised doubts about the usefulness of history and principles of education.[98] Perhaps the fact that such subjects had become too academic, in Russell's terms, played a part.

In the Carnegie study of 1920 the claims of foundational concepts, not immediately translatable into technique, were explicitly supported. This group tied their defense of educational theory directly to their concept of the broader role of the teacher, and argued:

> It is unfortunate that educational theory, of which psychology is a part, has suffered quite undeserved condemnation merely because of its inadequacy for prescribing techniques. There has been a very general failure to recognize that the study of theory exercises an important function that is quite independent of its influence upon the art of teaching. While the young teacher will depend largely upon imitation and practice to master the techniques of his art, and while the normal school in consequence must first of all provide abundant opportunities for the successful mastery of technique in this empirical fashion, it should not be forgotten that the teacher should be something more than a craftsman.[99]

The authors went on to emphasize the need for teachers to take a more active role in making educational policy and to argue that only by seeing education in its broadest focus could they intelligently meet the demands which modern society placed on the school. In order to provide this broad focus the claims of history of education, sociology, psychology, economics, and biology were discussed.[100]

The group did not recommend separate courses to provide instruction in all these areas. They advocated, in respect to psychology, an introductory course based on concrete, practical psychological topics having direct bearing on the classroom situation. Following this course it was suggested that the appropriate psychological observations should be made as they appeared in relation to other activities. Finally, at the end of the program, a systematic course in psychology was to be provided.

So far as history of education was concerned, the survey group doubted its value as a separate course in the short curriculum, though

[98] Koos and Woody, "The Training of Teachers in the Accredited High Schools of Washington," p. 255.

[99] Learned *et al., The Professional Preparation of Teachers,* p. 180.

[100] *Ibid.,* pp. 180–187. For summarized recommendations, see pp. 392–393.

they thought that it might have rich possibilities as a summarizing course at the end of a three- or four-year curriculum. They found that students at the junior college level lacked the necessary "maturity of mind," "breadth of interest," and adequate philosophical and historical background.

In the short curriculum, history of education, sociological implications for education, and other foundational materials were to be used to enrich professionalized general courses and methods courses. To illustrate, it was suggested that

The significance of the modern methods of teaching reading, for example, is much more keenly appreciated by the student if he knows something of the older methods of teaching reading. And the appropriate point, indeed the only effective point, at which to give the student this historical perspective upon the reading problem is in the specific course that deals with primary reading. Again the courses in arithmetic and in the teaching of arithmetic offer innumerable occasions for illuminating present practices thru references to the development, both of arithmetic itself and of the methods of teaching it to children. The modern conceptions of geography and history as component parts of the elementary program faithfully reflect the fundamental doctrines of the important modern educational reformers from Pestalozzi, Froebel, Herbart, and Herbert Spencer to contemporary leaders like John Dewey; in presenting these conceptions as they recur in the specific courses in geography and history, there is the best possible opportunity to give the student an initial acquaintance with the philosophy on which they rest. The study of school management and the technique of teaching is probably best approached by the same genetic method; the apparently trivial details of classroom routine, for example, take on a new meaning when their development is traced from the old days of individual instruction, thru the innovations of the Jesuits and the Christian Brethren and the contributions of the Bell-Lancaster schools. . . .[101]

This rather long quotation is included to illustrate the type and context of the history, sociology, biology, and philosophy which were intended to give the teacher the broad social vision needed to make him competent to guide the nation's social development and to make important policy decisions about education. It also gives the flavor of the professionalized academic courses which were recommended for the collegiate grade normal schools.

No courses were suggested in educational philosophy, but presumably

[101] *Ibid.,* pp. 186–187.

the course in general method or principles of education would include philosophical considerations not covered elsewhere.

As the period progressed, courses in educational theory were under increasing competition from the scientific and technical courses. Formal courses in educational history and philosophy increasingly failed to gain the approval of teachers who were polled, of the scientists, or of the curriculum people who, following the general principle suggested by Bagley in the Carnegie study, advocated that materials from these disciplines be incorporated into other courses.

A long list of studies revealed this loss of popularity. While most of these were based on an evaluation of practical values, some, such as those by C. O. Davis and by Wesley E. Peik, did try to recognize "theoretic" as well as "practical" value.[102]

Contrary to the trends in respect to history and philosophy of education, educational sociology seems to have gained ground in the early decades of the century.[103] The early approaches to courses in anthropology for educators and in aesthetic foundations of education did not take firm root in undergraduate programs of pre-service training.

The years between 1895 and 1930 were rich in the development of American thought. The literature of social protest has been cited and attention has been called to the extent to which educational leaders emphasized social considerations in their theory. Psychology became a respected university discipline, in spite of its growing pains, and even achieved the pinnacle of American success by being incorporated as a business.[104] Thanks to Edward L. Thorndike, Charles H. Judd, and

---

[102] See C. O. Davis, "The Training, Experience, Salaries, and Educational Judgments of 24,313 of the High School Teachers in North Central Accredited Schools," North Central Association of Colleges and Secondary Schools, *Proceedings, 1922–1923*, Part I, pp. 24–55; Frederick J. Kelly, "A Study of the Values Assigned to Courses in Education and Related Fields by 249 High School Administrators in Kansas," National Society of College Teachers of Education, Ninth Yearbook, *Studies in Education*, Educational Monograph, No. 11 (Ames, Iowa: Tribune Publishing Co., 1920); George P. Deyoe, *Certain Trends in Curriculum Practices and Policies in State Normal Schools and Teachers Colleges* (New York: Bureau of Publications, Teachers College, Columbia University, 1934); and Wesley E. Peik, *The Professional Education of High School Teachers*.

[103] See F. R. Clow, "Rise in Educational Sociology," *Journal of Social Forces*, 2:332–335 (March, 1924); and Harvey Lee, *Status of Educational Sociology in Normal Schools, Teachers Colleges, and Universities* (New York: New York University Press Book Store, n.d.).

[104] J. McKeen Cattell and others organized the Psychological Corporation to serve commercial clients in 1921.

hundreds of others, it provided a mine of significant information for the guidance of teachers.

The university study of history, anthropology, sociology, economics, and political science ranged over the whole field of human experience in the search for new insights. The influence of this scholarship briefly brushed the American teacher as he wandered through his general education program. If he happened to major in the social sciences in a good college perhaps it marked him deeply. When he moved into the professional sequence or the department of education he turned his attention to *practical* things. This was but partly as it should be.

If, perchance, he wondered about the connection between all this general knowledge in the social sciences and his professional work he found, with increasing frequency as the period progressed, rather little of such concern among many of the educationists.[105] The growing consensus as the period drew to a close was that liberal study designed to bring a rich set of understandings to problems could be left to the general education program while the professional program concentrated on the technical job of making skilled craftsmen. The educationists who held this opinion were following the evaluations placed upon offerings in the foundations areas by students who had sampled those offerings.

The development of new attitudes toward student-teaching experiences.—Everyone agrees that a technical concern is proper in respect to the training school or other direct-experience programs. That the teacher should there build up at least reasonable competency in the actual handling of a class is unquestioned. Nor has it been seriously doubted among educationists since 1895. Efforts to make the technical aspects of the training program more effective, as such, are not the primary concern of this study. Such efforts have received the tireless support of many educationists.

A deep concern to bring theory and practice together marked the

[105] This general evaluation of the over-all trend from 1905 to 1930 is clearly documented by Obed J. Williamson, *Provisions for General Theory Courses in the Professional Education of Teachers* (New York: Bureau of Publications, Teachers College, Columbia University, 1936). In respect to the treatment of historical materials it is even more thoroughly documented by Lawrence A. Cremin in "The Development of the History of Education as a Field of Study in the United States from 1918 to 1952," *The Role of the Historical Foundations in the Professional Education of Teachers,* an unpublished manuscript prepared for the Committee on Historical Foundations of the National Society of College Teachers of Education, 1952.

period here discussed. In most cases this meant that everything offered in the professional sequence must prove itself by improving classroom technique. There were, however, those who were also concerned that the training school carry the liberal theory into the broader professional life of the teacher. Since this latter trend marks a great deal of current activity in laboratory-experience programs, its early advocacy needs to be cited.

One of the most complete early statements of this attitude was made by John Dewey in 1904. He assumed agreement that the preparation of teachers required a certain amount of practical work. He pointed out, however, that there were two ways of looking at such work and that the two controlling purposes were significantly different, dictating totally different arrangements throughout. These two approaches he described in this manner:

On the one hand, we may carry on the practical work with the object of giving teachers in training working command of the necessary tools of their profession; control of the technique of class instruction and management; skill and proficiency in the work of teaching. With this aim in view, practice work is, as far as it goes, of the nature of apprenticeship. On the other hand, we may propose to use practice work as an instrument in making real and vital theoretical instruction; the knowledge of subject-matter and of principles of education. This is the laboratory point of view.

The contrast between the two points of view is obvious; and the two aims together give the limiting terms within which all practice work falls. From one point of view, the aim is to form and equip the actual teacher; the aim is immediately as well as ultimately practical. From the other point of view, the *immediate* aim, the way of getting at the ultimate aim, is to supply the intellectual method and material of good workmanship, instead of making on the spot, as it were, an efficient workman. Practice work thus considered is administered primarily with reference to the intellectual reactions it incites, giving the student a better hold upon the educational significance of the subject-matter he is acquiring, and of the science, philosophy, and history of education. Of course, the *results* are not exclusive. It would be very strange if practice work in . . . securing a more vital understanding of its principles, should not at the same time insure some skill in the instruction and management of a class.[106]

[106] John Dewey, "The Relation of Theory to Practice in Education," *The Relation of Theory to Practice in the Education of Teachers,* Part I, Third Yearbook of the National Society for the Scientific Study of Education, Charles A. Mc-Murry, ed. (Chicago: University of Chicago Press, 1904), pp. 9–10.

Dewey defended the laboratory concept. He pointed out that the objective was to give "control of the intellectual methods required for personal and independent mastery of practical skill." This, he granted, may have to be done at the expense of postponing the development of finished technical skill until after graduation.

Dewey argued that to put the student prematurely into the actual teaching situation was ineffective and undesirable. It immediately forced him to concentrate on external factors, e.g., classroom order, rather than to give attention to such internal factors as the use of the subject matter and the psychological reactions of the students. The result, he thought, was that teachers mastered the form of technique without understanding what was really involved.

Under the pressure of actual teaching, Dewey believed that the student who was not properly prepared turned to empirical tricks, which only seemed to work, at least to achieve order, and that these techniques were fixated, crowding out the more effective ones that might later be discovered. He argued that if basic psychological and philosophical considerations and the subject matter of instruction were so thoroughly mastered that they became second nature, the teacher placed in a challenging situation would instinctively turn to them. The premature placing of students into critical situations where they had to make crucial decisions Dewey held responsible for the separation of theory and practice.

Dewey felt that the practice experience should be pursued in reference to its making the professional pupil an alert student of education. Otherwise he thought that immediate technical skill was purchased at the price of the ability for continued growth. This did not mean that no experiences of an active nature were needed. He proposed a series of references to direct life and a series of graduated direct experiences in observation wherein the goal was to be, not to follow techniques, but to observe the psychological and socio-psychological reactions of students to each other, the teacher, and the subject matter.

Dewey emphasized strongly that the student teacher, before he entered actual teaching, must have a thorough understanding of subject matter in its organized form. This form, he thought, represented the distillation of human experience and the pattern of thinking toward which the maturing human mind naturally moves if it seeks to make its grasp of past experience effective. Again, however, he objected to the compartmentalization of disciplines and to the assumption that they had an end beyond making the solution of human problems more intelligent. The process of direct experiences, provided prior to actual teaching, should give the teacher an opportunity to study the way the student acquires this organized and effective store of experience.

In spelling out his recommendations in general form, specifically objecting to its being made a pattern, Dewey suggested, first, a graduated set of direct experiences to gain understanding of educational principles and subject matter, second, an opportunity to assist teachers, and, finally, a chance to exercise absolute control with a minimum of criticism of the early efforts at teaching.

Finally, Dewey pointed out that, in so far as conditions permitted, an apprenticeship program designed solely to sharpen skill was completely desirable, provided that the conditions of the type of laboratory program above outlined were first completed.

The contrary point of view, that there should be an early and long-continued apprenticeship type of program, requires no extensive documentation. Those favoring such a program were vocal throughout the period and were highly insistent. Typical statements of this general position included the demands that every normal school instructor prove the value of his ideas by applying them daily in teaching children in the training school [107] and that everything taught in the normal school be planned with a view to its use in practice teaching.[108]

That such an attitude dominated the practice of student teaching was attested by Thomas Alexander as late as 1930. He pointed out that "Recent studies in the field of student-teaching reveal quite clearly that the content of student-teaching is limited generally to classroom practice in a rather narrow sense of the word." [109]

In opposition to this tendency Alexander suggested a system of direct experiences falling more in the line suggested by Dewey. He indicated his belief that practice teaching should bridge the gap between the teacher training college and the job in such a manner that the teacher

[107] C. B. Robertson, "The Function of the Training School; Its Relation to the Department of Principles and Methods," National Education Association, *Proceedings, 1909,* p. 565.

[108] Merritt D. Chittenden, "The Oswego Normal and Training School Plan of Cooperation," Supervisors of Student Teaching, *Fifth Annual Session, 1925,* p. 21.

[109] Thomas Alexander, "A Wider Extension of the Content of Student-Teaching," Supervisors of Student Teaching, *Tenth Annual Session, 1930,* p. 33.

would learn to apply her total education most broadly in every professional decision and act. He argued that "Student-teaching of an adequate sort should provide contact with and practice in all of the major activities of the teacher's work." [110]

One very clear difference, however, between the position taken by Alexander and that taken by Dewey was the greater stress placed by the former on experiences of a nonintellectual nature. The Dewey statement that practice aims at "control of the intellectual methods required for personal and independent mastery of practical skill . . ." [111] was somewhat alien to the flavor of the Alexander article.

Between Dewey and Alexander there were, of course, a large number of men who expressed an attitude toward practice teaching which was in this general trend. At least one concrete plan seems clearly to have been inspired by the pattern of thought developed by Dewey. This was the plan worked out in some detail at the University of Wisconsin.[112]

Summary

The period from 1895 to 1930 had been one of fantastic expansion in every dimension of teacher education. The normal schools, besides increasing in size, had largely become teachers colleges; the collegiate and university training of secondary school teachers had mushroomed beyond all expectations; the teaching profession had not only expanded but had become highly organized; new materials for teacher education had filled thousands of volumes; and the universities, with their growing graduate schools of education, were turning up new material far faster than it could be absorbed or evaluated. There was critical need for a time of stability to permit a careful resurvey of what had happened and a dispassionate analysis of existing thought and practice.

The chaos that was teacher education became part of the chaos that was the great depression. The growing insistence of some educational thinkers, largely ignored before 1929, that all was not right with the world and that the schools must awaken to new responsibilities became

---

[110] *Ibid.*, p. 36.

[111] John Dewey, "The Relation of Theory to Practice," p. 11.

[112] H. L. Miller, "The University of Wisconsin Plan for the Preparation of High School Teachers," *The Professional Preparation of High School Teachers,* Part I, Eighteenth Yearbook of the National Society for the Scientific Study of Education (Bloomington, Ill.: Public School Publishing Co., 1919), pp. 7–165.

irresistible in the face of the shock which hit the American culture in the early 1930's.

The axis, along which attitudes about the relationship of general to professional education were placed in previous chapters, still held some meaning, although the educationists as a group were, perhaps, less inclined to argue about it. They were more concerned with problems within the professional sequence. The academic purists of the traditional liberal arts variety continued to hold essentially the previous position. In this they were joined by scattered university professors of education who were hoping to establish purely professional graduate schools of education and who accepted the dichotomy of liberal versus specialized education. Moreover, an occasional normal school man, in the earlier years, suggested that the attempt to provide collegiate general education for elementary school teachers was unrealistic.

So far as the majority of normal school people were concerned they were, throughout most of the period, engaged in converting their schools into teachers colleges. Since this involved the addition of academic courses they were logically compelled to advocate either the parallel position or that of professional treatment. In practice they seem to have generally assumed the former. A *modus vivendi* by which the departments of education and the departments responsible for general education lived side by side, with only an occasional acrimonious dispute, seems to have prevailed on most of the university and normal school campuses. Such an arrangement passed for what has here been called the position of the "harmonizers." However, there were important thinkers on both the normal school and university levels who insisted increasingly as the period closed that the two sequences must be planned as a logically related unit, and that neither narrow professionalism nor academic compartmentalization should become the criteria for organization. Among the educationists and their supporters, perhaps the synthesis suggested by John Dewey and some of the state university presidents was most popular. The instrumentalist position, as was noted, approached very closely in some respects that of the "integrators."

The group of "integrators," those advocating professionalized general education, continued to include some of the most influential spokesmen among the educationists. In the early decades it included a number of the leading Herbartians. In the middle period the position was accepted by the survey committee of the Carnegie study, which included several of the most widely recognized professors of education in the nation. The integrators continued to place great stress on the claims of subject matter, generally that to be retaught by their students, and on the necessity of incorporating instruction in method with instruction in content.

In the academic community at large, and in the thinking of many educationists, the need to study society and to see the interrelationship of its institutions was more often emphasized. This trend combined with the trend toward giving teachers an increasingly important role in determining educational policy to make the liberal function within the professional sequence more crucial. However, under the impact of the graduate school research attitude, every pedagogical discipline seems to have been concentrated rather exclusively on building its own techniques and departments of instruction. Consequently, the wholeness of the professional sequence tended to suffer at the hands of graduate school specialization much the same fate which had threatened the general education sequence. It thus became more difficult to place certain courses on the liberal–technical axis. To know, for example, when courses in the history of education, which ostensibly served liberal ends, became technically oriented courses for students treated as if they were preparing to be educational historians was difficult. Similarly, to evaluate courses in educational psychology or sociology which began to imply that they provided a sufficient methodology for attacking all major educational problems was equally difficult.

In the third decade of the century the emotional tenor of professional education seems to have reflected overwhelmingly that of the society at large. There was great confidence in the ability of educational scientists to engineer an educative process, and there was extensive "production" of educational research. Educational thought and organization were patterned increasingly on industrial and business models. Yet underneath there was a basic lack of direction. The expansion had been so rapid that new insights were unincorporated, and new theories often inadequately tested. Just as some of the more acute economists warned of soft spots in the nation's economy, some of the more perceptive educationists began to call for a reappraisal of basic assumptions about teacher education. Out of this concern was to come the National Survey of Teacher Education.

Finally, the doctrines of the new Gestalt psychologies and the stress on interest and activity in learning had suggested a new role for direct-experience programs. In contrast to the traditional normal school view of practice teaching as apprenticeship had come the laboratory-experience idea. It was argued that the prospective teacher should be given ever-widening contacts with children and with educational problems prior to the assumption of actual student-teaching roles and that these prior experiences should be designed to help the teacher gain control of underlying intellectual concepts and disciplines rather than directly to improve actual teaching technique. Moreover, this laboratory-experience idea was beginning to be broadened to include activities calling for a study of the policy, as opposed to the technical aspects of education in a complex society. By 1930, however, these concepts were almost entirely unimplemented.

chapter FIVE

The Search for New Guides to

Teacher Education, 1930—1952

One might as well state it in simple terms: we are in doubt as to our heritage—American in the narrower sense, "Western" in the broader.[1]

THE SIGNIFICANT EVENTS OF RECENT DECADES ARE FOR POETS. THE economist, the scientist, the sociologist, the student of world affairs, and the historian can well describe the tremendous changes in the world economic scene, the vital formulae, the battles and treaties, the shifts in class structure, and the new political and social theories, but this is not enough. One must relive the shock of depression with its obvious implication for old faiths in classical economic doctrine. One must re-experience the horror of Buchenwald with its implications for the old belief in eternal progress and the infinite perfectibility of man. One must again sense the elation and then the despair of the Yalta gamble on good faith and humaneness in international affairs. One must feel

[1] Henry Stuart Hughes, *An Essay for Our Times* (New York: Alfred A. Knopf, Inc., 1950), p. 4.

again the warmth of the dream of a "post-war" world and then experience the chill of the Berlin blockade. One must defend the ideal of free speech and free assembly in face of clear evidence of subversion, conspiracy, and espionage. One must see witch hunts in all their ugliness, at a time when there are really witches.

When one has again lived these conditions and recalled the anxiety and despair of people who watch one loved institution after another, and one ideal after another, proved somewhat inadequate, he is ready partially to understand the desperate search for new moral constructs. The traditional institutions and concepts not only *seemed* but *were* inadequate to the political and economic realities. This was true of the old concepts in international affairs, of traditional economics, education, religion, and even, in the face of new ideologies, of the old expectancies concerning honesty and good faith.

The search for new verities was made more urgent by the shadow of impending tragedy which hung over the world as the mid-century mark approached. This urgency led some to abandon tradition and history and even tomorrow in a pointless today. It led others back to authoritarian political, religious, and economic beliefs which denied the efficacy of doubt. The great issues of this century are moral issues, rooted in the new technology and the new science, but moral issues nevertheless. It remains an open question whether or not men have sufficient faith in each other to create a new moral persuasion by honest discussion and free inquiry. In education, as in every other branch of American life, the easy retreat to a faith already spelled out in the dogma of the past has been chosen with increasing frequency over the hard path to a new moral order hammered out in the forum of free thinkers.

General Forces Influencing
Educational Thought

All of this has had much to do with teacher education. At no time since the founding of the first normal school have teacher educators been more conscious of the involved social setting in which the school operated. They always placed the greatest emphasis on training in moral values, but in previous generations everyone assumed that the important value judgments involved supporting the Christian Church and the Ten Commandments and voting on Election Day. The changes in technology had been those which could be ignored until nearly the turn of the century. After that, as we have seen, some teacher educators became keenly aware of the social function of the school but conditions still permitted the majority to sleep until 1929. As the second decade ended, however, there were frequent calls for a restudy of the whole educational system in the hope of making it more adequate. As the following decades progressed a number of social trends having important implications for education became clear.

The widespread unemployment of youth in the early depression years made it clear that our technology had reached the stage where the continued employment of adolescents was no longer necessary, or in depression years even possible. The fact that vast new programs, such as the Civilian Conservation Corps, had to be set up outside the school raised questions about the responsiveness of our whole educational system to the needs of young people and of the society.

The increased mechanization of industry and the replacement of skilled labor by semiskilled labor created new conditions for vocational education. Adaptability, the ability to meet people and to work effectively with them, the ability to "sell" oneself, and a general understanding of the economic and social systems became more important on the job than did training in specific skills. More and more employers expressed the willingness to provide the technical instruction needed so long as the schools would provide quick-learning, well-adjusted, literate candidates. This meant that general education had become an increasingly more important part of vocational preparation.

Studies of the American Youth Commission indicated that very little specific training was required for initial employment in most occupations. Only 12 per cent of the occupations required specialized education beyond high school. Another 25 per cent required specialized training from a few weeks to six months beyond the general education provided in the lower schools.[2]

Moreover, the job played a much smaller part in the life of the

[2] American Council on Education, *Cooperation in General Education,* A Final Report of the Executive Committee of the Cooperative Study in General Education (Washington, D.C.: The Council, 1947), p. 22.

American. While the American worker had fought bitterly in the 1840's for a sixty-hour work week he worked from forty to forty-eight hours in the 1940's. And, while his life had once been lived within walking distance of the job, his radius of activity had spread over hundreds of square miles by 1950. The fine arts and recreational activities which once had been patronized largely by the property-owning classes were within reach of the new "proletariat" whose well-organized members were earning more than vast numbers of petty bourgeois and professional people. Moreover, this proletariat was becoming increasingly vocal in demanding an education which would not only give their children the adaptability needed to shift employment more readily, but also one which would give them the capacity to enjoy these higher things. One of their leaders, James B. Carey, argued:

> We need to decide whether we want a nation of merely well fed, clothed, and housed individuals, who have developed no sense of beauty, cultivated no taste for reading, pictures, music or other things which help differentiate human beings from lower forms of purely physical life. A really full standard of living must include more than material satisfaction. And unless our schools re-establish courses in other than immediately practical fields, which have been emphasized during the war, our long-range society will be impoverished in thought and feeling if not in merchandise.[3]

The problems which one had to face as a union man, unless he were willing to accept unquestioningly the dictation of his leaders, were alone so complex as to require a high degree of literacy and understanding. The problems of being an intelligent consumer were equally demanding. The issues which one must face in political life were even more overwhelming, so much so that millions of Americans voted for father-substitutes in presidential elections.

As the period drew to a close it seemed apparent that the activities of the professional traitors and the professional patriots were beginning to restrict the people's faith in other Americans, and in the American ideals of free association and free trials. Here, especially, one needed broad understanding and good judgment.

In many respects the crucial question was one of finding community. Economic, religious, political, and ethnic differences made it increas-

---

[3] "The Antioch College Institute on Conditions for an Enduring Peace," *School and Society*, 60:223 (September 30, 1944).

ingly difficult to agree, and differences in educational background made it almost as difficult to communicate. Even in the most highly educated circles each specialty had created its own language which tended to isolate it from every other specialty and particularly from the relatively unschooled. To the general public each man's specialty seemed like a forbidding cave in which, it was almost felt, some dark deed was being plotted. In the 1930's American educational leaders were trying to find the way to lead the American community; by 1952 they were trying to find the community.

Even literacy was beginning to be a threat in a sense. The extent to which the art of propaganda had been developed, in free society and totalitarian, had enslaved the literate population to the advertiser, the commissar, or the newspaper editor. The intellectual sophistication needed to cut through this propaganda was beyond that conceivable to uninformed men who spoke directly in terms of their honest intent.

The tremendous growth in school population was beginning to level off in 1930 and educators, seeing an era of decreasing demand for teachers, were discussing ways to use the situation to consolidate higher qualifications. But by the end of the period the search for teachers and facilities to handle a new boom had become frantic. What had been a serious surplus problem in the early years became a serious shortage after the war. In spite of this change in the demand situation, the qualifications of those being hired in 1953 had substantially increased. Whereas in 1931 only 12 per cent of the nation's elementary school teachers had the equivalent of a bachelor's degree or better, that number had grown to around 60 per cent by 1953.[4] The per cent of teachers with fewer than two years of college had fallen from 25 per cent in 1931 to 8 per cent in 1953. These higher standards were increasingly wiping out salary differentiation between elementary and secondary school teachers and increasing the prestige of the elementary school teacher. Since, in the early post-war years, the ratio of demand to supply was far higher in respect to the elementary schools, graduates from the liberal arts colleges were increasingly turning to teaching the younger children.

[4] These comparisons are made from *National Survey of the Education of Teachers*, Vol. 6. p. 37, and from "Teacher Supply and Demand," *Journal of Teacher Education*, IV:(1)3–46 (March, 1953), pp. 16–17. The samplings are not completely comparable nor are the categories identical. The figures here given must be considered only generally indicative of the true situation.

The Concept of General Education

The Committee of Ten in 1892 had recognized that the high school's major function was not to prepare people for college. They had, nevertheless, escaped the implication of this finding by concluding that, in any case, the function of education was solely one of intellectual development, and that, by a fortunate coincidence, those very subjects which were most effective in developing the mind were also best for college preparation.

By 1918, there had been a partial reorientation of secondary education. This resulted from greater social demand for behavior requiring education of a sort not strictly intellectual, and from new educational thought which had raised serious doubts about the old psychological theories. The Commission on the Reorganization of Secondary Education of the National Education Association, noting the changes in American society and the demands for a functional type of intelligence on the part of all citizens, composed the Seven Cardinal Principles.[5] Here, though the need to master "fundamental processes" was included, the focus was clearly shifted from the development of "intellect" for its own sake. The goals of education were oriented around function, and the end was clearly seen in a quality of living. The importance of providing the maximum development in every individual of his greatest "knowledge, interests, ideals, habits, and powers" was insisted upon as a social and personal need.

We have noted that as the first three decades of this century drew to a close there was a growing recognition on the part of many colleges that their programs were unsatisfactory. Reforms such as the Contemporary Civilization course at Columbia, in 1919, and individualized instruction such as that provided by Bennington, Sarah Lawrence, and Stephens, were under way. However, these were largely the more expensive colleges, and the reforms were intended to improve the education of the type of people who had always attended such colleges— people with strong interests in college life who could afford to spend four years in the pursuit of learning "for its own sake."

When the full impact of the depression hit, a new era was born.

[5] Commission on the Reorganization of Secondary Education, *Cardinal Principles of Secondary Education*, U. S. Bureau of Education, Bulletin, 1918, No. 35 (Washington, D.C.: Government Printing Office, 1918).

Young people, unable to find work, were anxious to go to college. Colleges, with decreasing enrollments and resources, opened the doors by lowering both expenses and standards of admission. The shock of seeing thousands of young people idling away their time was deeply disturbing to many Americans. By the mid-thirties the concept of the liberal college as a retreat for students most gifted verbally was under bitter attack. This attack included in its target the preoccupation with a detached intellect. The new general education movement was in direct line with the earlier demand, embodied in the Seven Cardinal Principles, that secondary education consider the whole needs of the whole people.

Looking back from the vantage point of a decade the committee on the Cooperative Study in General Education for the American Council on Education saw five factors characterizing the new movement which was clearly under way by the mid-thirties. In paraphrase these were:

1. A reaction against specialism which was permeating education at the secondary and collegiate levels.

2. A feeling that the subject-matter fields needed to be more adequately integrated to be meaningful.

3. A sense that more prescription was needed to provide a common body of shared experiences and skills which would characterize increased numbers of Americans regardless of their vocation.

4. The concern for a wider range of objectives. While no one denied the importance of training people to think clearly, there was a feeling that this was not enough—that moral, aesthetic, and emotional development were equally important.

5. An increased concern for everyday activities of human beings. "Those interested in general education advocate the development of instruction which begins with the immediate problems of life for the student who does not intend to pursue the subject into its upper branches." [6]

In 1939 Alvin C. Eurich had made a similar analysis of the movement. His description of the common purpose of these programs revealed how much they were a part of the basic quest for meaning which characterized the whole society. Eurich said:

Every program of general education designed to date stresses the *need for integration*. The word has, perhaps, through endless repetition and over-use, lost some of its forcefulness. Nevertheless, the constant emphasis upon it signalized a *quest* for some sort of *unity* now lacking

[6] American Council on Education, *Cooperation in General Education*, p. 205.

in educational matters. The quest is expressed in various ways. Some would achieve unity by having all students study basic areas of subject matter in order to give them common ground for understanding each other. Some think of unity as represented in great books that have stood the test of time and the attacks of critics. Some keep searching for first principles, great truths, that hold at all times and in all places; if we could only discover these, they argue, unity could readily be arrived at through a study of them. Some would center general education about the student's individual and personal problems, his adjustments and maladjustments; for, they say, integration is not really achieved unless it takes place within a student. Some think of integration as growing out of a study and an understanding of basic needs of the individual, such as food, . . . and all the activities in which he must engage to satisfy these needs. Some are firmly convinced that the quest for unity can be satisfied only through an emphasis upon the relationship of the individual to society; upon the activities in which he engages . . . in order to contribute to, and be fully part of, a social group.[7]

The patterns generally advocated took one of several forms, depending on the categories one uses to describe them. It will be recalled that the American Council on Education's Executive Committee for the Cooperative Study broke existing programs into five types (see above, pages 12 and 13). They noted that four of these assumed that the student could best prepare for life by studying subject matter not directly related to the areas and needs of everyday life and argued that a broad transfer from academic field to life situations would occur. In this respect they saw the functionalist as standing alone.

This committee did not see any fundamental differences of aim between the functionalist and nonfunctionalist groups. In respect to severe conflicts on philosophical issues and on the lower (or higher) level of basic educational policy they found the issues hard to resolve. However, by transforming these policy questions to a series of specific practical issues in which attention was clearly focused, they found a broad range of agreement possible. They suggested that both the functionalist and nonfunctionalist aimed to prepare essentially the same type of student for the same type of life in a democratic system. Both were concerned with essentially the same values and insights; both were anx-

---

[7] Alvin C. Eurich, "A Renewed Emphasis Upon General Education," *General Education in the American College,* Part II, Thirty-Eighth Yearbook of the National Society for the Study of Education (Bloomington, Ill.: Public School Publishing Co., 1939), p. 7.

ious to prepare students for effective ways of meeting the problems of daily living.[8]

While these efforts at cooperative action are important, and the techniques used to resolve differences are most valuable, there remain obviously severe differences of opinion about several important matters, some of which may be solved by the very wholesome experimentation with many types of general education programs.

One very important problem for purposes of this analysis is, of course, the attitude of people toward the relationship of general education to specialism, whether vocational or otherwise. In this respect the spread of opinion remained, in the period since 1930, as broad as ever. The classic position that consideration of useful knowledge destroyed the value of liberal education continued to be heard in many places. One of the most vigorous supporters of this position was Norman Foerster who wrote in the tradition of Irving Babbitt.[9]

This sharp distinction was not so clearly emphasized by all who continued to see liberal education as primarily organized around the humanities. For example, the committee appointed by the American Council of Learned Societies, under the chairmanship of Theodore M. Greene, took the traditional, conservative position on most issues of liberal education. That is, they insisted that while each of the traditional disciplines had a unique contribution to make none was sufficient by itself; that liberal education should be analyzed in terms of the traditional triad—truth, goodness, and beauty; that on the proper level of consideration there was a transfer of training, i.e., mathematics could be so taught that students received training in making logical inference which carried over; and that the humanities were, indeed, the core of any liberal education. Moreover, they were insistent that vocational and professional considerations not be allowed to push the liberal program "to the wall." They continued to insist that a very close relationship between liberal and vocational education was salutary to both: "Both types of activity can benefit from wise association; a liberal atmosphere can humanize vocational studies, and vocational pursuits can

[8] American Council on Education, *Cooperation in Teacher Education*, pp. 38–50, *passim*.

[9] Norman Foerster, *The Future of the Liberal College* (New York: Appleton-Century-Crofts, Inc., 1938), and *The American State University; Its Relation to Democracy* (Chapel Hill, N. C.: University of North Carolina Press, 1937).

orient liberal studies to the more immediately practical necessities of life." [10]

One consideration which began to weigh more heavily in determining the relationship of general to vocational education was the need for communication. This need for all Americans to have, so far as possible, a common background at least in kind of education was one of the central themes of the Harvard Report.[11] The same concern was expressed by the President's Commission on Higher Education which pointed to the failure of higher education to provide a core of unity as a cause for grave concern. They argued that:

> The crucial task of higher education, therefore, is to provide a unified general education for American youth. Colleges must find the right relationship between specialized training on the one hand, aiming at a thousand different careers, and the transmission of a common cultural heritage toward a common citizenship on the other.[12]

Neither group interpreted this need for a common background as implying that the same methods and curricular organization were necessary for all students. On the contrary, both denied such a conception.

Nor did they suggest that, in order to provide common experiences, a general education sharply separated from specialized education was necessary. Both saw the generalized and specialized programs as organically related. This continuity was implicit throughout the Harvard Report, while the President's Commission was explicit, arguing that "It is urgently important in American education today that the age-old distinction between education for living and education for making a living be discarded." [13]

After pointing to the aristocratic presuppositions of the tradition which insisted on keeping liberal education free from contamination with the servile arts, the Commission continued, "Our purpose, then, is to raise general education to a position of equal dignity and importance with vocational and professional education—to develop a program com-

---

[10] Theodore M. Greene, chm., *Liberal Education Re-examined; Its Role in a Democracy*, Report of a Committee appointed by the American Council of Learned Societies (New York: Harper and Brothers, 1943), p. 110.

[11] Harvard Committee, *General Education in a Free Society* (Cambridge, Mass.: Harvard University Press, 1946).

[12] President's Commission on Higher Education, *Higher Education for American Democracy, A Report of the President's Commission on Higher Education* (New York: Harper and Brothers, 1947), Vol. 1, p. 49.

[13] *Ibid.*, p. 61.

bining the two kinds of education in suitable proportions and making them interdependent." [14]

The problem of functionally organized courses is particularly important in the consideration of teacher education, not only because the idea of organizing the entire collegiate program around the vocational dimension is clearly a form of this, but because the role of "disciplines" in attacking educational problems is also at issue. To argue, as many teacher educators do, that the content of these disciplines will be brought into the discussion of each problem as it seems relevant presumes either (1) that a sensitivity to the methodology as such is not important in deciding the relevance and the effectiveness of the content, (2) that the teacher educator in charge of the problem approach will be adequately trained to use these disciplines in an effective way, or (3) that the student's previous experience has made him sensitive to the methodological issues involved.

In one form or another most of the positions respecting general or liberal education since 1930 have assumed that there is something peculiar about the methodology of each of the broad fields which deserves cultivation, aside from the value of the content or its application to the solution of immediate problems. The committee of the American Council of Learned Societies, as might have been expected, most nearly stated the traditional view, as amended to avoid the old arguments over faculty psychology. They argued:

> Historically some disciplines may be regarded as much more mature than others. They have been the subjects of instruction literally for centuries. In the course of grappling with those problems again and again, the methods of attack have been refined, fallacious techniques have been identified, ideas and insights have been reviewed, criticized, sharpened, and made more appealing and effective. That gives these studies, which are the substance of the liberal arts, a unique quality which other disciplines can acquire only after like periods of developing maturity. [15]

In a slightly different form, the Harvard committee argued that one could most adequately define areas of learning in terms of methods of knowing. [16] The natural sciences "describe, analyze, and explain"; the humanities "appraise, judge, and criticize."

[14] *Ibid.*, p. 63.
[15] Theodore M. Greene, *Liberal Education Re-examined*, pp. 8–9.
[16] Harvard Committee, *General Education in a Free Society*, p. 59.

The President's Commission, while urging new types of functionally oriented courses and defining its goals in terms similar to those of the Cardinal Principles, also placed emphasis on the development of such things as communication skills, scientific method, careful logical thought, and effective use of numbers.

Though they were concerned with aesthetic and emotional development they also saw the role of education as primarily intellectual. After criticizing the past preoccupation of the college with fact-gathering they argued:

More to the purpose and of much more lasting effect would be emphasis on the student's acquiring familiarity with the processes of inquiry and discovery. Insofar as education is not indoctrination it is discovery, and discovery is the product of inquiry. Arousing and stimulating intellectual curiosity, channeling this curiosity into active and comprehensive investigation, and developing skill in gathering, analyzing, and evaluating evidence—these should constitute the primary job of every teacher from the elementary grades through the university.[17]

The issue, then, was primarily one of approach. Among general education groups there seems to have been no strong tendency to deny the primacy of intellectual development—or the development of intelligent ways of handling problems. The general pattern seems to have been to rely on a number of courses of differing types. One point everywhere stressed was the danger of permitting the general education program to be dominated by specialist considerations which looked primarily to the development of intellectual disciplines as an instrument for further specialization.

Related to the problem of functional versus traditional approaches to the curriculum was the question of who should go to college. While the generalization should not be pushed too far there was, throughout the period, a tendency for the advocates of the discipline-centered type of organization to accept the "Jeffersonian" concept of rather high selectivity, based on measurements of intellectual (verbal) ability. If these people did suggest a semifunctional approach they tended to emphasize the organization of courses around major problem areas of a broad philosophical nature which would call into use a considerable number

[17] President's Commission, *Higher Education for American Democracy*, Vol. I, p. 57.

of "great books," though not necessarily those on the Hutchins–Adler list.[18]

This complex of ideas, emphasizing intellectual development as the sole serious concern of the college, placing great stress on the value of the disciplines, and urging greater selectivity and restriction was of great influence in the thought of the Commission on Financing Higher Education.[19]

On the other hand, there was an increasing concern with the larger group of students who, though not in the upper quarter intellectually, were nevertheless thought capable of profiting by higher education of some type. This belief was expressed in proposals that higher education organize programs around the interests of students for whom the traditional, highly bookish type of education seemed inadequate. There was a strong feeling that a high degree of functioning intelligence could be developed in a much larger group of students if the program were organized in terms of more clearly functional courses, giving greater attention to teaching aids other than the great books. This spirit which, though not careless of intellectual values, was definitely concerned with the broader interests of a greater group of students, was manifest in the report of the President's Commission on Higher Education.

One notable development of the general education movement was the support given it by representatives of a number of professional groups who came increasingly to feel that the extreme specialization which had previously marked their education was unwise. Earl J. McGrath, commenting on this fact, noted that it grew partly out of a recognition that the professional man needed education designed to fit him more effectively as a person and as a citizen. Other factors which he saw as influential were (1) the realization that in a society where changes occurred so rapidly the ability to readjust and learn new procedures was a prime requisite for professional success, (2) the recognition of the social bearing of the professions, (3) the discovery that students who had a broad general program were more successful in professional stud-

---

[18] Clarence H. Faust, "General Education: Its Nature and Purpose," *General Education in Transition, A Look Ahead,* A report of the Conference on Building a Program of General Education, University of Minnesota, 1949, H. T. Morse, ed. (Minneapolis, Minn.: University of Minnesota Press, 1951), Part V, pp. 56–68.

[19] See Commission on Financing Higher Education, *The Nature and Needs of Higher Education* (New York: Columbia University Press, 1952), pp. 14–18; and Byron S. Hollinshead, *Who Shall Go to College?* (New York: Columbia University Press, 1952), *passim.*

ies than those who had previously specialized, and (4) the belief that the ability to think and to generalize effectively was a basic prerequisite of success in any field. Representatives of law, medicine, engineering, architecture, business, nursing, and social work joined with McGrath in documenting these trends.[20] Throughout their statements ran the idea that general education was essential on professional grounds as well as of value to the individual in his nonprofessional roles.

General Education for Teachers and Its Relation to the Professional Sequence

Almost without exception the major documents on general education gave special attention to the strategic position of the teacher and to his need for a rich general education program. With similar lack of exception this emphasis was based on professional as well as general grounds. That is, the needs of the society for a particular type of public school teacher had come to dictate partially the program of general education. The efforts of teacher preparing colleges to meet this challenge were studied as part of the National Survey of the Education of Teachers.

The National Survey revealed the extent to which general education programs in the teachers colleges resembled those in the liberal arts colleges and universities, which by this time were found to be preparing a sizable proportion of the new teachers. It was noted that there were much greater differences in the general education program within a given type of teacher preparing institution than there were between types.[21] The similarities included the tendency in all types of institutions to concentrate general education largely in the first two years.

Moreover, the survey confirmed the feeling that college students were carrying specialization to a point which prevented adequate contact with large fields of knowledge. This was particularly noticeable in respect to subjects outside of the traditionally approved liberal arts

---

[20] Earl J. McGrath, "General Education and Professional Education," *General Education in the American College*, Part II, Thirty-Eighth Yearbook of the National Society for the Study of Education (Bloomington, Ill.: Public School Publishing Co., 1939), pp. 219–256.

[21] *National Survey of the Education of Teachers*, Vol. VI, pp. 76–78. Nearly one-half of the new teachers in 1930–31 were trained in multipurpose institutions, though there were obviously great differences from state to state and from level to level. Moreover, nearly half of the graduates of these colleges and universities entered some form of educational work.

course of study. Such areas as the newer social sciences, fine arts, health and physical education, and problems of the family were largely neglected. Edward S. Evenden concluded that ". . . prospective teachers from all types of institutions in 1931–32 had had a very limited contact with the principal fields of knowledge and also with fields closely related to the fields of major specialization." [22]

Another matter of grave concern about the general education of teachers, and its carry-over into the years after graduation, was the failure of teachers in training and in practice to read widely and to give evidence of concern with serious issues. Douglas Waples, after an extensive survey of reading interests and habits, discovered no significant difference between the sensitivity to social issues shown by some groups of teachers on the one hand and a cross section of the general public on the other.[23] In respect to problems which were of concern to the general public he found teachers to be less interested than other college-trained vocational groups.[24] He concluded that teachers were not concerned enough about social issues to give effective leadership to students faced with the crucial problems of the coming era. Evenden, in summarizing the findings in respect to general education, suggested that the serious shortcomings which were revealed were primarily due to the failure of the college to provide adequate guidance.[25]

Since the National Survey there have been extensive experiments with plans for general education sequences which blend harmoniously into the professional program. Until the recent experiments sponsored by the Fund for the Advancement of Education, most of the thinking of those positively interested in both the general and professional sequences has been along this line. However, solutions considered ideal have covered the continuum, ranging from those in which there is but occasionally contact between the two sequences to those involving professional treatment.

ARGUMENTS FOR PARALLEL AND HARMONIZED SEQUENCES

In 1939, Karl Bigelow, at that time Director of the Commission on Teacher Education of the American Council on Education, summarized

[22] *Ibid.,* p. 86.
[23] *National Survey,* Vol. V, Part V, p. 256.
[24] *Ibid.,* pp. 283–284.
[25] *National Survey,* Vol. VI, pp. 92–93.

general education programs in the teachers colleges. He cited the great diversity of patterns, but noted some common trends including:

. . . a broadening view of the curriculum; a functional emphasis on individual growth in capacity to meet personal–social needs in the various basic aspects of living; a stress upon student activity and upon individualization of instruction under guidance; a special, though not necessarily exclusive, concern with the contemporary problems of the individual and of society; an effort to enrich experience within and beyond college walls and to relate these experiences to each other; and, in general, a seeking after integration of various sorts. While the majority of teachers colleges are tending, along with the liberal arts colleges, to consider the freshman and sophomore years as constituting a period that should be pretty exclusively given over to general education, some oppose the sharp distinction between elements of general, and elements of professional training.[26]

At the Bennington Conference which touched off the Cooperative Study of Teacher Education in 1939, Bigelow again dealt with the problems of general education for teachers. He placed great stress on the importance in all general education of developing a sense of individual worth in relation to a sense of social responsibility and cohesiveness. He pointed out that if democratic presuppositions were at the center of the program a willingness to consider the student's needs and interests and to provide direct experiences must be demonstrated. "What I am pleading for," he insisted, "is that general education should recognize the importance of firsthand experience as well as of vicarious experience, that it should keep close to the earth and the common people thereof, and that it should unhesitatingly attend to any problem which is of genuine concern to students." [27]

Bigelow anticipated the possible charge of "anti-intellectualism" by pointing out that intellectual principles or insights are most apt to have repeated meaning if they are forged by the pupil himself out of his experience. Bigelow noted with some misgivings the tendency to distinguish too sharply between (1) general education, (2) instruction

[26] Karl Bigelow, "General Education and Teacher Education," *General Education in the American College,* Part II, Thirty-Eighth Yearbook of the National Society for the Study of Education (Bloomington, Ill.: Public School Publishing Co., 1939), pp. 274–275.

[27] Karl Bigelow, "General Education and Teacher Education," *Cultural and Social Elements in the Education of Teachers* (Washington, D.C.: Published jointly by the Commission on Teacher Education and the Educational Policies Commission, 1939), p. 14.

which was of general professional importance, and (3) specialized professional education. In the same spirit he raised doubts about the advisability of restricting the professional sequence to the last two years.

In 1946, when the Cooperative Study had virtually run its course, the Commission summarized its judgments concerning general education, as distinct from subject-matter specialization and the professional sequence. There was no intent to present any recommendations as authoritative, or as representative of everyone who had participated in the Cooperative Study. Nevertheless, since the Commission was composed of recognized leaders in higher education as a whole, in teacher education, in liberal arts colleges, universities, and teachers colleges, their considered judgments were important. These recommendations included the following special emphases:

> While general education may be usefully contrasted with special or vocational education, it ought not, as conducted, to ignore the implications of the special or vocational purposes of students; nor should professional education be carried on wholly without reference to students' more general needs; an integration of general and professional education should be sought. . . .
>
> At least three-eighths of the college experience of a prospective teacher should have as its primary objectives those properly ascribable to general education. . . .
>
> While elements of general education may well predominate during the first two college years they should neither monopolize nor be limited to this period: some educational experiences related to vocational purposes should be provided as soon as the latter are formed; and the idea that general education may be considered as "completed" at some particular time should not be encouraged. . . .
>
> The contemporary trend toward balance and integration in general education is significant and deserves support. This implies a basic pattern of broad courses, each developed with the special purposes of general education in mind, each requiring a fairly substantial block of time, and planned in relation to one another. . . .
>
> The trend toward the use of more in the way of nonverbal methods of instruction and student expression also deserves encouragement. First-hand experience, as well as motion pictures and the radio, should supplement books as tools of learning, and students should be helped to express what they have learned not only in words but through the arts and social action. . . .
>
> General education should be concerned with the body and the emotions as well as with the intellect. . . .
>
> Students should be given a more active, responsible role in the plan-

ning and carrying out of their own general education. This implies that instruction should be flexibly administered to provide for responsiveness to individual differences.[28]

These recommendations were in advance of actual practice, though generally consistent with the prevailing thought of educationists and presidents of liberal colleges, as revealed in the studies made by Warren Lovinger and Van Cleve Morris in 1947 and 1949.[29] Lovinger, for example, found that only one-fifth of the institutions holding membership in the American Association of Teachers Colleges could describe their present programs as designed to help each individual "develop all of his personal powers so that he may learn better to satisfy his own needs and share in caring for the needs of contemporary society." [30] The rest characterized their programs either in terms of the development of skills and knowledge common to educated persons and citizens in a free society (65 per cent), or of the "cultivation of the intellectual virtues" irrespective of whether or not it obviously helped the individual to adjust to his environment (9 per cent). Yet the majority of administrators of these colleges listed the development of all the student's powers as the ideal, while none of them so described the cultivation of intellectual virtues.

Similarly, though a very small group (4 per cent) believed that general education programs should be organized along departmental lines, a substantial majority reported that such organization still prevailed in their institutions. Thus, in terms of purpose, pattern of courses, and the relationship of general education to professional education, practice consistently lagged behind the thinking of the teachers college administrators who, in the majority of cases, so far as can be determined from Lovinger's evidence,[31] agreed essentially with the recommendations of the Commission on Teacher Education.

Morris' findings, which he compared with Lovinger's, indicated that

[28] American Council on Education, Commission on Teacher Education, *The Improvement of Teacher Education; A Final Report by the Commission on Teacher Education* (Washington, D.C.: The Council, 1946), pp. 82–84.

[29] Warren C. Lovinger, *General Education in the Teachers Colleges* (Oneonta, N. Y.: American Association of Colleges for Teacher Education, 1948); and Van Cleve Morris, *The Education of Secondary School Teachers in the Liberal Arts Colleges* (unpublished doctoral project, Teachers College, Columbia University, 1949; summarized in Association of American Colleges, *Bulletin*, 36:511–528, December, 1950).

[30] Lovinger, *ibid.*, p. 38.

[31] *Ibid.*, pp. 37–46.

there was broad agreement in important details between the liberal arts colleges which he had studied, and the teachers colleges studied by Lovinger. For example, both groups agreed that their present general education courses were departmentally organized and both hoped ultimately for a divisional or functional pattern.[32]

Both teachers colleges and liberal arts colleges concentrated professional education largely (not entirely) in the last two years. Over 40 per cent of each group hoped such an arrangement would continue, while substantial numbers in both groups hoped to see the programs parallel throughout. There was less enthusiasm for parallel programs among the liberal arts people (31 per cent as compared with 49 per cent of teachers college people). Finally, a majority of both groups hoped that the professional motivation would be utilized when it arose, so long as the general education program was protected from undue narrowing through professional considerations. It is interesting to note here that only one-fifth of the teachers college presidents favored a completely professionalized treatment.

The conservative approach to harmonizing the general and professional sequences has always been one of juggling courses in an attempt to create an integrated, continuous pattern. Since 1930, there have, however, been proposals and experiments looking to a more drastic reorganization of the entire teacher education program. A number of ideas which have recurred in these proposals were included in the theory of teacher education expressed by William H. Kilpatrick in 1933.[33]

Kilpatrick criticized the then prevailing scientific trend in education because of its atomistic psychology. He argued that this psychology assumed that each educational objective could be specifically isolated and achieved by techniques scientifically validated as providing a direct route to the goal. This psychology, he thought, implied that the total of specific skills so developed would make a whole and adequate human being. According to Kilpatrick, the movement had assumed, basically, that once the scientists had isolated the specific skills to be produced and the proved techniques for producing them the teacher had simply to learn to follow the blueprint.

[32] Morris, *The Education of Secondary School Teachers,* Tables XVIII, XIX, and XX.

[33] William H. Kilpatrick, ed., *The Educational Frontier* (New York: The Century Co., 1933). Chapter VIII, which deals with teacher education, was written by Kilpatrick.

Kilpatrick argued that the orienting principle of teacher education ought to be the building of a more inclusive, more critical, and more adequate social outlook. This involved, as he argued, an understanding of "the individual life process and how learning is essential in it to its continuous upbuilding; and, on the other hand, the social process and how education is essential in it also to its continuous upbuilding." [34]

It was argued that so far as possible ". . . the specific preparation of the prospective teacher, both broadly and narrowly conceived, should be carried on through the process of helping him educatively to raise to more adequate self-directive efforts his own life and work." [35] Moreover, the life and work of the student teacher were to be related as closely as possible to the surrounding social life.

Kilpatrick suggested that the student should increasingly participate in the actual teaching of children and that most of what he learned in the professional program should grow out of this experience. He believed that if the children were actually studying problems growing out of the surrounding social process, the student teacher, in helping his pupils to deal more adequately with these problems, would be progressively led to search out their basic implications. He was convinced that such a process would require the service of well-prepared professors and would tap the richest resources of the accumulated culture. In this manner he thought to utilize the disciplines and content of the traditional fields without organizing them in what he considered to be their traditionally deadening independence of living situations.

Kilpatrick dealt with the anticipated charge that he was neglecting the traditional disciplines by arguing that the imposition of logically organized materials on the teacher in training might result in their seeming illogical and meaningless to him. He explained:

Organization seems better conceived as the way of holding materials in such perceived relationships as to facilitate appropriate use. The crux here is perceived relationships. To acquire what someone else has put together need not mean perceived relationships; it may very likely mean vaccination against the desired perceiving. While the experience of others may be of great help in the matter, organization for effective intelligent use becomes thus almost the same thing as personally made organization. Certainly, unless it is so personally made and in answer to personally felt needs, we can have little if any faith that organization

34 *Ibid.*, p. 262.
35 *Ibid.*, pp. 271–272.

made simply by another will greatly facilitate intelligent use. To speak, then, of our organizing subject-matter for others to acquire comes dangerously close to treating subject-matter so that in the end it will probably not be organized for the learner. The best hope seems to lie in well-guided treatment of adequately varied problems.[36]

This, presumably, took care of the problem of the content of the traditional courses. Since some selection from the available material is, in any case, inevitable, Kilpatrick had suggested that the selection be based on the relevance of the material as it appeared to the learner who was led to consider a broad number of topics. So far as the disciplines, as methods of knowing, were concerned, Kilpatrick claimed to hold them of great value. He noted that the effectiveness with which the student analyzed problems depended on the intelligent use of "the best available methods of analysis and of knowing what past thinkers and workers have devised."[37] Each student was to be encouraged on every occasion to criticize his own results in the light of all the best evidence. By such a process Kilpatrick suggested that the very valuable techniques and procedures, which were deadening if allowed to dominate, would be reduced to their most fruitful role as means to be used when the larger purposes of life and education called for them.

There were a number of factors in the Kilpatrick position which ran through many of the proposals for an integrated general–professional program. These included (1) the suggestion that the professional program be organized around direct experiences, (2) the belief that the entire program should be problem oriented, (3) the feeling that an adequate grasp of disciplines could come indirectly from their repeated use in discrete problems of an immediate nature, and (4) the insistence that problems on which the elementary school, the high school, and the teachers college focus be socially significant ones whose urgency was such that they were clearly recognized and "felt" by the student. In practice these items were seldom found in the relationship which Kilpatrick gave them, but they characterize a major trend of thought.

One concrete experiment, which involved basic reorganization of the entire general–professional sequence in line with the spirit of the Kilpatrick position, was New College, conducted at Teachers College, Co-

[36] *Ibid.*, pp. 275–276.
[37] *Ibid.*, p. 278.

lumbia University, from 1933 to 1939. This experiment, directed in its major period by Thomas Alexander, placed great emphasis on individual guidance and on a curriculum organized around persistent problem areas.[38]

The program was built around a central seminar which in the early years of a student's attendance concerned itself with broad problems which might be thought to fall in general education. Phases of problems discussed in the central seminar were referred for further consideration to the divisional seminars of which there were four, each concerned with a subject area such as human relationships, natural sciences, arts, and philosophy. Service courses or units were provided to give students the knowledge and skills which they and their advisers thought were needed to supplement the seminars. These service courses tended to occupy about three-fourths of the student's time.

In the later years of the student's enrollment the central seminar gave way to an education seminar, and the divisional seminars were organized in terms of area of teaching specialization. In addition to this work on the Columbia campus the program included experience in community living at the New College Community in North Carolina, foreign travel, and a period of professional internship. As originally planned, the individual students were to move through the program more or less in their own peculiar pattern. The total program, including the internship, was designed to last five years after which a master's degree was to be awarded.

New College was closed in 1939 for budgetary reasons according to the official Teachers College Announcement. However, the experiment, which was closely watched by teacher education circles, provided an opportunity to try out a number of important ideas. Agnes Snyder, who participated in the New College program, became director of a somewhat similar program at Adelphi College, with the advice of Thomas Alexander, the former New College director.

There were, of course, other notable attempts to harmonize the general and professional sequences. The Supervisors of Student Teaching, in 1937, discussed plans in operation at Montclair, New Jersey; Stan-

---

[38] See Thomas Alexander, "The Significance of New College," *Twelfth Yearbook of the American Association of Teachers Colleges*, 1933, pp. 58–64; Karl Bigelow, "General Education and Teacher Education," *General Education in the American College*, pp. 271–274.

ford University; Towson, Maryland; and Terre Haute, Indiana.[39] Most of these programs were designed to ensure greater cooperation between different segments of the faculty or greater integration of the professional sequence itself rather than thorough integration of the total general and professional education programs, however.

THE PROFESSIONAL TREATMENT POSITION

The program at Montclair represented a frank attempt to make the professional dimension, broadly conceived, the integrating core of the entire general–professional curriculum. This represented the continuation of the professional-treatment position as it had developed. By this time the concept was being used to describe either a completely professionalized collegiate program or a plan to combine instruction in teaching with instruction in subject matter. The difference between these two meanings involves the extent to which the professional objective influences the general educational program. The Montclair plan professionalized the entire curriculum.

The discussion between John G. Flowers and Wesley E. Peik highlighted some of the major issues so far as educationists were concerned. Florence B. Stratemeyer, in reacting to these papers, sharpened the issues still further.[40]

Flowers pointed out that the whole general education movement had recognized the need of a central core around which to organize its work. For teacher education that core should be, he affirmed, the professional aim and organization. Cultural background, subject matter, personal growth of the student, professional ideals, knowledges, techniques, and administrative machinery were all concerned and must, as he thought, constantly be kept in mind. He insisted that a proper vision of the profession could prevent the loss of the liberal ideal and of scholarship, and could ensure the development of artists instead of artisans. He suggested that only a narrow view of the profession of

---

[39] John G. Flowers, ed., *The Integration of Laboratory Phases of Teacher Training with Professional and Subject-Matter Courses*, 1937 Yearbook of the Supervisors of Student Teaching.

[40] John G. Flowers, "The Integration of Subject-Matter and Education Courses with the Laboratory Phases of Teacher Education," *ibid.*, pp. 7–24; Wesley E. Peik, "Integration of the Pre-Service Curriculum for Teaching in Separate and Intensive Professional Courses," *ibid.*, pp. 25–35; and Florence B. Stratemeyer, "The Integration of Subject-Matter and Education Courses," *ibid.*, pp. 36–40.

teaching could justify the argument that a professionally oriented program must be illiberal.

Once the profession was properly conceived, Flowers argued (1) that its purposes should dominate the organization and administration of the college, (2) that they determine the curriculum, (3) that the subject matter should be professionally treated, (4) that instruction in psychology and techniques of teaching should be taught in connection with subject-matter courses, not as detached courses, (5) that laboratory experiences should be closely integrated with subject-matter and education courses, and (6) that the needs and problems of the service for which teachers were being prepared provided acceptable standards for determining objectives, techniques, and ideals which should be served. Flowers made explicit the obvious fact that such a program involved the "academic" professors as full partners in the "professional" program. They should teach methods classes, when appropriate, and participate in laboratory experiences.

To prove that the Montclair plan did not result in a loss of scholarship Flowers pointed to tests administered by the American Council testing program which indicated that Montclair students were well above the seventieth percentile of university and liberal arts college students similarly tested.

W. E. Peik's discussion was not a direct answer to that of Flowers. He did, however, take a vitally different position. He argued that the job of integration should fall to the special methods courses if they were properly handled. He suggested that, besides such courses, there were four significant parts of the teacher's education: general education including pre-college work, specialization in teaching fields, basic courses in education, and an elective program of studies taken for personal development. He considered the plan of professional treatment as a device to spread throughout the entire curriculum the work which he would concentrate in special methods courses.

Peik granted that the old special methods courses had been totally inadequate since they had been solely concerned with techniques rather than including all the relevant material. The material which he would add included some treatment of such items as philosophy, history, psychology, and trends related to broad fields. He believed that the existing inadequacy grew out of superficial and unsystematic treatment of such material. He doubted that the usual academic teacher could take the time or become adequately prepared to handle this type of work in addition to his other responsibilities.

Peik further objected to the professional treatment of subject matter on the grounds that to be effective it pulled the level of material down to that suitable for elementary or secondary school students, thereby failing adequately to challenge and develop college students.

In reviewing the history of teacher education Peik noted that the review of elementary subject matter had grown out of the inadequate general education of teacher candidates. He argued, further, that when competition between single-purpose normal schools and the colleges and universities had developed the professional treatment idea was conceived as a rationalization for continued elementary and secondary work and as propaganda material in the conflict. However, his assumption, that since professional treatment originated with respect to elementary material it necessarily remained so restricted, was challenged by Stratemeyer.

Peik was quite willing to grant the importance of special courses in children's literature, art, and music, and to see such courses integrated with instruction in teaching, but he insisted that, though this was necessary, it was not "higher education."

The point of view which Peik represented had particular bearing on multipurpose institutions where people with widely diverse occupational goals were educated together. He argued that the needs of different types of teachers were too varied to make professional treatment of subject matter practicable even for them. In the more or less general subject-matter courses all types of teachers were found, so these could not easily be professionalized. In the advanced and, therefore, more selective courses, the return to secondary or elementary materials would, in Peik's opinion, be especially unfortunate. Moreover, Peik felt that prospective teachers should share their general education program with students destined for other professions.

In analyzing the Flowers and the Peik papers Stratemeyer noted that two problem areas were involved: the relationship between the academic and professional programs, and the relationship of laboratory experiences to each. She saw five sets of issues in these areas: (1) the problem of how functionally to acquaint the student with broad fields of knowledge, (2) the question of whether or not learning was more functional when several relationships were simultaneously considered, (3) the problem of whether or not professional materials distributed over a long period become segmented parts whose relationships were not clearly seen, (4) the problem of how to make the professional emphasis effective when students are attending the course for different reasons, and (5) whether or not instructors adequately prepared to provide the professionalized program which Flowers had described could be found.[41]

Stratemeyer concluded by citing the need for (1) focusing attention upon the professional work for which the student was being prepared and selecting all materials in the light of the work of the student as an individual, a member of society, and a teacher; (2) remembering that such integration as actually occurred would take place within the individual; (3) recognizing the functional use of knowledge; (4) integrating the work through a study of societal problems; (5) differentiating the work in terms of individual or group needs; and (6) providing long and continuous contacts with people as they dealt with fundamental problems. It is quite clear that her basic position was in sympathy with that expressed by Flowers.

The Liberal and the Technical Functions
Within the Professional Sequence

Arguments such as that between Flowers and Peik inevitably involved differing opinions concerning the professional sequence itself. As Flowers had pointed out, one's conception of the teacher's function was crucial in designing the professional sequence as well as in relating it to general education.

PREVAILING CONCEPTS OF THE
ROLE OF THE TEACHER

The function of the teacher in respect to social change and stability was greatly emphasized during the depression and war years. Moreover, the concept of democratic school administration which made the teacher an active participant in making decisions about curriculum,

---

[41] Florence B. Stratemeyer, "The Integration of Subject-Matter and Education Courses," pp. 36–39.

discipline, and other crucial matters gained greater currency. These factors not only made a thorough general education essential, but also made it more important for teachers to receive a liberally oriented professional training.

One of the most unusual efforts to criticize constructively the school's program was made by the American Historical Association. Their Commission on the Social Studies published a number of significant volumes during the 1930's. This Commission, headed by A. C. Krey, was notable in bringing "educationists" and "academicians" together for an extended discussion and study of the problems of the public schools. For present purposes the significant thing about the Commission's work was the clear statement which it gave to the social responsibility of the school. The Commission cited the crucial changes which had occurred in American life and noted the passage of the individualistic frontier economy. They pointed to the rise of a collectivist society which involved both dangers and opportunities. They insisted, in light of these profound social changes, that the action or inaction of the school was critical, and that only by re-examining its philosophy and deliberately aiding the transition could education fill its role. This examination must, as they saw it, be made in terms of the unique character of American society which needed to be thoroughly understood. Viewed in terms of this framework, education was conceived as "one of the highest forms of statesmanship." [42]

The statement of the educational beliefs upon which the Commission based its report was drawn from the writings of George S. Counts, whose *Dare the School Build a New Social Order?*[43] had dramatically challenged educators to face their responsibilities; of Jesse H. Newlon who, among leaders of educational administration, placed greatest emphasis on education as social policy and on the importance of democracy in school administration; and of Merle Curti who, among academic historians, has been notable as a student of the role of education in American society. In the early years of the decade, these men joined with other colleagues in education to publish the *Social Frontier,* a periodical which not only carried high the banner of "education as a

---

[42] Commission on the Social Studies, *Conclusions and Recommendations of the Commission* (New York: Charles Scribner's Sons, 1934), p. 30.

[43] George S. Counts, *Dare the School Build a New Social Order?* (New York: The John Day Company, Inc., 1932).

social policy," but courageously and vigorously spelled out the type of social order which they conceived as necessary. Counts served for a while as editor.[44]

The same general emphasis, with the educational implications more fully spelled out, was contained in the *Educational Frontier,* published by some of the same group in 1933.[45]

There was growing support for the idea that teachers should participate more fully in making fundamental decisions about educational policy. This was accompanied by an emphasis on the educational supervisor as a "helper" rather than a critic. In these movements such men as Newlon and Ernest O. Melby were most influential.[46] By 1938 the Educational Policies Commission, representing the American Association of School Administrators and the National Education Association, had taken official notice of the importance of this teacher participation.[47]

It would seem that the growing importance and power of the teacher would lead to an emphasis both on general education and on a professional sequence more directly oriented around these leadership roles. And so it did for some educational thinkers. Others, however, tended to follow out the implications in one or the other, rather than in both sequences.

For example, Wesley E. Peik, in his proposals for the education of teachers in colleges and universities, made as part of the National Survey, noted as one of his guiding principles that

Teachers occupy a key position in the progress of a rapidly moving civilization. It is important that curricula for their preparation be given

---

[44] The list of those who participated included most of the leading educational thinkers of the Experimentalist school—John Dewey, William H. Kilpatrick, Boyd H. Bode, Goodwin Watson, Sidney Hook, John L. Childs, R. Bruce Raup, V. T. Thayer, Gordon Hullfish, to mention only a few, and such scholars from other areas as Charles A. Beard and Merle Curti.

[45] William H. Kilpatrick, ed., *The Educational Frontier.* The authors included Bode, Childs, Hullfish, Raup, Thayer, and Dewey.

[46] Jesse H. Newlon, *Educational Administration as Social Policy* (New York: Charles Scribner's Sons, 1934), pp. 170–202; Ernest O. Melby, "The Teacher and the School System," *The Teacher and Society,* First Yearbook of the John Dewey Society, William H. Kilpatrick, ed. (New York: D. Appleton-Century, 1937) pp. 119–144.

[47] Educational Policies Commission, *The Structure and Administration of Education in American Democracy* (Washington, D.C.: National Education Association, 1938), pp. 67–68.

much thought to keep them responsive to social change and social need.[48]

Apparently in keeping with this principle he suggested that the general education program place more emphasis on sociology, fine arts, economics, government, biology, and philosophy, and that the courses should be problem oriented. He even suggested a special course in the social function of education for *nonteachers* as part of their general education.

So far as the professional sequence was concerned, Peik recommended special-methods courses, courses in school organization, and courses in educational, social, and general psychology. He did not recommend any professional instruction specifically aimed at making the school more responsive to social issues except as it might come incidentally into one of the other courses.

THE PLACE OF FOUNDATIONAL THEORY

Peik, and probably every other educationist who made recommendations about the pre-service program, placed considerable emphasis on the importance of psychology as an essential element. That the prospective teacher needed some understanding of the processes of growth and of learning seemed evident. While such understanding contributed directly to technique it is apparent that most educational policy questions need also to be solved in its light.

However, at the beginning of the period here discussed, educational psychology was in a state of considerable confusion which amounted to a running war between varying schools of thought. By and large it seems to have been largely dominated by a mechanistic and individualistic bias. Apparently the text writers in the field were giving rather little attention to developments in social psychology and depth psychology. Walter S. Monroe, one of the outstanding students of educational research, was able to write a book covering developments in teaching–learning theory up to 1950 with only the barest mention of "field" theories, and with virtually no mention of either depth or social psychology as such.[49] As late as 1952 Harold Rugg was still complaining, un-

---

[48] Wesley E. Peik, "Teacher-Education Curriculum in Universities, Colleges, and Junior Colleges," *National Survey of the Education of Teachers*, Vol. III, Part III, p. 353.

[49] Walter S. Monroe, *Teaching–Learning Theory and Teacher Education, 1890–1950* (Urbana, Ill.: University of Illinois Press, 1952), *passim*.

doubtedly with exaggeration, that of those psychologists actively engaged in teacher education, only three had given serious thought to the social implications of their work.[50]

Throughout the period there seems to have been an increasing tendency to place less emphasis on minor differences between schools of psychology and to recognize the relatedness of this to other disciplines. This was noted by H. H. Remmers and N. L. Gage who, in a 1943 review of literature on child development, described the following as clearly discernible trends:

There is a continuing growth of the wholistic emphasis—the whole child interacting with a total environment; nothing is irrelevant and everything matters. There is thus coming about a greater integration of a number of disciplines, such as biology, anthropology, economics, and education. There is increasing awareness of the influence of cultural factors in the development of personality.[51]

Since 1930 the need for other liberalizing materials has been more frequently urged, though perhaps with little serious effect. However, the organization of the professional sequence into functional courses has made it a little hard to determine the extent to which these experiences were being provided. At the beginning of the period, Edward S. Evenden, director of the National Survey of the Education of Teachers, suggested that the professional sequence as a whole was concerned with seven functions: (1) providing professional orientation, (2) offering service courses from such areas as curriculum construction, science of education, educational history, philosophy and sociology, and the use of tests and measurements, (3) ensuring knowledge of students to be taught, (4) developing methods of teaching appropriate to each grade or subject to be taught, (5) giving an understanding of the organization and management of the type of school in which the teacher intended to work, (6) ensuring a safety minimum of technical skill, and (7) providing an opportunity to build an integrated philosophy of education and teaching.[52]

Of these components it would seem that materials drawn from the social sciences as applied to education should logically enter into the

50 Harold Rugg, *The Teacher of Teachers* (New York: Harper and Brothers, 1952), p. 93.
51 H. H. Remmers and N. L. Gage, "The Family, Education, and Child Adjustment," *Review of Educational Research*, XIII:(1)21–28 (February, 1943), p. 21.
52 *National Survey*, Vol. VI, pp. 93–94.

professional orientation, perhaps the service courses, and the final integration course which Evenden specifically described as drawing from history, sociology, and related subjects.

In 1940 Evenden summarized the findings of a subcommittee of the American Association of Teachers Colleges' Committee on Standards and Surveys, which gave some indication of existing practice. He pointed out that, in addition to the general education program aimed at a broad cultural background, 95 per cent of the colleges reported courses designed to give a "systematic overview of the social conditions under which children were living." A substantial number, he reported, gave attention to the differences between urban and rural life, and to an understanding of the American system of government. Moreover, he found that "an understanding of the relationships between education and society" was theoretically an objective of many courses, providing a median of seven semester hours of credit, which were typically given in the junior and senior years and required for all prospective teachers.[53]

Obed J. Williamson reported in 1936, however, that there was a continuing loss of interest in basic questions of educational theory. This was in spite of the vigorous agitation of educational frontier groups and others.[54]

In the later years of the third decade of the century the protest against this lack of interest continued to be strong. In 1937, for example, W. W. Charters charged education, as a discipline, with neglecting "its fundamental bases." He granted to the opponents of the professional sequence the point that its courses were primarily thin scatterings of information about methods of instruction and administration which could easily be learned on the job. He insisted that this should not be the case and pointed to the vast new body of material which ought to constitute the heart of the professional program. He cited, as some of the fundamental bases which were being ignored by the educationists, psychology, physiology, nutrition, and sociology. To these, he maintained, there should be added materials drawn from a more careful

[53] Edward S. Evenden, "Some Interpretative Comments on Curriculum Practices in Normal Schools and Teachers Colleges in the United States, 1939–40," American Association of Teachers Colleges, *Nineteenth Yearbook,* 1940, pp. 140–143.

[54] Obed J. Williamson, *Provisions for General Theory Courses in the Professional Education of Teachers* (New York: Bureau of Publications, Teachers College, Columbia University, 1936), p. 113.

analysis of American culture and civilization, from anthropology, and from biology.[55]

In the same year the National Society of College Teachers of Education gave their yearbook over to the rationale of, and argument for, what is here called the "foundations" approach.[56] In the introduction Charles F. Arrowood noted the general fear that the solution of educational issues would be hampered by a too narrow approach to them. He repeated the basic thesis that, though education was a special field of knowledge having its peculiar content, this content, nevertheless, interlocked with that of other fields of knowledge. He pointed out that the process of moving from a general understanding of the social environment to its implication for education was not simple or automatic. The job of selecting what of the general background was significant and of determining its relationship to education was, he insisted, a most difficult task calling for broad insight into both general content and the educative process.

Arrowood noted that in certain periods educationists simply assume a certain world view and give their attention to developing techniques of teaching, management, or community relationships. In other periods, according to Arrowood's observation, more basic issues arise, and the attention formerly given to the technical must give way to a more basic reinterpretation of educational purposes and of fundamental patterns of education. For these basic re-evaluations a more extended study of the findings in other areas of scholarship was, he thought, essential. He suggested that educationists had critically ignored fundamental developments in public law, the new history, anthropology, and the biological sciences. The only hope which Arrowood could see for the type of educational reconstruction most critically needed was for students of educational problems to widen the intellectual foundations of their fields and for scholars in the social and natural sciences, and in the humanities, to bring the resources of their fields of knowledge to bear upon the interpretation of educational issues.

Finally, Arrowood insisted that the employment of "chance-met gen-

55 W. W. Charters, "Education Neglects Its Fundamental Bases," American Association of Teachers Colleges, *Sixteenth Yearbook* (Oneonta, N. Y.: The Association, 1937), pp. 10–15.

56 Fowler D. Brooks, ed., *The Use of Background in the Interpretation of Educational Issues,* Twenty-Fifth Yearbook of the National Society of College Teachers of Education (Chicago: University of Chicago Press, 1937).

eralizations and bits of fact from the various fields of human knowledge" was completely inadequate. The yearbook attempted to emphasize some of the contributions which might be made by the various "foundational" disciplines. It included sections prepared by teachers from the academic faculties of universities as well as by educationists. Some of the specific areas which were briefly spotlighted included the exact and biological sciences, psychology, philosophy, political science, sociology, comparative studies, and history. In each area it was pointed out that the most recent developments—in methodology and in findings —had been largely ignored in the making of educational decisions.

The preparation of teachers having the capacity to use these background materials required an extended and reorganized general education, a fact noted by several of the contributors to the yearbook. These authors placed great stress on the development of patterns of organization which would bring the scholarship of other disciplines close to the study of education.[57] John S. Brubacher and Philip W. L. Cox, for example, in a statement approved by the yearbook committee as a whole, suggested that the background might well be given in the undergraduate years by the arts faculty, though with the professional use clearly in view. Such an arrangement was seen as providing for more rapid and comprehensive professional instruction at the graduate level.

Regardless of the pattern of organization, the contributors to the volume felt that a thorough understanding of these foundations in both their general and professional implications was essential to the adequate resolution of the most crucial educational problems. They recognized that students of short courses in the normal schools could expect only a minimal exposure but, to the extent that the teacher was accepted as a major participant in making educational policy, this background was seen as crucial. Contributors who specifically spelled out the professional functions of their areas included Edward H. Reisner on the role of history, Charles F. Arrowood on the importance of philosophical background, George W. Hartmann on psychology, and I. L. Kandel on comparative education.[58] Judd, Hartmann, Reisner, and Kandel all cited,

---

[57] See Charles H. Judd, "The Scientific Study of Social Trends as Background for the Interpretation of Educational Issues," *ibid.*, pp. 142–162; and John S. Brubacher and Philip W. L. Cox, "Making Background Available for Students Effectively to Interpret Educational Issues," *ibid.*, pp. 211–227.

[58] Edward H. Reisner, "The More Effective Use of Historical Background in the Study of Education," *ibid.*, pp. 186–210; Charles F. Arrowood, "Educational Issues in the Light of Contemporary American Philosophy," *ibid.*, 86–116; George

directly or indirectly, concepts taken from social psychology and anthropology.

The yearbook had been conceived to call attention to the pertinence of the foundational disciplines in making educational policy, and also to further the development of ways to organize them for use. The underlying task was to create a discipline of educational foundations in which educational practitioners and their academic colleagues could have confidence. A methodology for investigation, an organization for effective presentation of foundations insights in the teacher education program, and a series of techniques for applying them to the actual process of making educational policy were needed. The attempt to create such a discipline ran through the entire period.

For example, John Dewey had attempted to outline some rough guides for the process in his 1929 Kappa Delta Pi lectures on *The Sources of a Science of Education.* He defined "science" for this purpose as simply involving systematic methods of inquiry which permitted a better understanding of facts and a more intelligent, less haphazard, and less routine control of them. He noted that a scientific approach to education demanded the opportunity to get somewhat away from the urgency of a situation demanding immediate action. He insisted that "preoccupation with attaining some direct end or practical utility, always limits scientific inquiry." He argued that the desire of teachers *directly* to use findings presented to them invariably diminished the type of freedom which such knowledge should have given. Dewey explained the "practical" way in which scientifically validated facts ought to be used by teachers in this manner:

Facts which are so interrelated form a system, a science. The practitioner who knows the system and its laws is evidently in possession of a powerful instrument for observing and interpreting what goes on before him. This intellectual tool affects his attitudes and modes of response in what he does. Because the range of understanding is deepened and widened he can take into account remote consequences which were originally hidden from view and hence were ignored in his actions. Greater continuity is introduced; he does not isolate situations and deal with them in separation as he was compelled to do when ignorant of connecting principles. As the same time, his practical dealings become more flexible. Seeing more relations he sees more possibilities, more opportun-

---

W. Hartmann, "Contemporary Psychology," *ibid.,* pp. 60–85; and I. L. Kandel, "National Backgrounds of Education," *ibid.,* pp. 163–185.

ities. He is emancipated from the need of following tradition and special precedents. His ability to judge being enriched, he has a wider range of alternatives to select from in dealing with individual situations.[59]

Dewey went on to argue that there was no science of education as such; that the educative process simply defined the problems with which techniques and materials of other sciences contend; and that ". . . material drawn from *other* sciences furnishes the content of educational science when it is focused on the problems that arise in education." [60]

The sources of the science of education which Dewey specifically cited were biology, philosophy, psychology—including social psychology and psychiatry—and sociology which he defined as all the "social disciplines."

Some generalizations from the Dewey position are significant: (1) the facts and techniques for educational science were to be drawn from other natural and social sciences, (2) they must be organized in relation to problems set by the educative process, (3) they were meaningful as educational science only as they were organized in the minds of the teachers who would use them, and (4) their utility was not an immediate one, but was one growing out of a deeper and wider range of understanding which made the teacher's judgment more adequate by permitting him to see implications not previously apparent. In this same stream of thought, teacher educators working with Dewey organized, in 1934, the first systematic, multidisciplinary course in the "foundations of education." The program which they established at Teachers College, Columbia University, clearly gave impetus to some of the most promising present programs in the universities and teachers colleges. The Teachers College pattern grew out of years of discussion involving, in the earliest period, William H. Kilpatrick, Harold Rugg, George S. Counts, John L. Childs, R. Bruce Raup. Goodwin Watson, Jesse Newlon, Edmund deS. Brunner, I. L. Kandel, Edward H. Reisner, and F. Ernest Johnson.[61]

As seen by the faculty who created the program, this action, in coordinating the focus of previously isolated disciplines, represented a significant shift from a mechanistic and atomistic outlook on life to an organic one. They stated part of their rationale in 1941 as follows:

[59] John Dewey, *The Sources of a Science of Education* (New York: Liveright Publishing Corporation, 1929), pp. 20–21.
[60] *Ibid.,* p. 36.
[61] See Harold Rugg, *The Teacher of Teachers*, pp. 224–228.

The final outcome of this foundational study, if prolonged over some years, should be proficiency in the design, construction, and operation of schools. The staff . . . believe that this proficiency can be developed only through a thorough study of American culture itself. The modern conception of curriculum development is that the sciences, the arts, the skills, and other parts of the school program are made directly from the culture itself, that is, from (1) the problems of the young people and grownups living in our country today; (2) the traits, characteristics, and values of the people; and (3) the trends and movements of American and world history which brought these problems, traits, and values into being. The very stuff of the study of education, we think, is the life of our people as it is actually lived.[62]

The particular program designed for Teachers College was intended primarily for candidates for the M.A. degree, many of whom already had teaching service. It was not solely, therefore, pre-service, but its basic principles were conceived as applying to all teacher education. These principles included the beliefs (1) that the "stuff" of education should be drawn largely from the study of the American people and their culture, (2) that these materials should be organized in terms of educational problems as seen through the coordinated study of several instructors each of whom was well trained in at least one of the social or natural science disciplines, and (3) that the goal conceived should encompass the entire "design, construction, and operation" of the educational program rather than focus directly on techniques of teaching.

In a 1950 "statement to the profession," the Committee on Social Foundations of the National Society of College Teachers of Education restated the increasingly critical need for a discipline of educational foundations. They summarized the resources which were available in meeting that need, and asked the support of the academic community at large and of all professional educationists in the task.[63] The statement, which was the product of the collective thought of many minds in many colleges and universities and was in the form of a "first draft," does not

---

[62] Harold Rugg, ed., *Readings in the Foundations of Education,* Prepared by Division I, Foundations of Education, Teachers College, Columbia University (New York: Bureau of Publications, Teachers College, Columbia University, 1941), Vol. I, p. vi.

[63] National Society of College Teachers of Education, Committee on Social Foundations, *The Emerging Task of the Foundations of Education, The Study of Man, Culture and Education, A Statement to the Profession* (Ann Arbor, Mich.: The Society, n.d.).

lend itself to brief summation by a few well-chosen quotations. However, among the major ideas were the following:

1. The world today lives in the shadow of catastrophe, in an age of incredibly rapid social change.

2. The solution of the problems which confront mankind demands the maximum use of potential human resources, in the development of which the school and its teachers have an awesome responsibility.

3. The reconstruction of our educational system to make it more effectively responsive to these great demands requires the leadership of three professional groups: the leading thinkers in the university disciplines at large; the educators who deal with the technical problems of administration, curriculum, guidance, teaching, and supervision; the professors of education in the foundational areas of psychology, philosophy, sociology, history, anthropology, aesthetics, and international relations.

4. The professors in the foundational areas have a peculiar responsibility to lead in bringing the findings of the academic disciplines to bear on the underlying problems of education in the American culture.

5. The techniques and knowledge required to build an effective foundational program are now available as the result of recent and most significant developments in the university disciplines of psychology, biology, philosophy, and social sciences.

6. Important elements from these disciplines are and should be offered as part of the general education program, but this does not make it less necessary for them to be focused specifically on the problems of education in the culture.

7. While each of several disciplines has a unique function, they must be integrated at least to the extent that they focus together on the problems of man, culture, and education. Moreover, educational foundations as a whole is creating its own unique body of concepts.

8. If organized education is to meet the demands made upon it, then workers at all levels must come to have a common conception of its basic function in this society. To this end foundations understandings must be central in every teacher education program. They should not be scattered and diffused through other parts of the curriculum, nor taught by inadequately trained people who are primarily interested in other aspects of the curriculum.

The above ideas, though presented without context and in paraphrase, are indicative of the committee's thought. In addition to a general discussion of the role of educational foundations, the statement of the committee contained specific discussions of current trends of thought in several of the areas—social foundations, international foundations, psychological foundations, group dynamics, philosophical foundations, religion, and historical foundations. Some of the disciplines and some of the concepts discussed were historically rooted in teacher education and had been implemented to a considerable extent. Other points of emphasis were rather new.

For example, while comparative education received attention rather early in the development of university professional programs, Donald G. Tewksbury's concept of "international foundations" as an area rooted in the university study of international relations was broad and different. So was Harold Rugg's repeated demand for the development of an "aesthetic foundation" program to be based on the "expressive arts." It will be recalled, however, that some early professors of education had urged, and New York University had established, a course in "aesthetics in relation to education" (see above, page 113).

As the foundations concept has developed in recent years it has centered on the process of reaching decisions in areas where values are in conflict or in confusion. The areas of conflict in the American culture were seen as the focal points at which the various academic disciplines could be brought to bear. The process of making educational policy decisions in respect to these conflicts tended to define the central "discipline" of educational foundations, just as "problem solving" became, for many, the central discipline of general education.

In the period after 1942 the task of improving this methodology received much attention from a number of leaders in the foundations movement. One group of thinkers made the improvement of "practical intelligence" (the ability to judge more effectively in situations where those making the decisions hold conflicting values) their special interest.[64] One member of this group, William O. Stanley, of the University of Illinois, has suggested that teaching and leading the public effectively to make social policy decisions defines the central responsibility of professional educators.[65] This group operates out of the experimentalist orientation and accepts its faith in the scientific method. Nevertheless, they have considered previous formulations of the decision-making process inadequate, in overstressing techniques for making judgment of fact at the expense of finding ways to reach consensus on normative issues.

---

[64] R. Bruce Raup et al., The Improvement of Practical Intelligence, the Central Task of Education (New York: Harper and Brothers, 1943).

[65] William O. Stanley, Education and Social Integration (New York: Bureau of Publications, Teachers College, Columbia University, 1953), pp. 185–186.

CONFLICTING VIEWS OF
DIRECT-EXPERIENCE PROGRAMS

As direct-experience programs had developed in the Oswego Training School tradition their directors had tended to emphasize two factors:
(1) that the direct-experience programs must be the heart of the pre-
service professional sequence, and (2) that improved technique, as
demonstrated in the handling of the training school class, defined the
goal of this sequence. This "apprenticeship" theory began to be broadly
modified after 1930 as teacher educators investigated more closely the
implications of the "laboratory" theory as developed by John Dewey,
Thomas Alexander, and others in the early decades of the century
(see above, pages 177 to 181).

However, the apprenticeship theory continued to have advocates in
practice-teaching circles throughout the recent period. Ironically
enough, it seems to be gaining new support from some of the people in
the conservative colleges who, out of their desire to improve the quality
of general education for teachers, are working to create a professional
sequence apparently of the apprenticeship variety.[66]

In this tradition Albert L. Rowland defended the teachers colleges
against the liberal arts colleges in 1934. He pointed out that in the
former neither the teachers nor the students ever forgot the professional
purpose. He noted that in liberal arts colleges practice teaching was
treated contemptuously. "But," he added, "in the teachers colleges,
what a difference! For three years all student eyes have been turned to
the training school. . . . Practice teaching has in short been the focus
of all the courses of the college, and is recognized by the student as
the epitome of their work." [67]

Similarly, in 1935, J. Howard Payne described the "Teachers College Slant" as being such that the entire program was bathed with the
consciousness of method.[68] Payne developed the basic principles which

[66] It would seem that the experimental Ford Foundation–Arkansas fifth-year
professional sequence might, unless carefully guarded, be reduced to an apprenticeship in techniques of teaching. See "A Review of What's Happening in
Teacher Education Around the Nation," *The Journal of Teacher Education*, 4:326
(December, 1953).

[67] Albert L. Rowland, "The Teachers College Preferred," American Association of Teachers Colleges, *Thirteenth Yearbook, 1934*, p. 113.

[68] J. Howard Payne, "The Teachers College Slant," American Association of
Teachers Colleges, *Fourteenth Yearbook, 1935*, pp. 76–80.

have been discussed as the "professional treatment" position, including not only the idea that method would be emphasized throughout but also that material would be selected on the basis of its usefulness in the lower schools.

Also at this 1935 meeting L. R. Gregory expressed his pride in the fact that the entire education department of his normal school had "been virtually swallowed by the training school." In Gregory's case, however, the academic department had not been integrated. He suggested that he was quite content for his students to receive general education free from the professional slant. In a sense this was a return to the purist position of early normal school days.[69]

The significant thing about this position is that it continued to presume that only experiences directly relevant to the technical function have a place in the professional program. This is inevitable when the focus is solely on the training school, although as this century has progressed the practice-teaching program has widened its vision to include other aspects of the school program beyond simple classroom instruction. Yet even if participation in grading papers, advising extracurricular activities, and meeting with the faculty are included the program may remain only technical.

A contrasting position was discussed by W. Earl Armstrong in a 1939 address before the Supervisors of Student Teaching.[70] Armstrong pointed out that the preoccupation with methods had characterized the education of teachers from the beginning of the century. Such a concept he saw as reasonable in the eyes of those who believed in conditioning psychology and in the scientific determination of objectives and methods. He suggested, however, that the newer concept of the teacher as a guide to learning necessitated a change in teacher education.

This shift, according to Armstrong, radically changed the place of student teaching in the professional program and reduced it to a position coordinate with other elements. Like other parts, student teaching, rather than being the end in itself, should seek to contribute to "all the aims of teacher education." Armstrong defined these aims in terms of greater understanding of the place of the school in the community,

---

[69] L. R. Gregory, "Adventuring in Faculty Cooperation and Participation in the Training School," *ibid.*, pp. 37–43.

[70] W. Earl Armstrong, "Possible Approaches to Certain Problems in the Supervision of Student Teaching," *Supervisors of Student Teaching*, Nineteenth Annual Session, 1939, pp. 19–25.

greater sensitivity to the needs of pupils, a clearer appreciation of the scope of subject matter and its place in learning, improved competence in dealing with pupils, broader concepts of evaluation, experience in the use of techniques, and deeper understanding of the concrete use of abstractions.

Armstrong was implicitly supported by Goodwin Watson who also clearly shifted the focus from technique. Watson defined the objectives of teacher education, including practice teaching, in terms of such factors as (1) improved capacity for effective living, (2) more adequately developed personality, (3) skill in democratic leadership, (4) ability to contribute to the social, economic, and political life of the nation, and (5) capacity to grow toward broader outlook and richer interests.[71]

To achieve these objectives Watson pointed to the need to get away from the existing direct emphasis on book learning and verbal skills. He clearly implied that a well-conceived educational program, functionally centered on improving the quality of living, would lead to a greater interest in worth-while reading as well as to other desired ends.

Allen D. Patterson extended what he still called "student teaching," in the direction indicated by Watson. The extent to which the concept of student teaching had evolved from that aiming at technical skill as its sole objective is apparent from the principles stated by Patterson:

Experiences in student teaching should be so selected and utilized as to develop a deep concern for the social, economic, and spiritual tensions of the surrounding culture as they affect the development of children and establish some competence in using these cultural conflicts for instructional purposes.

. . . .

The dominating spirit in the student teaching program should be consistent with the spirit of experimentation, broadly interpreted, and developed in a manner consistent with the conception of supervision as "counselled self-direction."

. . . .

Student teaching, although directed by a cooperatively developed philosophy of education, should acquaint the student with the conflicting points of view and practice in educational philosophy, psychology, sociology, etc., and enable student teachers to function effectively as teachers in transitional public schools.

. . . .

[71] Goodwin Watson, "Redirecting Teacher Education and Its Implications for Supervisors of Student Teaching," *ibid.*, pp. 27–33.

Student teaching should provide for exploratory and responsible contacts with several different types and levels of pupil groups in the classroom, the extra-classroom program, the home and the community.

. . . .

Student teaching should include guided experience in the discovery, development, and creative use of professional and educational resources of the community.

. . . .

To enable student teaching to become a truly integrating experience some other patterns of experience must replace the present compartmentalization of theory courses, content courses, observation, and practice teaching.[72]

Patterson's concept of direct experiences was different from the training school tradition in being designed for a far more liberal function. The locus of problems which were to occupy the attention of the student teacher was no longer solely the classroom, but included the community and the culture as a whole. However, the selection of the direct-experience program as the integrating center of the entire professional sequence was in keeping with the tradition. Patterson implied that the responsibility of the supervisor of student teaching was (1) to "acquaint the student with the conflicting points of view and practice in educational philosophy, psychology, [and] sociology"; (2) to help him to develop a deep concern for the social, economic, and spiritual tensions of the surrounding culture; (3) to guide him in the discovery, development and creative use of community resources; and (4) eventually, to find a way to integrate theory courses, courses in the academic disciplines, and courses in practice teaching. This would seem to be a fairly demanding task.

In 1948 the American Association of Teachers Colleges conducted an extensive poll which indicated rather widespread agreement on a number of principles closely related to those suggested by Patterson.[73] By this time the old phrase, "student teaching," was giving way to a fancier title, "professional laboratory experience." The changed terminology recognized the idea that direct experience, prior to actual

---

[72] Allen D. Patterson, "Redefining the Values and Functions of Student Teaching," *ibid.*, pp. 38–43, *passim*.

[73] American Association of Teachers Colleges, *School and Community Laboratory Experiences in Teacher Education* (Oneonta, N. Y.: The Association, 1945), pp. 16–41. For the distinction between "student teaching" and "professional laboratory experiences," see pp. 321–323.

practice teaching, was needed to increase the student's understanding of concepts encountered in the general education and educational theory courses. This was essentially the principle involved in John Dewey's 1904 statement that "practice work thus considered is administered primarily with reference to the intellectual reactions it incites, giving the student a better hold upon the educational significance of the subject-matter he is acquiring, and of the science, philosophy, and history of education" (see above, page 178).

The American Association of Teachers Colleges poll revealed some consensus on nine principles. One of these, previously cited, pointed to the threefold function of laboratory experiences: (1) implementing theory by giving the student a chance to check its pragmatic value and his own understanding, (2) helping students to become conscious of personal and professional needs, and (3) giving them an opportunity for guided experience in actual teaching. A second principle insisted that laboratory experiences be closely tied to the guidance program so they could be made responsive to individual differences. A third insisted that the program provide contact with children of different socio-economic backgrounds and different maturity levels for a long enough period to permit an effective understanding of their growth and developmental patterns. Another principle suggested that professional programs should provide contact with all important phases of the teacher's work, both in and out of school. The fifth provided for the cooperative participation of the student and his laboratory-experience directors and college teachers in working out the program. The sixth insisted that all members of the faculty must jointly participate in developing the program in the interests of both general and professional needs of the individual student. Evaluation of the experiences, according to the seventh principle, was to be made on a functional base in terms of the requirements of a teacher working in the American society. The two final principles dealt with the need for adequate facilities and for continuity between the pre-service and in-service programs.[74]

The 1948 Yearbook of the Association for Student Teaching cited some of the more interesting experiments in providing such activities.[75] This review of laboratory-experience programs revealed the extent to

[74] *Ibid.*, pp. 16–34, *passim.*

[75] Association for Student Teaching, *Professional Laboratory Experiences; An Expanding Concept in Teacher Education,* Twenty-Seventh Yearbook of the Association for Student Teaching (Lock Haven, Pa.: The Association, 1948).

which they lend themselves to preparing teachers for the particular kind of community in which they will work. This became very clear when the program used in a metropolitan university, Wayne University, was compared with that provided in a state teachers college in Michigan, and when each of these was compared with the program provided for teachers in the elementary schools of Georgia's rural areas.[76]

Summation: Some Issues Recast

That some are born great teachers has never been gainsaid. By 1953 American teacher educators had tried for over a century to capture elements of that greatness and, through disciplined intelligence and instruction, to reproduce these elements in increasing numbers of teachers. This age-old quest for a discipline of education has been marked by conflicts, false starts, and disappointments. Most of the perplexing issues which arose in the early decades remain, though their form has changed somewhat and they have been complicated by a host of other factors rooted in the profound changes of American culture.

Not the least complicating factor has been what might be called an inflationary cycle in the realm of ideas. New insights, new disciplines, and new artifacts to cope with the problems of men—including those of education—have been developed so rapidly that we are embarrassed by as yet uncounted riches. But rapid as the increased production has been, it has failed to keep pace with growing needs. With our fabulous wealth of tested knowledge we feel inadequately equipped to meet the situation in which we find ourselves.

So it is with teacher education. The extent to which educational situations involve forces rooted in other cultural patterns, and to which educational decisions ramify into the larger culture, is increasing, and is increasingly realized. To judge wisely in these situations teachers must be prepared with integrity of personality, a broad grasp of intellectual disciplines, great human sensitivity, and a keen understanding of a complex social system and of students who face acute problems. Moreover, having judged wisely they need the skill to achieve in action the goals which are projected. To aid in this task many insights have been devel-

---

[76] See W. E. Lessinger, "How A Large University Provides Laboratory Experiences for Prospective Teachers," *ibid.*, pp. 39–44; Troy L. Stearns and Guy H. Hill, "An Adventure in Teacher Education—The Marshall Plan," *ibid.*, pp. 26–32; and Katie Downs and Grace Tietje, "Pre-Service Education of Rural Elementary Teachers at West Georgia College, Carrollton, Georgia," *ibid,* pp. 10–17.

oped by research in education and other disciplines. The problem is to organize the pre-service experience of potential teachers so efficiently that maximum understanding and control of the forces at work in educational situations are achieved along with a safe margin of technical skill. This is the issue of the liberal and the technical in teacher education.

To see the problem whole three areas must be kept in focus: (1) the concept of general education, (2) the relationship of the professional to the general education sequence, and (3) the balance sought between the liberal and the technical emphasis in the professional sequence. To make decisions concerning one area without considering their implications for the other two seems most unreasonable. However, the preceding historical survey indicates that such judgments are frequently made.

For example, it seems clear that many of the early normal school people were so concerned to create a professional sequence that they largely neglected general education and permitted it to develop chaotically. This lack of carefully planned attention to the general sequence, coupled with an excessively technical concept of the professional sequence, may well have been responsible for the widely cited obsession of teachers with tricks of the trade.

A second example of the type of danger lurking in the tendency to look at only part of the problem is seen in the failure of the early introspective "scientists" of education to transmit, by reports of their speculation, that liberal view of educational problems at which they aimed. It is interesting to note that in the case of early philosophical theory—Pestalozzianism, Hegelianism, and Herbartianism—the underlying assumptions were largely ignored while teachers borrowed the stereotyped methods presumably growing out of these assumptions. These basic theories were all rooted in northern European thought and in the ethos of European peoples, and were formalized by American scholars in terms of German thought and experience. It seems probable that educational theory growing out of the experience of American students, and closely related to their own general education program, would have been more meaningful and more influential. Indeed, it was to be expected that connectionist psychology, described by Edward L. Thorndike in symbols which paralleled those of American technology, and pragmatic philosophy, developed out of the indigenous culture by William James and John Dewey, were readily accepted and more nearly understood by

American teachers. Before educational theory could become meaningful to teachers in training it had to be mediated in familiar terms by men from the rocky soil of New England and the plains of the Midwest. Moreover, the scorn with which the early university educationists viewed technical problems of serious concern to classroom teachers inevitably biased the teachers against the theory.

The interrelationship of the three problem areas has been even more clearly seen in noting the extent to which one's ideas of general education, for example, have dictated his views of the relationship of the two sequences. There seems little doubt that the present insistence upon a harsh separation, in point of time, between the sequences grows out of the Aristotelian assumption that a concern with professional utility will narrow the scope of the general sequence and is, therefore, an illiberal factor. Here, too, the fact that such early university educationists as William H. Payne accepted the assumed dichotomy of liberal and technical clearly prejudiced them against technical instruction in the professional sequence for teachers.

Finally, in the thinking of those who specialize in foundational theory and of those concerned with laboratory-experience programs, the three areas have become critically interrelated. To determine, for example, how best to bring the disciplines of history, sociology, philosophy, psychology, and anthropology to bear on the solution of educational problems without reference to the student's general education in these areas is completely impossible. On the other hand, if one assumes that laboratory experiences are to be used in providing a grasp of the intellectual principles underlying the solution of educational problems, in addition to providing drill in technique, such experiences must also be structured in terms of the general as well as the professional sequence.

Historically, the clusters of ideas which American teacher educators have held can be plotted along two axes: one which takes its clue from conceptions of the ideal relation of the general to the professional sequence, the second which runs from an exclusive concern with technique —of thought or practice—to an emphasis on the broad interrelationships of knowledge and technique in human living.

Along the first axis we have seen that positions have always included that of the purist, who insisted that each sequence be focused strictly on its own peculiar ends and freed from other concerns. We have seen that this position has been held by both academicians and educationists

—usually, in the first case, to free the general program from professional dictation, and, in the second case, to free the professional school from general education responsibility. At the other extreme has been the position of the integrators who have tried to organize the total program in terms either of professional demands more broadly conceived or of the ideal of liberal education softened to permit some instruction in the liberal art of teaching. Between these two extremes have been those who, seeing general and professional objectives as separate and deserving of explicit consideration, have, nevertheless, tried to develop an adequate concept for a parallel and harmonized pursuit of both. As the prevailing concept of the roles of the school and the teacher has broadened it has become increasingly difficult to distinguish between the position of the integrators and that of the harmonizers on this axis.

In higher education the search for an ideal relationship between the specialized or professional sequence and the general education program has been pervasive. The central concern in most of the colleges has been with the relation of graduate faculty professionalism to general education. But those supporting parallel or integrated programs to prepare students for such other callings as engineering, agriculture, and business have also wrestled long with the problem. Educationists, however, have tended to view their history and their problems as divorced from this larger struggle. In so doing they have often permitted themselves to be isolated from their natural allies in the other faculties.

In respect to the second axis, that involving the search for perspective and the necessity to improve technique, present positions also draw from a long tradition. Here the issue is concerned with ways of relating techniques of many types to whole problems. The issue within the professional sequence has paralleled that within the general. In both cases the development of an adequate sense of the wholeness and interrelatedness of all experience has seemed to demand a focus on general ideas or problems, while the development of specific intellectual skills, or techniques of teaching, appears to have required the isolation of a specific situation calling as purely as possible for a concentration on a particular method of treatment.

To a persistent minority throughout the history of American teacher education these two axes have been one. If the specialized knowledge required of a teacher is limited to instruction in pedagogy, the technique of teaching, then its relation to the general sequence is simply the relation of one set of techniques to the whole. Whether the axes be considered one or two depends on the value one places on the efforts of the last century to liberalize the professional sequence. Historically some thinkers from academic departments and from departments of education have seriously discounted these efforts.

But to return to the second axis, we have noted several attempts to create a single concept of the educative task which would provide for the development of individual arts in a program which simultaneously ensured their being adequately related to each other and to life. Two of these have reached their maximum developments in single-purpose schools.

The more venerable of these was the classical tradition in the liberal arts college. Here was a curriculum the content of which was carefully selected to perfect the classical intellectual arts. The great ideas or books of its tradition were such that they called into play precisely those disciplined ways of approaching knowledge which had been most vigorously developed for many centuries. The knowledge considered of most worth and the tools of learning considered most valuable grew naturally out of a commonly accepted course of study. The prevailing faculty psychology seemed adequately to explain how well-mannered men with strong character and leadership ability could be prepared in such a program. While the old psychology has been under long attack and new disciplines and knowledge have assumed relatively greater importance, the ideal of a single conceptualization of the college program which will ensure vigorous discipline of the parts and unity of the whole remains powerful.

The trouble is that each of the arts or disciplines requires a particular type of problem in terms of which it may be perfected. To train a novice in the methodology of history, or physics or anthropology, it has seemed necessary to select the problem at which he will work in terms of its suitability for illustrating and developing the techniques of the discipline. While the traditional problems of philosophy and literature seemed effective in developing the older arts they seemed to be less than ideal in respect to the modern exact and social sciences. Consequently, in lieu of the prescribed traditional curriculum there came the system of providing discipline-oriented courses in the hopes that the student will relate them. In respect to general education a program made up solely of such courses marks the end of the axis opposite that of the traditional liberal arts ideal.

Moreover, with the growing realization of the extent to which human behavior is influenced by nonrational factors, new experiences, involving guidance and opportunities for more rewarding interpersonal relations as well as for aesthetic expression, have had to be devised to ensure the education of the whole man. The general education movement has become an attempt to create a more inclusive concept of the old liberal arts ideal. Outside of some such unifying concept which ensures both discipline and wholeness the only remaining alternative is the continued strife and competition of the departments.

The second major effort of this type, even more ambitious in some respects since it hopes by a single concept to order the professional and the general education sequences, has been that which we have considered as the professional treatment position in the single-purpose teachers colleges. It has been noted that this position has a considerable history and evolution of its own. When it was developed in respect to elementary school subject matter it was largely unconcerned with the methodology of the liberal arts. The emphasis until comparatively recent times has been on integrating only methods of teaching with instruction in subjects to be taught. The question of whether or not the new conception of the professional objective is broad enough depends on the prior question of the adequacy of the present problem-solving approach to education as a whole. Since professional treatment, general education, and other attempts to find a way of ensuring discipline and wholeness tend increasingly to focus on this approach as a unifying factor, it demands further consideration.

The unity of the traditional liberal arts was partly a function of their being jointly suited to a consideration and analysis of the historic problems of philosophy. For every person, however, these problems took their meaning from his experiences in a specific historic culture developed on a specific material and technological base. As new arts of gaining understanding were perfected in the form of the exact and social sciences the old problems were redefined. The type of issue around which training in the new as well as the old intellectual arts could be organized increasingly involved a specific social and material situation. The methodology of science as popularly understood, if turned to the solution of the problems faced by particular societies, seems to offer a set of principles around which to organize a curriculum, adequate for the application of most of the arts and sciences.

However, out of the romantic tradition of Rousseau, Pestalozzi, and Froebel, the child study movement, and the insights of depth psychology has grown a different concept of the type of problem which ought to be at the center of the curriculum. This is the concept of meeting, as they arise, the developmental and personality needs of the student as he feels them. There is, it seems, a tendency to equate all of education with the acquisition of an adequate self-concept. The ordering of the curriculum is, in this tradition, provided by the natural maturation process. Hence it must be different for every student, and any ready-made ordering, it is argued, will lack psychological meaning or importance to the learner. The Deweyan argument that the logical organization of the disciplines, having been worked out by many human beings over many years and having proved repeatedly fruitful, should provide an end-in-view toward which the student is led to modify his approach to problem solving, is still largely ignored by many educationists. One reason for this is apparently the belief that such disciplines still give inadequate recognition to the importance of nonrational factors.

In this context, the suggestion that education be coordinated around problems which demand choice and action among several possible alternatives, each of which has broad ramifications and deeply involves the psychological imperatives of students, seems interesting. If an adequate methodology for reaching and implementing such decisions could be perfected it might provide the end-in-view toward which students are led. To be effective as the central core of the educational program such a methodology would have to find a place for using many different tested approaches to human knowledge and life. The problems in terms of which it operated would have to ramify broadly into the social system and have significant bearing for many vocations. The quest for such a discipline of education has been the central pursuit of educators for centuries. It is a quest which one dare not ignore in an age when in spite of an overwhelming growth of specialized knowledge man finds himself unable to solve effectively his most threatening problems.

But while the search for the whole continues, and even if it is successfully consummated, it seems clear that there will have to be a standing off from the whole to discipline and improve the parts. To make certain that none of the crucial parts are neglected it seems important that their defense be institutionalized. It becomes irritating when some too loudly insist that the whole of the teacher education program be organized in terms of the concepts or disciplines to which they are particularly attached. Yet while some are stressing the whole and the interrelationships, it seems important that others perfect the techniques for knowing, apply these techniques broadly to the problems of education, develop methods of teaching, and improve ways of ensuring a minimum safety of teaching skill. Each of these parts has its own peculiar contribution to make, and must make it in terms of its own discipline. It seems doubtful if any one person, or any like professional group, can determine how each can most effectively help to ensure teachers who are both liberally and technically competent.

Selected References

ADAMS, CHARLES KENDALL. "The Teaching of Pedagogy in Colleges and Universities." New England Association of Colleges and Preparatory Schools, *Addresses and Proceedings of the Third Annual Meeting, 1888,* pp. 17–29.

AMERICAN ASSOCIATION OF TEACHERS COLLEGES. *School and Community Laboratory Experiences in Teacher Education.* The Association, 1945.

AMERICAN COUNCIL ON EDUCATION. *The Improvement of Teacher Education: A Final Report by the Commission on Teacher Education.* Washington, D.C.: The Council, 1946.

AMERICAN NORMAL SCHOOL ASSOCIATION. *American Normal Schools, Their Theory, Their Workings, and Their Results, as Embodied in the Proceedings of the First Annual Convention of the American Normal School Association.* New York: A. S. Barnes and Burr, 1860.

ASSOCIATION FOR STUDENT TEACHING. *Curriculum Trends and Teacher Education.* 1953 Yearbook of the Association for Student Teaching, prepared by Jesse A. Bond and John A. Hockett. Lock Haven, Pa.: The Association, 1953.

ASSOCIATION FOR STUDENT TEACHING. *Professional Laboratory Experiences: An Expanding Concept in Teacher Education.* Twenty-Seventh Yearbook of the Association for Student Teaching. Lock Haven, Pa.: The Association, 1948.

BARNARD, HENRY. *Normal Schools, and Other Institutions, Agencies, and Means, Designed for the Professional Education of Teachers.* Hartford, Conn.: Case, Tiffany and Co., 1851. Two volumes.

237

BUTTS, R. FREEMAN. *The College Charts Its Course: Historic Conceptions and Current Proposals.* New York: McGraw-Hill Book Company, Inc., 1939.

CHARTERS, WERRETT WALLACE. "Education Neglects Its Fundamental Bases." Sixteenth Yearbook of the American Association of Teachers Colleges, pp. 10–15. The Association, 1937.

COOPERATIVE STUDY IN GENERAL EDUCATION. *Cooperation in General Education: A Final Report of the Executive Committee of the Cooperative Study in General Education.* Washington, D.C.: American Council on Education, 1947.

DEARBORN, NED H. *The Oswego Movement in American Education.* New York: Teachers College, Columbia University, 1925.

DEWEY, JOHN. "Culture and Professionalism in Education." *Education Today,* edited by Joseph Ratner. New York: G. P. Putnam's Sons, 1940.

DEWEY, JOHN. "The Relation of Theory to Practice in Education." *The Relation of Theory to Practice in the Education of Teachers,* pp. 9–30. Third Yearbook of the National Society for the Scientific Study of Education, edited by Charles A. McMurry. Chicago: University of Chicago Press, 1904.

DEWEY, JOHN. *The Sources of a Science of Education.* New York: Horace Liveright, 1929.

DEYOE, GEORGE P. *Certain Trends in Curriculum Practices and Policies in State Normal Schools and Teachers Colleges.* New York: Teachers College, Columbia University, 1934.

ELIOT, CHARLES W. *Educational Reform, Essays and Addresses.* New York: The Century Co., 1898.

ELSBREE, WILLARD S. *The American Teacher: Evolution of a Profession in a Democracy.* New York: American Book Company, 1939.

GORDY, JOHN P. *Rise and Growth of the Normal School Idea.* United States Bureau of Education, Circular of Information, 1891, No. 8. Washington, D.C.: Government Printing Office, 1891.

GRAY, THOMAS J. "Report of the 'Chicago Committee' on Methods of Instruction and Courses of Study in Normal Schools." National Educational Association, *Proceedings, 1889,* pp. 570–581.

GREENE, THEODORE M., chairman. *Liberal Education Re-examined: Its Role in a Democracy.* Report of a committee appointed by the American Council of Learned Societies. New York: Harper and Brothers, 1943.

HALLECK, REUBEN POST, chairman. "Report of the Committee of Seventeen on the Professional Preparation of High School Teachers." National Education Association, *Proceedings, 1907,* pp. 523–668.

HARVARD COMMITTEE ON THE OBJECTIVES OF GENERAL EDUCATION IN A FREE SOCIETY. *General Education in a Free Society.* Cambridge: Harvard University Press, 1946.

HINSDALE, BURKE A. "The Teacher's Academical and Professional Preparation." National Educational Association, *Proceedings, 1891,* pp. 713–724.

KILPATRICK, WILLIAM H., editor. *The Educational Frontier.* New York: The Century Co., 1933.

LEARNED, WILLIAM S.; BAGLEY, WILLIAM C.; *et al. The Professional Preparation of Teachers for American Public Schools: A Study Based Upon an Examination of Tax-Supported Normal Schools in the State of Missouri.* Bulletin No. 14. New York: The Carnegie Foundation for the Advancement of Teaching, 1920.

LOVINGER, WARREN C. *General Education in the Teachers Colleges.* Oneonta, N.Y.: American Association of Colleges for Teacher Education, 1948.

MANGUN, VERNON. *The American Normal School, Its Rise and Development in Massachusetts.* Baltimore: Warwick and York, Inc., 1928.

McCOSH, JAMES. *The New Departure in College Education: Reply to President Eliot's Defense of It in New York, February 24, 1885.* New York: Charles Scribner's Sons, 1885.

MEIKLEJOHN, ALEXANDER. *The Liberal College.* Boston: Marshall Jones Co., 1920.

MONROE, WALTER S. *Teaching–Learning Theory and Teacher Education, 1890–1952.* Urbana: University of Illinois Press, 1952.

MORGAN, THOMAS J. *What Is the True Function of a Normal School?* Prize Essay: Award of the American Institute of Instruction. Boston: Willard Small, 1886.

MORRIS, VAN CLEVE. *The Education of Secondary School Teachers in the Liberal Arts Colleges.* Unpublished report of an Ed.D. project, Teachers College, Columbia University, 1949. Summarized under the same title in *Association of American Colleges Bulletin,* 36:511–528, December, 1950.

NATIONAL SOCIETY OF COLLEGE TEACHERS OF EDUCATION. *The Use of Background in the Interpretation of Educational Issues.* Twenty-Fifth Yearbook of the National Society of College Teachers of Education, edited by Fowler D. Brooks. Chicago: University of Chicago Press, 1937.

NATIONAL SOCIETY OF COLLEGE TEACHERS OF EDUCATION, COMMITTEE ON SOCIAL FOUNDATIONS. *The Emerging Task of the Foundations of Education, The Study of Man, Culture, and Education: A*

240 SELECTED REFERENCES

Statement to the Profession. Ann Arbor, Mich.: Lithographed for The Society, n.d.

NATIONAL SOCIETY FOR THE STUDY OF EDUCATION. *Changes and Experiments in Liberal Arts Education.* Thirty-First Yearbook of the National Society for the Study of Education, Part II. Bloomington, Ill.: Public School Publishing Company, 1932.

NATIONAL SOCIETY FOR THE SCIENTIFIC STUDY OF EDUCATION. *The Education and Training of Secondary Teachers.* Fourth Yearbook of the National Society for the Scientific Study of Education, Part I. Bloomington, Ill.: Pantagraph Printing and Stationery Company, 1905.

NATIONAL SOCIETY FOR THE STUDY OF EDUCATION. *General Education.* Fifty-First Yearbook of the National Society for the Study of Education, Part I, edited by Nelson B. Henry. Chicago: University of Chicago Press, 1952.

NATIONAL SOCIETY FOR THE STUDY OF EDUCATION. *General Education in the American College.* Thirty-Eighth Yearbook of the National Society for the Study of Education, Part II. Bloomington, Ill.: Public School Publishing Company, 1939.

NATIONAL SOCIETY FOR THE SCIENTIFIC STUDY OF EDUCATION. *The Professional Preparation of High School Teachers.* Eighteenth Yearbook of the National Society for the Scientific Study of Education, Part I. Bloomington, Ill.: Public School Publishing Company, 1919.

NORTON, ARTHUR O., editor. *The First Normal School in America: The Journals of Cyrus Peirce and Mary Swift.* Cambridge: Harvard University Press, 1926.

OGDEN, JOHN. "What Constitutes a Consistent Course of Study for Normal Schools?" National Educational Association, *Proceedings, 1874,* pp. 216–229.

PANGBURN, JESSIE M. *The Evolution of the American Teachers College.* New York: Bureau of Publications, Teachers College, Columbia University, 1932.

PAYNE, WILLIAM H. *Contributions to the Science of Education.* New York: Harper and Brothers, 1887.

PRESIDENT'S COMMISSION ON HIGHER EDUCATION. *Higher Education for American Democracy: A Report of the President's Commission on Higher Education.* New York: Harper and Brothers, 1948. Six volumes in one.

RANDOLPH, EDGAR D. *The Professional Treatment of Subject Matter.* Baltimore: Warwick and York, Inc., 1924.

SMALL, ALBION. "The Demands of Sociology on Pedagogy." National Educational Association, *Proceedings, 1896,* pp. 174–184.

STOWE, CALVIN E. *Common Schools and Teachers Seminaries.* Boston: March, Capen, Lyon and Webb, 1839.

SUPERVISORS OF STUDENT TEACHING. *The Integration of Laboratory Phases of Teacher Training with Professional and Subject-Matter Courses.* 1937 Yearbook of the Supervisors of Student Teaching, compiled and edited by John G. Flowers.

TARBELL, H. S., chairman. "Report of the Sub-Committee on the Training of Teachers." National Educational Association, *Proceedings, 1895,* pp. 238–259.

UNITED STATES OFFICE OF EDUCATION. *National Survey of the Education of Teachers.* United States Office of Education, Bulletin 1933, No. 10. Edward S. Evenden, associate director. Washington, D.C.: Government Printing Office, 1935. Six volumes.

WAYLAND, FRANCIS. *Thoughts on the Present Collegiate System in the United States.* Boston: Gould, Kendall and Lincoln, 1842.

Index